BEYOND THE NEW MORALITY

The Responsibilities of Freedom

Beyond the
New Morality
The Responsibilities of Freedom

THIRD EDITION

GERMAIN GRISEZ

and

RUSSELL SHAW

University of Notre Dame Press
Notre Dame, Indiana

Library of Congress Cataloging-in-Publication Data

Grisez, Germain Gabriel, 1929-
  Beyond the new morality.

  Bibliography: p.
  Includes index.
  1. Ethics.   I. Shaw, Russell B.   II. Title.
BJ1025.G7   1988   171'.3   88-4805
ISBN 0-268-00678-4
ISBN 0-268-00679-2 (pbk.)

Manufactured in the United States of America

The authors affectionately dedicate
this work to their wives:

Jeannette Grisez
and
Carmen Shaw

Contents

Introduction

We are proposing an ethics. But what is *ethics*? As we use the word, it means a philosophical study of morality, of the foundations on which morality is based, and of the practical implications of a systematic moral outlook.

We believe ethics must start by clarifying the fundamental notions of freedom, action, and community. Then it can go on to examine the question "What is the ultimate distinction between moral good and moral evil, between action which is right and action which is wrong?" An answer becomes useful in practice, however, only after one has worked out a satisfactory way of thinking through concrete moral issues—"Should I do this or that?" Thus we next turn to the problem of establishing basic moral principles. Finally, once one is in a position to take a reasoned view of moral issues, it is possible to ask and try to answer the question "To what extent can I close the gap, in my life and in society, between the way I think things ought to be and the way they are?"

History studies human actions, but it looks at particular actions which have actually taken place; ethics is concerned with human action in general or with possible kinds of actions. Psychology and the social sciences also have somewhat the same subject matter as ethics, but they are mainly concerned with how human beings actually do act and societies actually do work; ethics concentrates on how persons ought to act and societies ought to be formed and reformed.

Theological ethics (moral theology or Christian ethics) deals with many of the same questions which are treated here philosophically. The principal difference is that theological ethics

1

takes for granted, as a point of departure, the doctrines of a religious faith, while a philosophical approach does not take for granted any particular set of beliefs. Although it is impossible to question everything at once, the philosophical approach regards every belief and viewpoint as in principle subject to questioning.

In trying to answer the questions which it asks, philosophy points to facts which anyone can observe and proposes arguments which any reasonable person should accept. "Arguments" here does not mean contentious disagreements, however. Ethics argues mainly in the sense that it proposes clarifications of the meaning of certain basic notions, such as "doing an act" and "morally good," and then draws out their implications.

A. The Roots of the Ethical Problem

The central problems of ethics readily present themselves to a philosopher today in a historical context. Although it would take us too far afield to go into that context in detail, it is necessary at least to indicate the deep historical roots of the ethical problems with which people today continue to grapple.

These roots are twofold. On the one side is the Judeo-Christian religious tradition; on the other, the Greco-Roman humanistic tradition.

The belief that God is the creator of all things is part of the Judeo-Christian religious tradition. The act of creation is pictured neither as an accident, nor as something God had to do, nor as an effort on his part to fulfill some sort of need, but as a completely free act. Also part of this religious tradition is the belief that human beings are made in God's image and somehow possess a freedom resembling the freedom by which God creates.

The Judeo-Christian tradition is based on the belief that God freely reveals himself to humankind and, in doing so, extends to human beings the offer of a special, personal relationship, an offer to which they in turn freely respond. Jews believe they are free to accept or reject the Covenant proposed through Moses; Christians believe they are free to accept or reject the Gospel of Jesus Christ. Of course, both Jew and Christian also believe they ought to accept the Covenant or the Gospel.

The ethical significance of this lies in the fact that according to the Judeo-Christian tradition human beings have freedom of self-determination. They can make or break their whole existence by their own acts, their own free choices, just as God was able to create—and could as well not have created—by his own free choice.

When, however, the Bible deals with moral good and moral evil, with what is right and what is wrong, it undertakes no general explanation of these concepts. The Covenant and the Gospel contain specific commands, which are represented as God's will; and the Bible always assumes that acting in accord with divine commands will be in the best interests of human beings. But it makes no extended attempt to explain why this should be so, beyond emphasizing that the well-being of human persons depends upon their friendship with God, their creator.

The Greek philosophical tradition worked out various conceptions of what a human being is. Each of these conceptions of human nature served as the basis for an ideal of human life. Having developed ideas about what a human being should be, the Greek philosophers then went on to discuss how individuals should live their lives in order to measure up to the ideal.

Although disagreeing considerably in the details of their views of ethics, the Greek philosophers did agree on several points. 1) There must be one ideal pattern of human life. 2) Rational inquiry should be sufficient to reveal this ideal. 3) The ideal is rooted in human nature, not in individual preferences or divine commands. 4) Individuals fall short of the ideal either because of lack of knowledge of what is good, or because of hereditary defects (slaves, for example, are just naturally inferior), or because of bad upbringing (children brought up in a barbarian culture can only be semihuman).

In short, the Greek philosophers developed quite definite ideas about what a human being must do to live a good, fully human life. While proposing these ideas on rational grounds, as corresponding to the requirements of human nature, they overlooked freedom of self-determination.

Throughout the history of Western culture thinkers have been trying to join elements from the Judeo-Christian religious tradition and the Greco-Roman philosophical tradition into one harmonious whole. If one takes from the Judeo-Christian tradition the idea that human beings have freedom of self-determination and from the Greco-Roman tradition the idea that there must be a reasonable basis for judgments of moral good and evil, right and wrong, one has the parts of the puzzle which ethics confronts.

Divine commands cannot serve as the point of departure for philosophical ethics, since it cannot proceed by taking for granted particular religious beliefs. In saying this we are not rejecting religious morality or denying the possibility that there are moral truths which must be accepted on the basis of religious faith. We are merely saying that such moral truths, if they exist and important as they may be, are not part of the concern of philosophical ethics. Similarly, such ethics today no longer assumes much of the permanence of human nature which the Greco-Roman philosophic tradition took for granted. Instead, we now take for granted the creative capacity and dignity of the individual person.

An adequate solution to the puzzle of ethics must therefore do full justice to two facts. First, human beings have freedom of self-determination; they determine what they make of their own lives. And, second, human beings have real moral responsibilities; there can be good reasons for judgments of right and wrong. The solution does not lie in denying human freedom or in treating moral requirements as the result of either arbitrary human preferences or humanly inexplicable divine commands.

B. Why Ethics Is Important

All children are brought up according to particular moral viewpoints, conveyed to them as much by actions as by words. Small children take for granted the rightness of the morality in which they are being raised; they may not always obey it, but it does not even occur to them to deny its reality and validity. At some point in adolescence or youth, however, most people in our culture become aware that it is open to them to keep, amend, or even replace the moral outlook in which they were raised.

These options are extremely important. Herein the framework of one's whole life is at stake. It is unfortunate if, as sometimes happens, so basic a decision is made whimsically, or simply in rebellion against the viewpoint in which one was raised, or merely by conforming to the prejudices of one's social class and age group. A person's basic moral stance should be the subject of his or her most careful inquiry and most critical judgment.

The study of ethics provides an opportunity for such careful inquiry and critical judgment. To avoid turning one's life over blindly to an old morality or a new morality, or to the opinions of friends or the demands of feelings, it is necessary to think things through. The only way to do this properly is to do it for oneself and from the ground up.

This book is not a substitute for such personal thinking. The viewpoint which it advances is proposed as one alternative, among many, to be considered seriously. We think it deserves consideration; it is the outcome of our personal inquiry and reflection, and we are convinced of its soundness. But we do not ask anyone to believe what we say; we ask only that the reader examine the questions discussed here and consider the reasons given for the views which are expressed.

People with deep, personal religious faith may feel that it is not necessary for them to undertake the sort of reflection in depth which we are proposing—they already have an altogether satisfactory moral framework for their lives and need look no further into the questions with which philosophical ethics is concerned. We cannot agree with this point of view, even if the religious faith in question should happen to be one we share. Religious persons need not reduce everything they believe to reasons, but they do need to assure themselves that their act of faith is itself morally defensible in human terms. Furthermore, one can hardly think out a sound theological ethics unless one has worked through the problems the philosopher must face.

The study of ethics has, moreover, an importance which goes beyond the individual and his or her personal life. We live in a society which is pluralistic, a society in which there are disagreements about basic issues. When we find ourselves at odds with our fellow citizens on matters of public policy, we cannot rest on an appeal to beliefs which they do not share. In this context we must be ready to give good reasons for our judgments about right and wrong.

Only by thinking through our own fundamental outlook are we in a position to articulate the strongest possible case for our judgments. Of course, it is altogether possible, even probable, that even if we have good reasons for our moral judgments, we shall be unable to convince others by philosophic arguments alone. But where fundamental issues are at stake, it is worth the effort to try. For what is the alternative? Propaganda, which is a kind of violence to reason. And when the universal use of propaganda renders all propaganda ineffective, the final "argument" becomes coercion and outright physical violence.

People who care for others and respect themselves do not want to use violence to back up their views. Thus, even if ethical reflection does not seem very likely to lead to agreement in a pluralistic society, it is worth trying. The fact that one falls short of total success does not necessarily mean that nothing has been accomplished. In our society many disputes are settled by means of compromise short of violence and without fundamental agreement. To negotiate the compromises most acceptable to our own convictions, we need to understand our own positions and our reasons for them.

Thus philosophical ethics has a vital role to play in our individual lives by helping us really to take possession of ourselves; and it also has an important place in our lives as members of a pluralistic society.

C. The Nature of This Book

It will be clear to any reader, and especially to professional philosophers, that this is not a technical work of philosophy.

That is said not defensively, but only as a caveat to those who might otherwise approach the book expecting what it does not pretend to offer. One of the authors, Grisez, has set forth his ethical theory at length and in the language of technical philosophy and theology in other publications. Professionals in the field are urged to consult these expositions for a statement of the theory and examples of its application, in terms to which they are accustomed.

For whom is this book intended? The primary audience is the general ethics class, where a teacher can supplement the book's presentation with the degree of technical and professional sophistication he or she deems appropriate. The work has also been used successfully as a foundation in courses in ethics in particular fields: for example, business ethics, health care ethics, and so on. In the authors' minds, however, the audience is by no means limited to students in formal classes. Others, such as adult study and discussion groups, will find it useful. It is also the authors' hope that the serious reader, reading independently, will study and reflect on it.

The present work does not attempt to set forth a variety of views; it is not a history of ethics or an overview of the field. Rather, it seeks to state clearly and simply, in language comprehensible to the nonprofessional, a particular approach to ethics. For this reason it may well be read in conjunction with other works which propose other approaches.

For all audiences the "questions for review and discussion" after each chapter and the list of readings at the end of the book provide an additional dimension. The questions are not meant to catechize readers but to encourage them to engage in further exploration of the issues raised and further evaluation of the answers offered here (as well as other answers offered by other ethical systems). As for the suggested readings, they do not comprise a comprehensive bibliography of ethics since such bibliographies are readily available elsewhere. Instead they identify two kinds of sources: those which complement and/or develop at greater length particular points made in the text and those which illustrate points of view with which the theory proposed here takes issue.

D. *The Plan of the Book*

The best way to see how the argument is developed is, naturally, to read the book. What follows is meant only as a brief look ahead for those who may wish such assistance.

We begin with freedom, since the question of moral good and moral evil involves the question of freedom—how it is used or abused. Freedom, however, cannot be understood apart from action; and our analysis distinguishes three distinct levels of action, with a particular "freedom" associated with each. Our principal concern is with the third level of action (self-determination) and its corresponding freedom, since it is at this level that one can speak most properly of moral good and moral evil. We note, further, that the individual as a moral entity does not exist in isolation; relationships with other people are part of the fabric of life, and ethics must therefore deal with the community dimension of living.

All this, however, is only groundwork for identifying principles by which one can determine whether an action is morally good or morally evil. Rejecting the solutions of relativism and subjectivism, we propose that morality is rooted in the manner in which choices and actions relate to the fulfillment of human persons, as individuals and communities. This fulfillment has a number of diverse aspects which provide the basic reasons for all human actions. We call these aspects of human fulfillment "basic human goods" and argue that the fundamental criterion of morality is the manner in which one makes free, self-determining choices. Having seen that the first principle of morality concerns choice which is consistent with integral human fulfillment, in chapter nine we identify two ways of choosing—one completely reasonable, the other somewhat less than completely reasonable—and conclude that the former is morally good because it leaves one open to continuing and ever greater growth as a person, as this is measured by the ideal of integral human fulfillment.

Next we move to the identification of guidelines which help people to choose rightly. First, approaches to choice which focus upon weighing and measuring among goods are rejected because, although they seem plausible at first sight, they turn out to be useless for solving real moral problems. Instead, eight "modes of responsibility" are identified (in chapters eleven through thirteen) as guidelines for choosing as well as for analyzing action. The problem of "ambiguous" action is examined in chapter fourteen, and a solution proposed in terms of the modes of responsibility.

The final section of the book applies what has gone before to several matters of particular concern, such as education, social reform and revolution, and theories of individual and social progress. The special role of religion in regard to morality (Is it a help or a hindrance?) is considered at some length. The book ends with a brief description of how persons who wish to do what is morally right might structure their lives.

It will be apparent at many points that this book is concerned in a special way with the "new morality." The new morality means different things to different people, but the general idea is that traditional morality placed too much emphasis on inflexible general rules, on obedience, and on abstract ideals of right and wrong; whereas the emphasis of the new morality is on the concrete situation, on love, and on the person.

On the whole we are sympathetic to the intentions of proponents of the new morality. But we are not satisfied with the positions they have worked out. We do not suggest a return to the old morality; that is in any case no longer possible. Rather, we suggest an advance beyond the new morality toward a sounder and more humane ethics. The new morality is only a halfway house.

The ethics we propose here takes full account of the concrete situation, of love, and of the person—including other persons and the community of persons to whom we all have many moral responsibilities. But it also seeks to put the concrete situation into the context of the whole of a person's life; it seeks to show how love requires a free response to human goods, a response which generates responsibilities; it seeks to defend the person and the community of persons against the implications of theories and attitudes that would make of them mere objects, mere means.

E. Story of the Book

A work resulting from collaboration naturally raises questions in reader's minds. Who is responsible for which ideas? Who wrote what? Does the book reflect thoroughgoing agreement or a series of compromises?

One of the authors of this book, Grisez, is a professional philosopher; the other, Shaw, is a professional writer interested in ethical theory. The ethical theory set forth here is, properly speaking, Grisez's. The authors have, however, discussed ethics with each other frequently and have arrived at a substantial harmony of view. In addition, they have worked together on several other writing projects involving ethics.

The book came about in the following way. Grisez's ethics course for an entire semester was recorded and transcribed. Grisez also drew up an outline of a short book on ethics, more or less this book. Working from the transcript and the outline while retaining considerable independence as to the ordering of the material and the manner of stating and illustrating concepts, Shaw produced a manuscript. The authors conferred and revised, added and subtracted. The result was the first edition of this book, published in 1974. In preparing the second edition in 1980 a less exhaustive but similarly collaborative process of discussion and revision was employed. In addition, the authors took into account—and here gratefully acknowledge—reactions and criticisms of teachers, students, and other readers who worked with the first edition.

In 1978 Grisez began full-time work in the field of moral theology and undertook a complete and systematic work on Christian moral principles. This entailed a thorough review of the ethical theory he had previously worked out. Although remaining the same in its main lines, it underwent considerable development in detail, much of this due to work done by Grisez with Joseph Boyle and John Finnis. And again the two authors conferred and collaborated in incorporating the results into this new version of the text.

The result is *Beyond the New Morality* as it now stands in this third edition. The authors regard it as a joint enterprise, for which they are willing to share not only blame, but (they continue to hope) also praise.

1. Freedom Means Responsibility

Freedom. Everybody wants it. Poets praise it. Politicians promise or proclaim it. Some people have given their lives to win it for themselves or others.

But what is it?

The word "freedom" can have many different meanings. It can refer simply to the lack of physical restraints. It can mean the absence of external social pressures and demands. And it can signify that capacity by which individuals are able to form their own lives—in a sense, their own *selves*—through their choices.

It makes a difference what kind of freedom one is talking about. True, there are common elements: for example, as applied to persons the meaning of freedom includes at least someone acting, the activity, and something else—a factor potentially in opposition to the activity. Common elements aside, however, the various meanings of freedom are significantly different. Furthermore, the freedom to determine one's self by one's own choices is the freedom most proper to a human being. It is the freedom with which ethics is most concerned.

Because there are different kinds of freedom, and because some are more properly human than others, it is worth looking at them in some detail in order to see where they are different and in what each consists.

11

A. Freedom Is Physical Freedom

The simplest kind of freedom is the absence of physical coercion and constraint. This is what is called physical freedom. Even inanimate objects can have it: we speak, for example, of "freely falling bodies." It is also the kind of freedom enjoyed typically by wild animals in contrast with those in captivity. However, a prisoner in a cell does not have freedom in this sense (or else possesses it only to a limited degree and in a highly circumscribed way) because he is physically prevented from doing many things, including leaving the cell. Someone forced to perform a physical action, or physically prevented from doing so, is not acting freely in performing or not performing the action.

Physical freedom corresponds to the simplest kind of action, that which can be performed even by an animal or a small child. A dog chases a rabbit. A baby crawls across a room to get a red ball. In such action the meaning of the behavior comes from its culmination. And the behavior and the meaning are closely united. The behavior only makes sense in terms of the culminating performance (catching the rabbit, getting the ball).

Freedom is present in such action in the sense that the behavior cannot take place unless the individual is not physically constrained. Where there is constraint, there can be no action; where there is no constraint, the action can be performed. The latter situation represents physical freedom.

This kind of freedom is always a matter of degree. Some measure of physical freedom is essential if one is to act morally. (Acting morally here does not mean doing what is right. It only means acting in a way that *counts* as right or wrong in moral terms.) At the same time, however, absolute physical freedom is not required for moral responsibility. In fact, it is nonsense to speak of "absolute physical freedom." Everyone is subject to some constraint; the law of gravity would see to that if nothing else did. Freedom in the sense of physical freedom is always more or less.

B. *Freedom Is Doing As One Pleases*

Freedom can also mean doing as one pleases in the absence of social demands and restrictions. A slave's basic condition is not one of freedom in this sense, because what the slave does and does not do is determined by someone else, his or her master. (Slaves may also be deprived of physical freedom, though this need not be the case.) By contrast, Robinson Crusoe was totally free to do as he pleased until Friday's appearance on the scene injected social obligations into his situation. Since there was until then no one else to impose societal demands and restrictions on Crusoe, he enjoyed complete freedom to do as he pleased.

As is the case with physical freedom, so freedom to do as one pleases corresponds to a particular sort of action. This kind of freedom is proper to action performed as a means to some end which is separate from the performance itself, an end not included in the culmination of the behavior. An example of this kind of action is planting seed in order to obtain a crop. Obtaining the crop is the end which is sought, but it is very widely separated, not only in time but in other ways as well, from the performance of sowing seed.

At this level of action persons are free to do as they please to the extent that they desire the end to be achieved and that certain means are necessary to achieve the end. The grain-crop example clearly meets the second condition because there will be no crop unless the seed is planted; as for the first (desiring the end) it is fulfilled in the case of a farmer who plants seed because he wants a crop; it is not fulfilled in the case of a slave who plants seed only because his master tells him to.

Several things are characteristic of action at this level. Calculation—reflection on what means to employ in order to achieve particular ends—is both possible and necessary. Also, it is clear that at this level doing as one pleases and responsibility are in opposition to each other. Responsibility in society is something which is imposed on one by other people. Freedom to do as one pleases lies in the absence of such imposition. Individuals would be totally free at this level of action if they had to do only those things necessary to achieve the ends *they* wanted to achieve.

Immature people tend to think that this is the highest kind of freedom. Adolescents seeking to shake off the requirements imposed on them by authority typically are seeking freedom of this sort. Doing what one pleases appears to be the very highest expression of what freedom is, and this is the opposite of doing as one is required by parents, teachers, or others in authority.

A more mature view of the matter, however, suggests that merely doing as one pleases is neither the final word on freedom nor an unqualified good. Some degree of freedom to do as one pleases is certainly essential to moral responsibility. But unlimited freedom of this sort is impossible—and would be undesirable even if it were somehow possible—for anyone living in social relationships with others. Even animals live in groups and are moved by instinct to care for their young. As for human beings, we understand that we can hardly pursue, serve, or enjoy any good except with other people. Thus once we begin to do anything to fulfill ourselves, we must take into account what pleases others, and this inevitably limits our freedom to do as we please.

More important than unrestricted freedom to do as one pleases is that individuals be able to participate in appropriate ways in setting up and directing their relationships and the communities which make demands and place restrictions on them. People have a right to a voice in setting the rules of the societies in which they live. But this is a very different thing from, practically speaking, opting out of societies and the demands they make in order to have maximum freedom to do as one pleases.

C. Ideal Freedom, Creative Freedom, and Political Freedom

Before passing on to the kind of freedom most important to ethics, it is worth mentioning several other kinds of freedom: ideal freedom, creative freedom, and freedom in the political sense.

"Ideal freedom" refers to the freedom possessed by individuals and societies which are able to act in accord with an ideal. This is the sense in which the word "freedom" is used by such different thinkers as St. Paul and Freud. St. Paul considered the sinner not to be free because on account of sin he or she is bound to fall short of the ideal of uprightness. By contrast, he held Christians to be free because their redemption from sin by Christ freed them for uprightness. Similarly, for Freud the neurotic is not free, but the cured patient, who has been liberated from neurosis, is to that extent free to behave in accord with an ideal of psychological health.

Ideal freedom and freedom to do as one pleases may sound at first like complete opposites—shaping one's actions to conform to an ideal as against acting without constraint—but they can be compatible. Ideal freedom means that the individual is not blocked from doing what ought to be done; freedom to do as one pleases means that the individual is not blocked from doing as he or she wishes to do. But underlying most ideals of behavior is the assumption that, once reached, they will be found easy and pleasant to fulfill, and people will actually wish to fulfill them.

Not all ideals, of course, are equally valid. The validity of various versions of ideal freedom depends on the truth of the worldviews underlying them. Although passing judgment on the truth of worldviews is not the task of ethical theory, we shall have something to say about this matter in the final chapter.

In practice, in any case, the content of ideal freedom varies widely. There are diverse conceptions of the ideal condition of the human agent and diverse views of the obstacles to the fulfillment of the ideals. Karl Marx, for example, considered the ideal human condition to be attainable not by isolated individuals but only by society as a whole. Yet whatever the particular content, the general concept remains the same: human beings will have ideal freedom when they can act as they ideally ought to do. And if one's ideal for human beings includes their realizing themselves by their own free choices, then ideal freedom will be closely related to freedom of self-determination, to be discussed below.

"Creative freedom" refers to the freedom present when

circumstances and factors which tend toward repetition are overcome and that which is new emerges. This is the freedom peculiar, for example, to a creative artist, inasmuch as the artist does not merely repeat what has been done before but creates a work possessing an element of genuine newness. Some philosophers have gone so far as to liken the whole of reality to the creative process of art, seeing reality as an ongoing process in which there regularly emerge novelties which are not attributable to antecedent conditions and laws.

Freedom in this sense is distinguishable from physical freedom, since the latter resides in the agent able to engage in a behavior, whereas creative freedom can involve the emergence of something new and distinct from the agent. Creative freedom is also different from freedom to do as one pleases: the latter can be as repetitive and noncreative as the desires which shape the content of what "one pleases," but new desires can be part of freedom as the emergence of novelty. Finally, creative freedom is not the same as ideal freedom, for the latter takes for granted the prior existence of an ideal of behavior, while creative freedom can involve the emergence of novel ideals and principles.

"Political freedom" suggests a kind of freedom to do as one pleases which applies to peoples rather than to individuals. In this sense a colony revolts and fights for its freedom.

There is, however, another sense of political freedom: namely, the participation of individuals in directing their own polity, which we mentioned at the end of the previous section. This concept is sometimes expressed by the phrase "government by the consent of the governed."

Although political freedom in this sense is closely related to individual freedom to do as one pleases, the two things are not identical. The difference is one of emphasis. In individual freedom to do as one pleases, the emphasis is on the absence of requirements set by others. In political freedom the emphasis is on the fact that persons act according to laws which they somehow share in making. In this sense children in a typical Western democracy are not politically free, but virtually all adult citizens are. In addition, political freedom is concerned, not with the whole of one's life, but only with that part of it in which one acts as a citizen.

D. Freedom Is Self-Determination

As we have suggested, freedom also refers to self-determination—the shaping of one's life, one's *self*, by one's choices. This is the kind of freedom most closely related to questions of morality. To the extent that we can determine for ourselves who we shall be, we are responsible for our lives. This kind of freedom does *not* assume or require the absence of all external pressures and prior causes. Self-determination refers instead to the state of affairs in which, despite external pressures and prior causes which can and do influence our choices, we retain at least some options of choosing or not choosing, of choosing one thing rather than another.

In cases where there is no such option there is no real choice and no self-determination. In such cases it is not a question of "moral" action at all. When people do things without really having chosen to do them, they are not acting either morally or immorally; their action simply has no moral quality in itself. (People may, however, have considerable moral responsibility for previous freely chosen acts by which they placed themselves in the position of being unable to choose freely and so have some responsibility for the consequences of their unfree behavior.)

It is certainly possible to act in this way—without choosing to act—and in fact people often do. But it is also possible for people to act on the basis of real choice and, in doing so, to be self-determining.

The experience of free choice is a familiar one. It begins in conflict, the awareness that one is in a situation where it is not possible to pursue all the goods one is concerned with. This leads to conscious deliberation about the alternatives. Even so, choice may *not* be necessary; this happens when, upon deliberation, only one alternative seems really appealing. But deliberation commonly leads to the conclusion that one is confronting real and incompatible possibilities. At this point one says in effect, "It's really up to me to choose." As that suggests, one does not encounter choices; one *makes* them.

Like physical freedom and freedom to do as one pleases, self-determination corresponds to a particular kind of action. Action at this third level derives its meaning from a good in which one participates by performing the action. The meaning does not come from the completion and consummation of the action (first level: physical freedom) or from a specific goal which the action is meant to achieve (second level: freedom to do as one pleases). Instead the meaning comes from a good in which one hopes to participate precisely through performing the action. The purpose of sharing in the good is not achieved at the end of the action or sometime after it but is present in the performance throughout, at every stage, and one realizes such a good by participating in it.

Consider an example: studying simply for the sake of learning. Studying is the action. Learning is the good. Learning is not something which occurs or is achieved only at the end of studying. It goes on all the time one is studying. One participates in this good for as long as one performs the action.

From this same example it is apparent how one and the same action can, simply by a change of perspective—or, more accurately, a change of intention—move from one level to another.

All actions, even the most complex, can be broken down into their individual first-level components. In studying—reading a chapter in a book, for instance—the eyes move from one line of print to another, and from one page to the next. This simple process of looking at words on a page is activity at the first level of action.

The same act of studying can also be an action at either the second or the third level. It will be an action at the second level if one is studying simply as a means to an end, for example, to pass an examination. But it will be an action of the third level if it is done not merely to achieve an ulterior objective (passing a test) but for the sake of participating in a good (learning) which is intimately and inextricably linked to the action itself. Furthermore, as the example makes clear, the same act can simultaneously be an action at the second level and at the third level if, for instance, while studying for an exam, one is also learning for learning's sake and is concerned about both purposes at the same time.

E. *Determinism*

Some theories of human behavior, which go by the general name "determinism," hold that there is really no such thing as freedom of self-determination. They argue that all behavior is determined by factors prior to choice. Many philosophers of the past three centuries, and especially of the nineteenth century, considered belief in self-determination unscientific. Many thought that a free choice would violate the physical laws articulated by Newton.

Determinists in the English-speaking tradition have generally been identified with what is called "soft determinism" or "compatibilism." In this view human acts can be attributed to the person who performs them, inasmuch as he or she is not coerced, yet the acts are determined by a cause and are not expressions of self-determination.

Determinism of one kind or another has had great impact—for example, the psychological determinism associated with Freud and his followers and the sociological determinism of Marx. Starting with the basic idea that there are fixed laws of nature which exclude the indeterminacy required for freedom, Freud and Marx claimed to find in the psyche and society mechanisms analogous to those found by Newton in the realm of physical nature. Determinism is still influential in sociology and psychology; and most compatibilists are in fact psychological determinists who hold that people necessarily choose the alternative which seems best to them. However, this way of thinking no longer has much support from contemporary physics and logic. Indeed, post-Newtonian physics is notable for replacing the model of nature as a vast machine operating according to a determined plan with a model which includes contingency and indeterminacy in the flow of nature's processes.

Basically, determinism comes down to saying that every action is determined in advance: everyone has to act as he or she does (for instance, because of psychological makeup) and could not choose to act differently. While we do not consider this to be a true or adequate explanation of human action, it does reflect some perfectly accurate observations about certain aspects of human behavior. For one thing, it is entirely true that antecedent factors play an extremely strong role in much behavior, a stronger role than perhaps many people are ready to admit. Some of what passes for free action is probably not really as free as it seems. This point has come to be understood only with growing insight into psychological conditioning—how it occurs and how it exerts its influence.

The concept of self-determination—freedom at the third level of action—does not mean that action takes place without causes which precede it or that the causes do not have a conditioning influence on the action. But it is important to be clear about what, in the case of free choice, the determining conditions do in fact determine. Essentially they determine two things: first, that there are at least two possibilities; second, that everything required, including the motivation for one to choose either (or any) of the possibilities, is present.

Prior determining conditions quite commonly exclude a large number of actions which might hypothetically be possibilities but which, concretely, are not possibilities here and now for this individual facing a choice. This so impresses many people that they conclude that antecedent conditions have excluded the possibility of choice itself.

This is a typical explanation of criminal acts: they are entirely accounted for by poverty, a bad family life, and similar factors which have deprived the individual of the capacity for free choice. Without ignoring or denying the powerful role of poverty, family influences, and other such factors in crime, we note that it cannot be taken for granted that such antecedent conditions, though sharply limiting the options open to an individual, have removed the possibility of free choice itself. Not everything people do is a free, self-determined action, but for the average individual it is possible at least sometimes to perform such actions.

Antecedent conditions do explain two things: the limited options available to some people—either because of objective conditions or because of their lack of vision and hope—and the feelings, inclinations, and temptations which people experience. With regard to the latter, freedom of self-determination does not mean that we have a direct way of controlling our feelings, desires, and temptations—indeed, one often finds oneself unable to get rid of unwanted feelings. But even if one has no choice about feeling, say, anger and hatred toward another and being tempted to take revenge for some wrong, still one does have a choice about whether to act on these feelings and succumb to this temptation.

Experience points to the truth of this. If all our actions were determined in advance by antecedent factors, we would not have the experience, often very intense and uncomfortable, of unsettledness and indecision in making a choice; there is no reason for deliberation about actions which are already determined. Furthermore, when people make choices, they do not experience choice as *happening to* them but as something they *do:* "I made up my mind." The experience of choice is an experience of acting, not of undergoing. Determinism must try to explain away our experience that what we do is really ours to decide.

It is reasonable to take such experience at face value unless one has a reason for doing otherwise. The data of experience should be accepted as genuine in the absence of a good reason for rejecting them. The burden of proof rests with determinism.

And, as it happens, determinism does not provide grounds for rejecting the validity of the experience of choosing freely. In fact, every attempt to prove the case for determinism is self-defeating. Consider the fact that any argument for determinism appeals to us to be loyal to the pursuit of truth. This appeal occurs when, in trying to prove their case, determinists take for granted our reasonableness and try to show that we *ought* to accept their position and concur with their view that the experience of self-determination is an illusion. The difficulty, however, is precisely with this *"ought,"* which itself contains an implicit reference to freedom. For it makes no sense for determinists to tell us what we *ought* to do—using "ought," as they must, to appeal to our loyalty to the pursuit of truth—if we have no choice about it anyway.

We are left, then, with the conclusion that determinism, as a self-defeating theory, is unable to supply reasonable grounds for rejecting our experience of choosing in a free, self-determining manner. So it is reasonable to accept this experience as valid. Sometimes at least we do make free choices and, in making them, exercise our freedom of self-determination.

Questions for Review and Discussion

1. Several meanings of "freedom" are distinguished here. Make up examples, or find examples in other sources, to illustrate each.

2. "Responsibility" has different meanings corresponding to three of the senses of "freedom," namely, physical freedom, freedom to do as one pleases, and freedom of self-determination. What are these three senses of "responsibility"? For instance, what is the difference between saying that a pet cat is responsible for the scratches on a table top and that you and I are responsible for our own lives?

3. What kind of freedom do we have in view in feeling that we do not want others bossing us around?

4. We shall see later that morality is more than just a set of rules to be obeyed. But supposing that *were* all there is to it, would morality then be incompatible with freedom of self-determination?

5. Do you think it is very important to you personally whether you do or don't really have freedom of self-determination? If you think that you do have such freedom, are there times when you wish you didn't?

6. Some psychological determinists argue that since we always choose something inasmuch as it is good, we are only free until we see what is the greater good (or lesser evil), at which point we necessarily choose that alternative. What do you think of this argument for determinism?

7. Many who deny freedom of self-determination—Marxists, say, who hold that everything is determined by the dialectic of history—nevertheless maintain that we ought to be socially responsible: for instance, by engaging in revolutionary activity to bring about a new and better society. Are they being consistent? If you think not, why do you suppose intelligent people who hold such theories either do not see their inconsistency or are not bothered by it?

2. Being a Person Is a Lifelong Job

In the last chapter we looked closely at freedom, particularly in order to distinguish freedom in the sense of self-determination from freedom in other senses. Self-determination is at the heart of the matter which concerns us in ethics. Now we are ready to take a closer, longer look at freedom of self-determination: what it is and how it works.

Everyone has special problems, but there is one problem which is common to the lives of all of us, a problem whose solution gives meaning to life. It is how to be a person—how to be who one is.

In raising this question we are not being merely paradoxical, much less whimsical. There are, after all, false notions about human life which go to the fundamental question of what life is all about. When one says that the problem, the challenge, and the meaning of life lie in being a person, one is also rejecting several contrary views about life.

One of these is that the basic problem shared by all people is how to *remain* persons. Another is that the fundamental challenge is how to *become* persons. Our contention is that it is a question, not of remaining or becoming, but of being.

A. Remaining a Person Is Not the Problem

Nonpersons have a definite, given character. They are not self-determining but determined. To be fully themselves, they need only remain themselves, and they usually have little trouble doing so. As a writer once remarked, "a rose is a rose is a rose." A rose remains a rose; it is in no danger of becoming a dandelion or a turnip.

The same is true even in the case of nonpersons which are capable of acting and changing. Chemicals act and react; plants grow; animals perform in many different ways. In none of these cases, however, is real choice involved. Even animal behavior, which can be very complex and, as people say, "almost human," is not self-determined action. Instead it is a series of determined processes whose meaning comes from the naturally given consummations to which the behavior leads (action at the first level).

Thus an animal does not enjoy freedom of self-determination. It does not choose how it will act; its "choices" are entirely determined for it by its own instincts, by training, and by other circumstances over which it has no control, so that in a true sense it cannot act other than it does. Nor is an animal self-conscious; it has no self of which to be conscious.

The point is that a nonperson (a rock, a plant, an animal) perfectly fulfills itself by remaining what it is and by undergoing whatever changes happen to befall it. It does just what comes naturally, but since it has no freedom in the moral sense, its actions cannot be called morally "good" or morally "bad," "right" or "wrong."

For persons the situation is very different. For them it is not simply a question of remaining what they are or experiencing change without choice. Doing what comes naturally is not enough, even if it were possible just to relax and simply *be*. Rather, persons face the constant need to make choices and, in doing so, to determine themselves. How to use our freedom of self-determination—how, in other words, to *be persons*—is the challenge which continually confronts us.

B. Becoming a Person Is Not the Problem

The challenge of being a person is, however, by no means the same thing as becoming a person. Persons *are* persons; the question for them is how to be what they already are. If the problem were how to *become* a person, it would mean that personhood was some sort of definite, well-defined goal or objective toward which one could work by action at the second level. But this is not the case. Personhood, as we shall spend much of this book seeing, does not have this character. Moreover, it is something we already possess. We are not working toward the goal of becoming persons; we are coping constantly with difficult but fascinating problems of how to *be persons.*

Clearly it is true that one can become a better person or a worse one. But this is something entirely different from becoming a person. When we say that the question facing us is how to become better persons (or to avoid becoming worse ones), we are saying in effect that the fundamental problem we face is how to be persons. Questions of better and worse, good and bad, are questions of how to be.

Thus personhood is not something we achieve, as if it could be the objective of exclusively second-level action by which one labors in a calculating manner to achieve a well-defined goal. The self-made person is a myth, and a confusing one. The question of how to be a person is never settled once and for all in anybody's life. It is the basic question with which we all wrestle every day, and all the days, of our lives.

C. The Problem Is How to Be a Person

It requires no effort for a person to remain a person. One cannot do anything else. Nor does a person face the challenge of becoming a person. One cannot very well become what one already is.

But for a person the problem of *how to be what one is*—or, perhaps better, *who one is*—is an engrossing challenge. It is a constant question. It is also a lifelong task. The responsibility cannot be evaded. It involves the continual necessity of making choices. One thing about which we have no choice is the absolute imperative of choosing.

It might be objected that suicide offers a way of evading this responsibility. But this is not the case. Suicide is merely one way of responding to the challenge to be a person. Even if one looks at suicide as a kind of choosing-not-to-choose, an attempt to return to the uncomplicated existence of that which just *is*, it still remains true that this attempt itself is a choice. (Of course, this is true only of suicide when it is freely chosen; if suicidal behavior is a product of determining causes, then it is not a free choice, and neither is it a human action in the sense of being an action which registers on the moral scale.)

How to be a person is a problem of self-determination. Basically it is a problem which we resolve for ourselves by our choices at the third level of action. It is sometimes supposed that in choosing to do something we are only determining our action, not ourselves. This is not true. When we act at the third level—something we all must do at some time or other—we are not just determining our action; we are determining ourselves. In a real sense we are choosing how we will be persons. We are taking ourselves in hand and shaping ourselves through the exercise of our freedom of self-determination.

Not only individuals but groups of persons make choices. For example, when two people decide to get married, they make themselves an engaged couple. Many of our most important choices are choices made with others to do communal acts. In such choices the community determines itself, and so does everyone who shares in its choice and action. Thus, to appreciate the self-determination of any individual in all of its dimensions, one must take into account not only the large commitments and the smaller choices that he or she makes individually—more or less in isolation, as it were—but all the commitments and choices which that individual makes with others in diverse relationships ranging from intimate friendships to business associations, from participation in the politics of a civic community to participation in the worship of a religious community.

As we have seen, actions are of three kinds. At the first level are those whose meaning comes from the natural consummation to which they lead. If the action is performed, it naturally ends, barring some physical mishap, in this particular result. We do not give the action its meaning. The meaning is already there. In acting at this level we are not doing anything essentially different from what an animal or a small child could do. We are not determining ourselves; we are simply remaining the sort of thing we already are.

This is not to suggest, however, that persons can simply act instinctively—at the first and simplest level of action—and thereby absolve themselves of moral responsibility. As we have seen, all actions, including those at the third level, can be broken down into their units, and these units are actions at the first level. (A student engaged in study turns the pages of a book, moves his or her eyes from line to line of print, and so on.) But these simple units of action do have a moral significance when they are, as it were, the building blocks or the concrete embodiment of action at a higher level. This is not the case with animals and may not be the case with very young children unable to choose freely. But it is inescapably the case for persons who can make choices. Even a decision always to act instinctively would itself have moral significance which would color all the actions performed on the basis of this decision.

At the second level of action we act in order to achieve specific, limited goals which are separate and distinct from the action. The meaning of the action is derived from its goal. (The student in the example cited studies hard in order to pass an examination; passing the exam gives meaning to the studying.) We are not determining ourselves by acting at this level either. For the meaning of the action is derived from its goal, and the goal is outside oneself. Even if it is something very important to the person performing the action—even if passing this particular examination is going to determine whether the student does or doesn't pass the entire course—it is still external to him or her: it is not an aspect of the person's *self*. Action at this second level does not involve self-determination.

It is, however, not possible to choose to act always or even usually at the second level. Where choice is involved, there has to be some third-level action, some commitment to participate in a good. Even if one sought to orient one's life to the pursuit of limited, specific goals, leaving out as much as possible participation in fundamental values, one would be determining the cast of one's life by doing so. And this would be a sign of a fundamental commitment, a real act of self-determination, which itself would be a third-level action serving as a sort of umbrella for many actions at the second level. Like actions at the first level, actions at this second level also derive their moral significance from their relation to purposes that go beyond the limited objectives of the second-level actions themselves.

D. Self-Determination

Self-determination occurs at the third level of action. Here it is no longer a question of action whose meaning comes from the consummation to which it naturally leads; nor is it a question of action whose meaning comes from the specific, definite objective at which it aims. At this level the meaning of the action is derived instead from the anticipated benefit—the participation in the good one hopes for in performing the action. The student in our example studies in order to participate in the good of learning—or, perhaps, in order to pass an examination as part of a complex series of steps on the way to becoming a physician in order (now comes the good in which participation is sought) to work in the service of human life and health. It is at this level that morality properly enters the picture, that the problem and opportunity of being, or failing to be, fully a human person exist.

Notice that at this level of action we speak of "participating" in a good, not "achieving" a good. When we refer to achieving something, we are speaking of a limited, definite objective which we can, in effect, grasp and possess as a result of our activity. In speaking of participating in a good, however, we imply that we never fully realize or exhaust it; we also imply that this participation is not something which occurs only at the end of our activity and as a result of it, but rather that it takes place all the time we are performing the action.

Technique and precise calculation are possible at the second level of action, where we are concerned with achieving specific objectives, but they are not possible at the third level of action, where it is a question of participating in goods. For example, technique and calculation are necessary and appropriate to study well; random, haphazard study in distracting surroundings and circumstances is not likely to pay off in success on an examination. But there is no way of calculating how to participate in the good of learning, how to make study a worthwhile experience in itself without reference to a payoff for studying well.

In third-level action the benefit one seeks is indefinite and always extends beyond what is done to achieve participation in it. Unlike the second level of action, where one can calculate what and how much to study in order to pass a certain examination, on the third level it is nonsense to suppose that one can study just so much and then consider oneself to have exhausted all further possibility of participating in the good of learning.

Self-determination is possible only when precise calculation is not: that is, only at the third level of action. When we act in this way, we are truly determining ourselves because we are defining ourselves in relation to the fundamental goods which correspond to the capacities of our human personhood.

E. Character and "Fundamental Option"

As we shall see later, the fundamental human goods involved in third-level action are in fact aspects of the human personality; thus we form our characters by the choices which we make at this level. Character might be defined as the result produced in and upon a person by the total impact, for good or ill, of making and carrying out his or her choices. This is far-reaching indeed: it includes self-determination in the will, an impact upon the individual's way of thinking about things, the orientation of emotion, a distinct coloration to the way things are experienced, and even bodily changes.

When people choose at the third level, this is how they *are* until they change their minds: the orientation thus given to one's life remains until it is changed. And it can be changed only by a new act of self-determination. That is why even small actions, if they are third-level ones, are important to character formation. When an action, whether large or small, involves self-determination, it contributes to the formation of character.

An analogy with intellectual knowledge helps make this clear. Once we have come to know something, the knowledge doesn't go away when we stop thinking about it, for we continue to be people who know something about calculus or the history of the French monarchy in the seventeenth century even though we may not be adverting to our knowledge here and now. The next time one thinks about the same thing, one starts where one left off, and what one already knows opens the way to new questions and expanding knowledge. Similarly, a choice determines the self unless and until another, incompatible choice is made. Like knowledge, choices last.

There are two ways in which people make themselves the persons they are by their choices. First, by some large choices an individual accepts a certain status, undertakes a certain way of life, enters into a certain relationship. Second, as we have already said in various ways, choices actualize and limit the self in relation to the fundamental goods which fulfill persons and so shape one's orientation toward further possibilities.

It is important to see actions in this context. Often we think of them as units of transitory behavior, with little or no relationship to our *real* selves. This is a common attitude for us when we commit immoral actions and feel uneasy about them: we prefer to think of our deeds as something apart from ourselves—something we can do and enjoy but then easily discard like an empty beer can or a pair of dirty socks. But this is not so—at least not with actions that really come from the heart, really are the carrying-out of self-determining choices. Such deeds are part of the process by which we both determine and express who we are. It is in this sense that Karl Barth says, "One is what one does."

As we have suggested, moreover, choices are constitutive not only for individuals but for communities. A certain social choice in which two individuals participate constitutes a married couple; another social choice in which a great many more persons participate constitutes the political society called a nation (to the extent, that is, that the political society is a true community rooted in the common commitment of its members to certain goods; often, however, political societies lack essential features of real community).

These considerations suggest why ethical theories are mistaken which say that in ethical terms it is only the overall orientation of one's life which is important and not individual actions. Certainly the overall orientation of one's life is of crucial importance. This orientation comes about, however, both through the large commitments which we make and also through our smaller choices to implement (or fail to implement) our commitments.

Some theories of so-called fundamental option posit a mysterious, comprehensive exercise of freedom—an opting of which we are never even conscious—which is supposed to determine the overall orientation of our lives. Leaving aside anything else which might be said of this, we make only two remarks. First, it is impossible to verify the existence of a freedom which, by the theory itself, is never accessible to consciousness. Second, it is entirely possible to account for the overall orientation of our lives by our conscious exercise of freedom of self-determination, without positing the existence of anything so mysterious as a "fundamental option."

In summary, then, we can say that although the overall orientation of one's life is indeed most important, this overall orientation is self-determined by one's choices. Among these the large choices, such as major commitments, count for most; but the smaller choices also are of great importance, since it is by them that one fulfills (or fails to fulfill) one's commitments and settles one's moral identity: the faithful (or unfaithful) spouse, the industrious (or lazy) student, the honest (or corrupt) judge, and so on. Through a unique blend of large and small choices each one of us self-determines himself or herself as the unique person he or she is.

F. Giving Meaning to Life

Lastly, it is appropriate to point out that life has more meaning when one sees the good which is at stake in situations and chooses and acts for the sake of participating in that good. Some acts which are, from one point of view, second-level actions can, by a change of intention, become actions at the third level. In the example of studying, at the second level one studies in order to pass an exam, whereas at the third level one studies in order, say, to learn for the sake of learning itself.

Lest all this sound moralistic with respect to third-level action, we hasten to point out that it is precisely at this level that one can be guilty of moral evil as well as moral good; that efficient, well-planned action at the second level is a necessary, important, and in itself commendable element of human life; and that, as we have already remarked, one seldom if ever acts *only* at the second level but almost always performs actions which partake in some way of third-level commitment.

Nevertheless, it is fair to say that a person who is concentrating on acting at the second level is, to that extent, necessarily looking to the future—to an objective which is to be achieved by the action—whereas a person acting at the third level is living meaningfully in the present, participating here and now in a good through the action which is being performed. And there is a certain absurdity in habitually concentrating on the second-level aspect of what one does—always focusing on future objectives. This robs life of its present meaning, because it situates meaning in something which is always yet to come rather than in something now present in which one is at this moment participating.

The point is not that one should always make the best of any situation, however bad. There are some situations one should bend every effort to change. We are speaking, however, of deriving the most meaning from one's present action, whatever it may be. Action has more meaning—more content, one might say—when it is action at the third level.

And just as habitually acting at the third level gives more meaning to life, so it also gives more meaning to death. A person who habitually acts at the third level, the level of self-determination, has participated in human goods throughout the course of life. Such a person's life is a meaningful whole at no matter what point it happens to end. By contrast, the life of one who habitually gives preeminence to the second-level aspect of action, emphasizing limited objectives and paying little attention to the challenge and opportunity of participating in fundamental goods, will be deprived of meaning to the extent that death finds such a person, as it must, with objectives yet to be achieved. This analysis of action helps us to understand self-determination better. It is not a matter of achieving specific, limited goals, although doing so is in itself proper and necessary, but of participating in fundamental human goods.

Next we shall turn to the question of happiness. Everyone wants to be happy, but at least sometimes most of us are uncertain about what being happy really means. In considering this question we shall stress the notion of fulfillment, meaning by this the most authentic and satisfying happiness of which people are capable. But by no means is it immediately apparent what "fulfillment" means either. Thus we shall begin by examining some inadequate notions and then seek, in chapter four, to determine in what fulfillment really consists. To anticipate what we shall discover, we shall see that authentic fulfillment corresponds to action at the third level.

Questions for Review and Discussion

1. What is the difference between "person" as we use the word here and "personality" as it is used in psychology or everyday conversation?
2. How does the idea of "person" held by someone who thinks the fundamental problem of life is how to remain or become a person differ from the idea of "person" developed in this chapter?
3. To engage in sexual intercourse as animals do is an action at the first level; to engage in intercourse as a prostitute does is an action at the second level; to engage in intercourse as a deeply loving married couple does, simply to express and celebrate their love of each other, is an action at the third level. Give other examples of actions at different levels, including, if you can, cases in which the outward behavior remains the same.
4. The three levels of action correspond to three senses of freedom distinguished in chapter one. Why are there not distinct levels of action corresponding to political freedom, ideal freedom, and creative freedom?
5. Do you think that people in our culture, in thinking and speaking about action, usually have in mind second-level or third-level

actions? What difference does it make to a person's view of life as a whole which of these two levels of action is his or her customary model of action?

6. If third-level action is really determinative of the self, what do the characteristics of this kind of action—for example, the impossibility of calculation—indicate about the sort of reality a person is?

7. The concept of self-determination is sometimes criticized as individualistic. Here, however, we argue that self-determination is also relevant to communities of persons. Besides the examples cited in the text, find and develop some other examples which show this process at work in communities.

8. If character is the result of self-determination and self-determination is all it's cracked up to be, how can one account for the fact that there are evidently some persons of authentically bad character?

9. The three levels of action are related to time in different ways. The motto of the first level might be "Live for the present." The motto of the second level might be "Invest in your future." How is the third level of action related to time?

10. Sometimes it is possible to change what one is doing from second-level action to action at the third level simply by a change of intention. But is it always easy to do so? And is it always a good idea?

3. What Fulfillment Isn't

Everyone wants fulfillment, but the obstacles are formidable. Although it would be naive to suppose that the lack of a correct intellectual understanding of fulfillment is the only obstacle (for one could know perfectly well what fulfillment consists in, yet not be fulfilled), it would be no less naive to suppose that misunderstandings play no part. At the very least people are more likely to reach fulfillment, whatever it may consist in, if they have a clear and accurate notion of what it means to be fulfilled than if they confuse some other experience or state with this one.

Many people's ideas of fulfillment are dominated by one or the other of two experiences. One is the experience of intense pleasure, typically felt upon reaching the consummation of a first-level action (for example, that first sip of cold, clear water after a hot and dusty hike). The other is the experience of seeking a future objective, working toward it, and finally attaining it. This is the experience of satisfaction upon reaching the goal sought in a second-level action. While either of these experiences can be, and often is, mistaken for fulfillment, neither provides a good point of departure for understanding it. Both fall short of the fulfillment which we would all like.

A. The Problem with Pleasure

One difficulty in equating intense pleasure with fulfillment is that the experience of pleasure is a value only for a part of the self. In saying this we do not mean to suggest that pleasure is identified with the "lower," "animal" part of human beings and fulfillment with the "higher," "spiritual" part. (We would not accept such a division of the human person into two parts.) The point, instead, is that pleasure, whenever and however experienced, is limited to consciousness and does not take into consideration the living whole of a human being.

To take an extreme example which makes the point quite clear, it is at least conceivable that a person could derive a great deal of pleasure from eating poisoned food—and die as a result of doing so. However pleasurable the individual's state of consciousness might have been while the food was being eaten, one can hardly conclude that the experience was good and fulfilling for this person. This is scarcely what we mean when we speak of fulfillment.

Another illustration, this one out of the realm of science fiction, similarly dramatizes the problem with pleasure and makes it clear why pleasure does not meet a reasonable expectation of what it means to be fulfilled.

Suppose it were possible to keep a human brain alive in a laboratory and feed it a continuous stream of artificial brain waves in order to give it the experience of a constantly pleasurable life. The brain would be in a kind of self-absorbed nirvana, insulated from all pain and at all times enjoying the consciousness of intense pleasure. Would this be worth doing (not from the point of view of scientific experimentation but from the point of view of bestowing fulfillment upon this particular brain)? Hardly. There would be no point in creating a merely pleasurable state of consciousness, apart from real experience and action in a real world. Even if the thing could be done, it would be meaningless, would make no sense. Whatever else one might say of the pleasure-experiencing brain, no one would call its condition one of human fulfillment.

This points to the fact that states of consciousness, even pleasurable ones, have no meaning and no value in themselves apart from the life which they reflect. A state of consciousness only has meaning in relation to the life of which it is consciousness. If there were really no lived life (as would be the case with the brain in the laboratory), the state of consciousness would be meaningless.

Moreover, because pleasure is limited to consciousness, it is private and can be no more than private; none of us has direct access to another's consciousness. This points to the inescapably individualistic tendency of pleasure-seeking, even when people seek pleasure together. In such cases the experience joins them in mutual self-absorption, each attending mainly to his or her own satisfaction. Real fulfillment, by contrast, is not and cannot be individualistic, since no one is truly fulfilled except with others. Evidently, though, this must involve something which can be shared, and this rules out pleasure as a state of consciousness with an inherent privacy. Rather, what can be shared are a joint undertaking, work together for a purpose, and common commitment to and service of goods in which people can participate together.

Consider two tennis games. One is a match involving two intensely competitive players, each intent on nothing but the satisfaction of outdoing the other; the second game is a good-natured encounter between two friends playing for the fun of the sport and the enjoyment of each other's company. The first two players are seeking individualistic pleasure; the second two, joined in communion, find satisfaction in all the benefits of playing the game, which otherwise would be beyond the reach of either alone.

In thinking out an ethics, then, it simply confuses matters to talk about pleasure, as a state of consciousness, as if it were a norm for action. Fulfillment, in the sense in which we shall explain it below, provides such a norm, but pleasure is incapable of doing so. Pleasure pertains to action at the first level. And although such action is part of life, the meaning of life cannot be reduced simply to this level.

B. Fulfillment Isn't Looking Ahead

Other thinkers who have sought to understand the meaning of fulfillment have taken as their starting point the experience described earlier: identifying a goal, working to achieve it, and at last attaining it. This approach locates the ultimate meaning of life in the outcome of action at the second level. St. Augustine interpreted the Christian promise of heavenly beatitude in light of the experience of working to achieve an objective. Today many people who no longer believe in God, heaven, or hell still identify happiness with the pursuit and attainment of goals and seek fulfillment in this experience.

The notion is admittedly attractive, not least because this kind of action is indeed a necessary and important part of life. Still, the idea that authentic fulfillment lies in the pursuit and attainment of goals is not really satisfactory either. As we have noted earlier, once people achieve one goal, they immediately begin the pursuit of another. Fulfillment lies always somewhere in the future, and that which lies perpetually in the future does not meet our expectations of what it should mean to be fulfilled here and now.

Several considerations make this clear. One problem with identifying fulfillment with the pursuit of future objectives is that the objectives *are* future, and a person who lives mainly for the future has to a significant degree robbed the present of meaning. Living in this way, one in effect makes the present a mere means to an ulterior end, whatever that may be. In this view of things the present has little or no value in itself; its value comes instead from what it contributes to or takes away from the achieving of the objective.

A life lived in this way is a life half lived. Take the case of a man whose whole life is devoted obsessively and totally to the goal of climbing Mount Everest. Let us suppose that in literal, cold fact he cares only about success in reaching his goal, toward which everything else in his life is directed. He spends years in rigorous training and preparations: scaling lesser peaks, developing his skills, organizing his expedition, planning his assault on the final objective. At last the time comes. He and his party set off up the slopes of Everest. Halfway up, the mountain climber falls from a ledge and is killed. Everest remains unclimbed.

One's natural reaction to such a story is that the tragic accident robbed the mountain climber's life of meaning. His life was built around the fanatical pursuit of a clearly defined objective, scaling Mount Everest. He never achieved the objective; therefore his failure to achieve it emptied his life of significance. But is this really the case?

Looked at more closely, it appears that the accident cutting short this life spotlighted a glaring fact about it: the life was empty and meaningless all along. How, after all, could reaching the peak of Mount Everest have given retrospective significance to everything that had gone before? For the fact about what has gone before is that it has *gone*, and either there was meaning there all along or there was never any meaning. If the mountain climber's death, short of his goal, makes us conclude that his life was without meaning, this must be because there was never any meaning in it. Even the successful ascent of Everest could not have invested meaning after the fact in the years preceding that event.

Not only individuals but groups, even whole societies, sometimes make the mistake of locating fulfillment in a future state of affairs. Marxism, for example, views the members of the present generation as mere means to be used and sacrificed in bringing about a wonderful new world which will emerge from the ashes of the revolution. It is the same error—sacrificing the present to the future—that individuals make when they radically subordinate their present selves to future objectives.

As we have said before, we do not intend an indictment of second-level action, by which one identifies specific goals, calculates ways and means of reaching them, and works to achieve them. This way of acting is necessary and appropriate. Failure to perform well at this level can result in a chaotic and ultimately disastrous kind of life, one reflective of its own particular kind of immoral orientation (a fondness, say, for "spontaneity," meaning a pattern of erratic and self-indulgent behavior, or an ineffectual commitment to "ideals" without the seriousness which causes responsible persons to take practical steps to realize the ideals to which they are committed). Nevertheless, the pursuit of specific goals cannot, by itself, make for a satisfactory and meaningful life; it does not represent an adequate understanding of fulfillment.

If our lives have meaning, it exists here and now. Making their meaning hinge on something in the future is tantamount to draining them of meaning. What the man who wished to climb Everest needed was a way of living his life which would have made it rich with meaning whether he succeeded, failed, or died before even setting out on the expedition.

There is another, even more fundamental difficulty in identifying fulfillment with the pursuit of future objectives. It is that, as far as we know, there is no finally satisfactory state. If fulfillment lies somewhere ahead, then—at least in our experience—fulfillment is never reached. It is a universal human experience that no one goal gives lasting satisfaction. At the instant we possess one thing, we begin to crave something else. If this is fulfillment, then fulfillment must consist in the frustrating experience of never being really satisfied and always seeking something more, something beyond what we already have.

C. A Goal to Be Achieved after Death?

A theologian in the tradition of St. Augustine might reply that this is an accurate enough description of this life, but this life is not all. The experience of lasting satisfaction, such a theologian would say, is always denied us in this world but is enjoyed after death, in eternal union with God.

Even theologically this is not a satisfying position. For such a theologian also holds that God does nothing useless and depends on nothing to achieve his purposes. But if eternal union with God is all that counts, and if this union is altogether future, then what use does human existence in this world have? Either it has none (in which case God *has* done something useless in causing it to be), or it is a necessary means (in which case God *needs* it for his end), or it has value in itself— which the theologian in the tradition of St. Augustine is not prepared to concede.

Thomas Aquinas, incidentally, took an important step toward resolving the problem by explaining that the value of our present life lies in the fact that in it we share in God's causing of the future, and in doing so we are more like him than if we shared only in his happiness without living through the process of attaining it. One might also argue that it is a mistake to think of *eternal* life as a purely *future* objective, since this is to treat eternity as if it were only another aspect of time.

In any case, to say that our present life derives meaning only from our experience after this life is beside the point as far as ethics is concerned. Ethics deals with this life. It asks whether and how fulfillment can be ours here and now—whether and how actions which we perform at the present time can also make us fulfilled at the present time. As human beings we live from moment to moment. Our lives are made up of these passing moments. To say that fulfillment cannot somehow be found in the unique, passing moments of our lives is to say in effect that human life is meaningless.

Still another very common approach to life is to combine pleasure-seeking and the pursuit of future objectives. For people who do this, life is not all one thing or all the other, but a combination of, or an oscillation between, the two. A crude instance is provided by the unlettered soul who slaves all week in order to earn the money to go on an enormous bender over the weekend; yet in their own ways more sophisticated people often manage to act in a not dissimilar manner. An approach to life along these lines combines the weaknesses of both pleasure seeking and the pursuit of future objectives.

The problem of fulfillment, then, comes down to this: How can we be fulfilled continually and how can we be fulfilled now? Fulfillment cannot be mere pleasure, because pleasure is a sometime thing; even as we experience it, it slips away—and we have all had the experience of feeling pleasure while knowing in our hearts that we are not really fulfilled. Nor can fulfillment lie in future objectives. If it did, fulfillment would be always deferred, always in the future, and never now. Even as we reach one goal, we immediately begin to crave another. Yet we live our lives now, not in the future, and *now* is where we must find meaning and fulfillment if we are to find them at all.

To put our conclusion in terms of levels of action: Neither the pleasure that arises from first-level action nor the pursuit of future objectives and the sense of satisfaction in reaching them which are involved in second-level action can give meaning to human life. We must look toward fulfillment as a fullness of life corresponding to third-level action. Human life derives meaning from participation in fundamental human goods through third-level action; if such a life is also morally good, its goodness will arise from doing what has just been described in a morally good manner. Next we shall begin to see what this means.

Questions for Review and Discussion

1. Although "pleasure," "joy," "satisfaction," and "happiness" are closely related in meaning, they have diverse connotations. Explore the differences, beginning by thinking of cases which exemplify the special sense of each word.

2. Our argument against identifying pleasure with fulfillment rests on the premise that pleasure is limited to consciousness and consciousness is not all there is to a human being. If personality is equated with consciousness, what is left out?

3. Does someone engaging in an act for sheer pleasure tend to identify himself with consciousness alone? Compare this with an act in which one engages with another person or persons and in which real communication occurs.

4. There is a conflict in our culture at present between middle-class ideals of achievement and success and the demand for instant gratification. Discuss this conflict in relation to the ideas about fulfillment developed in this chapter.

5. Marxism condemns religion as the opium of the people—"pie in the sky when you die." At the same time it argues that the present generation must be sacrificed for the sake of bringing about a perfect society in the future. Are these positions consistent?

6. Much education is future-directed, organized as a preparation for later life. Discuss the demand for relevance in education in light of this chapter's criticism of identifying happiness with future objectives.

7. Why is it that no one goal a person reaches in life gives lasting satisfaction?

8. If you knew you were going to die—in one year, one month, one day, or one hour—what difference would that knowledge make to you? Does the answer tell you anything about the way in which you find meaning in life at present?

4. Fulfillment Is Being a Complete Person

What is fulfillment? In the last chapter we examined two suggested answers and found them wanting. Fulfillment is not the same thing as fleeting, intense pleasure—an experience limited to consciousness alone. Nor is fulfillment identified with seeking future objectives which, even if achieved, provide only a momentary satisfaction before one sets off restlessly in pursuit of yet other goals.

In seeing what fulfillment is not, however, we have also achieved some insight into what it does mean to be fulfilled. It must be something continuous and here and now, present in each unique moment of our lives, yet not limited to any one. Obviously, though, such a general notion leaves many questions unanswered, including the question of how to *be* fulfilled. We need to look much more closely now at this notion of fulfillment in order to see what it really entails.

A. A Whole Life

Aristotle developed a theory of fulfillment (often translated "happiness") which avoided the mistake of identifying it either with pleasure or with the pursuit and attainment of specific, limited objectives. Fulfillment for Aristotle is a whole life in which a human being's peculiar capacity, the ability to reason, is realized both in theoretical knowledge and in rationally guided action.

There is much truth in Aristotle's analysis. He was correct in locating fulfillment in a whole life (rather than in isolated episodes or in future expectations). However, he neglected to consider two other important pieces of the puzzle: the role of self-determination and the fact that other human capacities besides reason make their unique, irreducible contributions to what it means to be fulfilled.

Aristotle looked at human beings from a particular perspective and concluded that their peculiar excellence—that which distinguishes them from every other kind of being in the world—is their reason. But if we consider humans as beings who constitute themselves through their own self-determination, it is clear that other areas of life are equally necessary to the fullness of the person. A person is not a disembodied intellect; a person engages in other kinds of activity besides intellectual activity, and these other spheres of experience also make their special contributions to personhood.

Each aspect of human nature, along with the activity corresponding to it, is properly personal. So, for example, human bodily functions are not animal behavior but truly and properly human, personal behavior. Aristotle and his followers go wrong in part by not seeing that the so-called "lower" levels of the rational animal are different from their counterparts in animals without reason, not just because they are organized and integrated under rational direction but, more basically, because they are aspects of a person.

If we could identify ourselves exclusively with the ideal of rationality, then self-realization and self-fulfillment would lie exclusively in rational activity. But the same is true of other purposes and ideals: aesthetic experience, play, even the day-to-day activities necessary for physical survival and well-being. All of these are valid, necessary areas of human activity and experience, and all offer opportunities for self-realization and fulfillment to the extent that they involve and express our freedom of self-determination.

But none of them encompasses the whole of human life and experience. Each is part of the story, but no one of them sums up in itself what it means to be a person. To be a person one must respect the unique demands made by each and all of them.

We see then that it is not enough to say that fulfillment lies in the use of reason. Indeed personal fulfillment *does* lie in the use of reason, but it also lies in the use of our human faculties for physical survival and well-being, for play, and for aesthetic experience. All are aspects of a human being.

Thus to be fulfilled will, as Aristotle suggested, mean living a whole life. In order to do this, however, one must take a comprehensive view of what human life is. It is not limited to one area of human capability. Instead it embraces all aspects of the person.

True, no one person can realize to the full what it means to be a person in all areas of life (or, for that matter, in any single area). But that is not the point. The point is that to be fulfilled we must, minimally, remain open to all our possibilities as persons and to all the possibilities of other persons as well. This requires that we refrain from treating one part of the person, one category of activity, and one sort of fulfilling good, as taking precedence over all the rest, so that all the rest are reduced to the status of mere means for the realization of the supreme good.

Aristotle's theory of fulfillment led him to conclude that people who cannot rationally regulate their own activities are natural slaves. Our theory of fulfillment leads to the conclusion that no one is a natural slave because everyone is a person. Whatever truly fulfills any person's human capacities is important, not solely insofar as it is regulated by reason but also and in the first place insofar as it is freely chosen.

B. The Question of Commitment

Mere openness to our possibilities as persons, however, is not enough. Being a person is not something passive; it involves self-determination. Choices are necessary. We must settle for ourselves the issue of how to be the persons that we are.

Self-determination is only possible when calculation is not. Calculation is a necessary part of life, but it does not enter into the action of self-determination (although precise, correct calculation is frequently required to achieve the goals and objectives which make it possible for one's self-determination to express itself in practical, efficacious ways).

Helen wants to buy a reliable used car; therefore she calculates what is necessary to achieve the objective (how to raise the money, how to select a dealer, how to pick out a car, and so on) and performs the required steps in sequence. Her calculations may or may not be correct, and, depending on their correctness, she will or will not achieve her objective: purchasing a reliable automobile at a reasonable price. But the process of calculation is a comparatively simple matter (even though mistakes can be made) because the only question that need be answered about a particular action is whether it contributes to achieving the goal. In other words, the various alternatives can be measured by a common denominator: their effectiveness in reaching the objective. They are accepted or rejected, on the basis of calculation, by how they stack up in relation to the common denominator.

In the case of buying a used car one can literally approach the task with a checklist of criteria which must be met—price, mileage, condition of the engine and the tires, and so forth— and which, if met, guarantee successful achievement of the goal. Suppose, though, that Helen is a mother who needs a car to carry out a number of her responsibilities in that role. While it is certainly possible to identify specific goals and objectives, such as buying a reliable used car, which both support and express her commitment, it is clear that the self-determining commitment in question here, that of being a mother, is not subject to the same calculation. Calculation is necessary and important to accomplish many of the specific things which mothers need to accomplish, but on a more profound level calculation cannot tell a woman whether or how to *be* a mother.

Self-determination is possible and necessary in situations where there is no common reference against which to weigh and measure alternatives. In such situations each alternative is appealing in its own way and in its own frame of reference. One could choose any one of the alternatives without being mistaken about facts or in one's reasoning. For in a situation like this, one is not simply making a choice of appropriate means to a limited, well-defined end. Instead, one is choosing among various goods which underlie the whole structure of personhood. In choosing this way—to pursue one purpose rather than another—we really decide what will constitute ourselves. We determine the kind of persons we will be. These acts of self-determination can extend very far; they can in fact control and shape our lives for an indefinite future. An act of this kind is "commitment" in a strict sense.

We shall have a great deal to say about commitments in this book, since they are of enormous importance to the question of self-determination lying at the heart of ethics. Here in summary form we note only some of the principal characteristics of this kind of free choice. First, commitments bear in one way or another upon purposes involving harmony, either among elements of our personhood or in our relationships with other persons. So, for example, a decision to reform one's life, a marriage promise, and an oath of allegiance are all instances of commitment. Commitments, however, are not only to purposes but to the persons with whom we hope to share in some fulfillment by pursuing these purposes. Thus, while a commitment requires undertaking service to a good, it also involves willing to realize the good in others for *their* sakes, not merely as a means to one's own participation in the good.

Commitments have a cumulative character, with no definite end to the accumulation of the particular good. Within a commitment there will undoubtedly be a nested sequence of lesser acts which are consistent with and partially fulfill the overarching commitment. Yet no one of these by itself totally fulfills the commitment—in no single action does Helen, the woman from our earlier example, totally realize what it means to be a mother—and in fact all of her acts together do not exhaust the commitment (there always remains some further way of unfolding the meaning of motherhood), which is essentially open-ended and always capable of being realized further. Making a commitment, then, involves much more than simply setting a long range goal for oneself. Goals can, and should, be pursued efficiently, with foresight and calculation; but the process of carrying out a commitment is essentially a voyage of self-discovery and self-determination through continued exploration of the many facets of a basic human good.

Friendship is a good example of such a commitment. In a friendship there is no point at which the friends can say, in effect, "So much and no more. We have now fully achieved this friendship and need do nothing more about it." They can of course break off the friendship, but then they are ending the commitment. As long as the commitment—and the friendship—endures, there is no point at which they have finally achieved friendship and can stop acting in ways which fulfill their mutual commitment.

The life of scholarship provides another example. As long as a person is committed to such a life, he or she goes on accumulating knowledge, without ever being able to feel that scholarship has finally been achieved and learning can now stop. A person who did decide to stop accumulating knowledge would in effect be deciding to withdraw from the commitment to a life of scholarship.

Marriage provides one of the very best examples of commitment. Jokingly or not, people often say of their marriages, "We didn't realize what we were getting into." Joking aside, they are entirely correct. People never know what they are getting into in making such a commitment, since it is absolutely impossible to foresee (that is, to calculate) all the actions that will be required in living out and living up to the commitment. It is impossible for a couple to know what, in specific terms, the reality of their marriage will be until they live it.

These examples suggest several other important things. First, "commitment" as it is used here is not an ideal; it is very real, even commonplace. For better or worse everybody makes commitments of one kind or another. Second, however, commitments *are* "for better or worse"—the mere fact that one has made a commitment does not mean that it is commendable and good. We shall see more about this later; here it is sufficient to remark that one can, for example, be committed to a life of crime, committed to corrupting and mutually destructive friendships, committed to the pursuit of knowledge for selfish and self-centered reasons, and so on. Even in such cases, no doubt, the individual is serving some aspects of real human goods; yet the fact remains that there is something morally flawed about such commitments.

Finally, it would be false to suppose that the process leading up to a commitment is always fully self-conscious and explicit. Many commitments, even fundamental ones like marriage and choice of career, are backed into by people who do not advert very clearly to what they are doing right up to the moment of truth itself—and at *that* moment they feel themselves so boxed in by the many small, careless choices which they have already made leading up to this point that there is no alternative except to follow through and commit themselves. Such commitments are real ones, yet the process which leads to them is poor, and prospects for their future fulfillment are not very bright.

In other cases people drift into life-orienting situations without making any commitment at all. For example, students sometimes pursue a particular course of study because it amuses them, because it makes their parents happy, because they would rather not go out and get a job, and so on—and then one day they wake up to find themselves professionally engaged in that line of work without having really chosen it. At that point they *can* make a commitment to what they are doing, but there is no guarantee they will.

To repeat: In large commitments which organize our lives, we never quite know at the start what we are getting into. Only gradually, through creative effort and experience, do we begin to understand the meaning of the commitment. And only gradually do we work out in practice the implications of the self we have constituted by making the commitment. What we are to be does not exist at the time the commitment is made; what we are to be is what we *become* through individual actions performed under the umbrella of the fundamental commitment and in response to what is required to carry it out.

There are, in short, two aspects to self-determination within the framework of a commitment. What we are to be depends, on the one hand, on our commitment to a purpose which transcends us and, on the other, to the creative working out of the implications of that initial commitment in the circumstances of life which we encounter.

One other thing needs to be said here about calculation. Calculation is definitely possible within a commitment. In fact, it is not merely possible: it is highly advisable to use calculation and technique, as in the case of Helen, the woman buying a used car, in order to achieve particular objectives which are consistent with and serve one's commitments. Acting merely on the basis of impulse and emotions, rather than rationally, does not give a more human character to activity, nor is it more likely to be an apt way of realizing one's commitments in practice. Commitments require projects—second-level acts— to carry them out, and projects require technique and calculation for their successful execution.

So, for example, having decided on an appropriate gift for a friend, one needs to bring calculation into play in order to carry out the project of gift-giving successfully. Where can I get the best quality without wasting money? How can I ensure that the item has the proper guarantee or warranty? What must I do to make certain that the gift is delivered on the right day at a convenient time? Here calculation is directed toward an objective (the giving of a gift) which is itself directed toward participation in and realization of the good involved in the commitment (the relationship of friendship between my friend and me).

C. How Self-Determination Works

Actions in and by which we truly constitute ourselves have a number of special characteristics. We have already seen what some of these are, but it is helpful to make a list here in order to get a clearer understanding of self-determination. Among the characteristics of such actions, then, are the following:

1. When acting in this way we cannot calculate what behavior will be appropriate for our purpose. Calculation comes into play, quite appropriately, in seeking specific, well-defined objectives outside ourselves. But when it is a question of determining ourselves, technique and calculation will not do the job.

2. We cannot act efficiently in carrying out our commitments. There is, for instance, no efficient way to fulfill the commitment to a friendship or a marriage. Of course people can and should act efficiently in pursuing goals which are consistent with and help to realize their basic commitments.

But these goals do not sum up the whole of a commitment, which serves as a sort of overarching umbrella under which many specific goals are embraced and many individual actions performed.

3. We cannot force anyone else, nor can we ourselves be forced, to act in this way. To be sure, it is possible to force somebody else to perform an action, but, by definition, that which one is forced to do is not fully an act of self-determination. This is not an argument for never forcing people to do or refrain from doing certain things: small children should be required to brush their teeth, emotionally disturbed people should be restrained from jumping out of windows. But people cannot be forced to determine themselves; they can only determine themselves on the basis of their own choices.

4. Often, in doing what we must, we can personalize the activity—make it an act of self-determination—by consciously locating and choosing in it a purpose to which we are or can be committed. One can, for instance, study simply in order to pass a course—period. Or one can study in order to pass a course in order to get a degree which will make it possible to pursue a profession to which one is truly committed. Or one can study just for the sake of increasing one's knowledge (with passing the course a kind of desirable by-product). In the latter two cases the act of studying has become more personally meaningful, because it relates to a commitment which expresses one's self-determination. We can frequently make the necessary events and activities of our lives more meaningful in this way. That is not to say one should not try to change unsatisfactory conditions in one's life and society that can and should be changed. It is only to point out a way of deriving the most meaning from parts of life that cannot or should not be changed.

5. Observation of outward behavior by itself cannot decisively establish whether or not a person is acting through commitment. To go back to our example, the student studying simply to pass a course will very likely *look* the same and perform the same external actions as the student studying out of love of learning for its own sake. The difference is not in their outward behavior but in their intentions.

6. Although it is possible for an individual to make a commitment which no one else shares in making, commitments are generally made not only to but with others. Very often, too, those *to* whom and those *with* whom a commitment is made are the same. (Marriage is a case in point.) Thus the self-determination of commitment most often has a communal character: through these acts of choice and the implementing choices which follow we constitute ourselves not alone as persons but as persons in community.

These characteristics have one thing in common: all illustrate the fact that self-determining action for a purpose intrinsic to the action is quite different from action which is determined by its orientation to an extrinsic goal. However much alike such actions may look from the outside, they are in fact radically different on the inside.

In determining ourselves through commitments we shape our lives. We establish our way of looking at things. We determine the meaning of the experiences we will have. Thus, we really create situations in a moral sense, because we give the events of our lives and the facts of the world the unique meaning which they have *for us*. This is in sharp contradiction to the argument of so-called situation ethics, which implies that the meaning of a situation is something given, over which we have no control and which we can only passively accept.

How then are we complete persons? This will be the case if our commitments meet certain criteria (which we shall discuss later), if they all fit together to form a harmonious whole, and if we live out our lives in accord with such a harmonious set of commitments. Then we shall be complete persons. And this is what fulfillment is.

But, as we have indicated repeatedly, we are not and cannot be "complete persons" in isolation from others. Many of our most important commitments have a communal character: we join with others to participate in human goods and in this way, with them, to bring about our fulfillment and theirs. In the next chapter we shall look further at the implications of this fact.

Questions for Review and Discussion

1. Explain how Aristotle's notion of fulfillment resembles but is also significantly different from the one presented here.

2. What are some possible reasons why Aristotle overlooked the capacity of self-determination as central to the human person?

3. What implications might the differences between Aristotle's position and ours have as far as issues involving "mere life" are concerned, for instance, the question of capital punishment or the question of euthanasia for the senile or insane?

4. "Choice" has two senses, corresponding to the second and third levels of action. Distinguish these two senses from each other.

5. Make a diagram representing the relationship between the subordinate ends, intermediate ends, and a final goal in second-level action. Make a different diagram expressing the relationship between subordinate acts and the overarching commitment in third-level action.

6. To what extent can expressions like "subjective" and "objective," "fixed" and "indeterminate," apply to diverse aspects of a commitment?

7. Why (in terms of the analysis of commitment in this chapter) do newly married couples often begin to experience difficulties as soon as the honeymoon ends?

8. Some people talk about an "art of living" as if there were an applied science (such as psychology) which could give us directions for living a good life. If the position developed in this chapter is correct, can there be an "art of living" in this sense? Leaving aside what is said here, what arguments can you think of for or against the possibility of devising an art of living?

9. We cannot force anyone else to make a commitment, nor can we ourselves be forced to do so. How, then, can people have any effect at all on one another's commitments?

10. Sociologists dealing with topics involving religion often experience serious difficulty in finding objective criteria by which to measure how "religious" different people are. Why do you think this is so?

11. It may be impossible to tell the outward behavior of a person acting for an intrinsic goal from that of another person committed to doing something for its own sake. But if you know them well, it's likely that you will see certain signs of their true attitude. Apart from what they say if asked, what might such signs include?

5. Persons Complete One Another

"No man is an island," wrote John Donne. "Hell is other people," according to a character in a play by Jean-Paul Sartre. For better or worse (sometimes better, sometimes worse) each of us is linked to many other people by an intricate network of social relationships. Sociologists, political scientists, and other specialists make this evident fact an object of constant study and analysis. For the student of ethics, too, it raises great and lasting issues. What sorts of relationships are possible between individual persons? And what moral significance do these relationships have?

For some philosophers a human being is primarily a self-seeking individual; they see society as an artificial creation—a framework for the operation of individual selfishness, an arena within which the powerful can exploit the weak or the many can control the few. Others take a radically different view and hold that the community is the central reality, while individual personality is only a sort of abstraction. Here we shall maintain that neither of these extremes is correct. The truth about human relationships is situated in a middle ground.

A. Others As Objects

Not all human relationships are the same. The relationship between two strangers sitting side by side on a bus is not the same as the relationship between a husband and wife. Nor is the relationship between either of these pairs the same as that between a bank teller and a holdup man who has just delivered the ultimatum "Hand over the money, or else!" But it is not saying a great deal to state merely that these relationships are not the same. We must look more closely and see where the basic differences lie.

In many human relationships people treat each other as objects. We are all conditioned to regard that as a bad thing, and in fact the consequences can be grim, as can be seen in such things as wartime body counts and the gas chambers in the Nazi concentration camps. Yet for all that the others-as-objects approach is not necessarily immoral. Sometimes it is entirely appropriate. An engineer seeking to determine the capacity of an elevator sets the limit at a certain number of passengers, based not on their peculiarly individual character-istics but simply on the average weight of the bodies to be carried. It would not help the engineer—indeed, it might make his task impossible—if he had to take into consideration the personalities of the unique individuals who would actually ride in the elevator.

There are also other human relationships, somewhat more complex and intimate, which involve a degree of recognition of human potentiality but still do not constitute genuine com-munity. In ordinary circumstances two strangers sharing a bus seat do not, and need not, enter into a relationship of commu-nity, but each does need to recognize the other's human needs and rights to the extent of allowing him or her enough room to sit comfortably.

Many formal contractual relationships are largely of the same kind. The parties to the contract do not need to share common interests, commitments, and points of view beyond the limited area covered by their agreement and a mutual commitment to the fair conduct of their business. And the arrangement works when the objectives which drew the parties together in the first place are achieved.

However, such arrangements do not always work. One bus rider can take up more than his or her fair share of the seat. One party to a contract can manipulate the terms of the agreement, or violate them, in such a way as to injure the other party or parties. In such cases, where the minimal necessary commitment to fairness is lacking on one side or both, the others-as-objects approach is not only dominant in the relationship but has become exploitative and unjust.

No doubt it is already clear from this analysis that this sort of relationship, in which other persons are viewed and treated as objects, is appropriate to action at the second level: action, that is, directed to achieving some specific, extrinsic goal. It should also be apparent that this way of dealing with others, although it can be abused, is a necessary, important, and entirely proper part of human life in society. Some human relationships, however, are based not on the seeking of particular limited objectives but on mutual commitment to the same value or values. Such a relationship is what we call "community."

B. Others As Community

Whether a community be very large or very small, at least some of its members continue to perform their individual, separate, third-level actions—basic, self-determining acts of commitment and also the acts by which they express and realize their commitment in concrete situations. This is necessary to the community's continued existence. But there is also more to a community than simply the sum total of the actions of the individual community members. When two or more people unite for the joint realization of a basic good to which they are committed, a community is constituted by their common social act—an act which is more than the individual actions of the community members.

We should mention that although we are concentrating here on a particular kind of community—that in which many people together make a common commitment—there is also another sort of community, no less real and valid, in which some person or persons make a commitment to the good realized in others without those others themselves making a commitment in return. A clear and common example is the community constituted by parents in relation to their young children, where the commitment is all on the parents' side, while the children are simply incapable of making a commitment. Obviously, though, this parent-child community can be and often is transformed into a community of the first kind—involving mutual commitment to common purposes on the part of all concerned—as the children grow and mature.

The members of a genuine community of the kind we are mainly concerned with here truly overcome their individual isolation, since, understanding and endorsing one another's commitment, they become common agents of a single action. It may very well be that each community member acts differently, doing what is appropriate to his or her own special role in the community, but the unity of meaning, the shared commitment, underlying these different actions flows into a single action, in whose performance the community members become one.

We do not wish to romanticize community as it is considered here. There is a popular sense of the word "community" which takes it for granted that it means commitment only to good purposes, besides involving only mutually loving relationships among the community members. This may be a true picture, more or less, of some communities, but it is not necessarily true of all. A band of terrorists or a fanatical religious cult is also an example of community as we are using the word. Good community implies proper commitment to good purposes expressed in suitable behavior; a bad community is one in which there is something morally wrong with the commitment, the purposes, the behavior, or some two or all three of these.

Each member of the community need not engage in all of the community's behavior, but the behavior of each member should be appropriate to his or her role in the community and should embody a working-out of the commitment shared with all the other members of the community. Ideally, at least, a college provides a good example of this. We do not need to be reminded that many schools are very imperfect embodiments of "community," where the reality has more to do with the self-interest and self-seeking of the individuals involved than with their common commitment to a shared purpose. At its best, nevertheless, a college is a community constituted by the

commitment of many individual persons to the good of knowledge in themselves and one another; the different members of
the academic community—students, faculty, administrators,
alumni—contribute to and participate in the realization of the
good in diverse ways according to their roles and functions in
this community.

Many communities are far larger than even a college. A
nation is also a community. In the United States the Preamble
to the Constitution is a verbal expression of the common action
constituting the community, an attempt to express in words
the values and the commitment to realize those values shared
by the members of this national community.

The example of the nation as a form of community underlines the complexity of this whole question. Thus, for instance,
the individuals who originally participated in the formation of
the particular community called the "United States" died long
ago; yet the same social act continues to exist today with new
individuals participating in it.

The example also makes it clear that much more is needed
for true community than simply a shared commitment to a
value or a set of values. Individual members of a national
community must perform many different, highly specialized
roles and tasks for the community as a whole to realize the
values to which its members are committed.

Furthermore, in a very large community, such as a nation,
there is need for an extremely complicated intermediate structure—laws, institutions—between the joint social act constituting the community and the multitude of individual acts performed by the members as they work to realize their shared
commitment. In large communities the alternative to such a
rational, intermediate structure is chaos.

Another evident fact about large communities such as nations is that it is unrealistic to think of them only in terms of
third-level action. To be sure, third-level action is central to
community: there must be a basic commitment to some fundamental human value or values, coupled with a determination
to realize the value or values through concrete action in concrete circumstances. But this necessarily calls for the calculated

pursuit of goals which express and are instrumental to the realizing of values: it calls, in other words, for second-level action, directed, at least immediately, not to participation in some basic human goods but to the achieving of limited, specific objectives.

This is not a criticism of communities. Individuals often do, and must, act for limited goals; and so do, and must, communities if they are to survive—if, indeed, they are to realize their basic commitments. The important thing for both individuals and communities is that the specific objectives and the means chosen to achieve them be shaped by, or at least not be in contradiction to, the basic values to which the individual or community is committed. Yet second-level action *may* tend to lessen the communal character of communities. That is so because in practice it is often directed to individual objectives which violate the common purposes of the community as such, as when a college becomes little more than a diploma mill with no serious interest in scholarship or a religious group devotes itself so heavily to political action or to fund-raising that its religious purposes are shunted aside.

C. Individual, Society, and Societies

Most people act most of the time as officials, in the root meaning of that word. This may sound like a surprising statement, but it is evidently true, provided one understands "official" to mean anyone acting in his or her capacity as a member of a community. To put the matter another way, most of what we all do is done as an expression of our roles in one community or another. All of us belong to many different communities, and we are constantly acting as members of them.

Consider some communities to which a typical person may belong: the community called "marriage," the community called "the family," the community called "the company," communities called "the church," "the nation," "the university," "the team," "the club," "the gang," "the neighborhood," "my best friendship," and so on. One could continue indefinitely.

With a little reflection anyone can put together an extremely long list of his or her own—and will probably forget some communities in the process.

The point is that each of us has not merely a few social roles but many, depending on which particular society or societies are in question at any given time. In the normal course of events almost everything we do is done by virtue of membership in one or another of these societies. It is a tendency of human action to be communal and social in nature.

We belong to some societies because we have chosen to belong and to others without really having made an explicit choice. Most people, for example, become citizens of a particular nation, and therefore members of that particular national community, by an accident of birth, not as a result of their own deliberate choice.

This is a practical convenience in many ways, but it can also present grave difficulties. By reason of membership in a particular community one can become involved in a communal act without actually making any decision, and perhaps without even knowing of it (as happens, for instance, in the case of infants and children who are involved in the actions of the various communities into which they have been born). But what if a community to which one belongs undertakes a communal action with which one cannot conscientiously agree? Suppose one's country becomes involved in a war which one regards as unjust. Very hard choices, imposed by membership in that national community, must then be faced.

An individual's role in society consists of the various things that he or she may do—and some of which he or she is obliged to do—in virtue of participation in the society. Roles are not catalogs of things which individuals actually do; rather, they can be thought of as lists of things persons can do and in some cases should do because of the positions they occupy in the community.

For its continued existence, as we have said, a society or community requires that its individual members fulfill the requirements of their various roles. In a sense, therefore, each member of the society depends on every other.

True, an individual can fail to meet some requirements of

his or her role without destroying the social act and, thereby, the society. A marriage can continue to exist even if one or both partners are something less than punctilious in carrying out their respective marital roles. A nation can continue to exist even if some citizens neglect some or all duties of citizenship. Yet every society has its own minimal level of role fulfillment which is essential for it to continue to operate. If a significant number of members (the significant number will be different for different societies) fall below this level, the community will no longer function as such.

We have already seen that everyone belongs to many different societies and, as a result, has a number of different social roles. This, too, can raise problems for an individual as far as self-determination is involved. The first and fundamental necessity is to opt for membership in morally good communities—those committed to good purposes pursued in good ways—and avoid membership in vicious and corrupt ones. But assuming that to be so, people still face the significant challenge of selecting their communities in a way that makes their lives unified wholes.

If membership in one society requires a commitment and forms of behavior in conflict with the commitment and behavior demanded by membership in another, something has to give. Normally a man cannot be a functioning member of both the community called "marriage" and a community of monks; it is difficult to be a participating member of a pacifist organization while also being a participating member of the armed forces.

These are extreme examples, but more subtle and complicated ones often arise. The demands of certain jobs—long hours, frequent travel—can be in almost intolerable tension with the requirements of stable marriage and family life for some people. An individual may simply not have time and energy to keep up membership in both a volunteer community service group and a worthwhile professional association. In times like ours, when people ordinarily enjoy many opportunities and options—to belong or not to belong to a variety of societies—the problem of harmonizing social roles and avoiding conflicts of duty can be pressing and quite serious.

D. *Community and Human Purposes*

Community is not an optional luxury, it is absolutely necessary. Human beings cannot live and flourish in Robinson Cru-
soe-like isolation, for most human goods simply cannot be
realized by individuals acting alone. Justice and friendship
require at least two persons practicing justice and friendship
toward each other. Life can only begin in some sort of family,
can only be sustained with the help of others (we must cooperate to eat, to fight diseases, to have shelter and warmth), and is
served by most people in others when as parents they hand on
life to their children. Knowledge is fostered by a process of
education in which some teach others what they know. And so
for all the other human goods.

In a real sense, then, community compensates for our individual limitations by making possible the realization, or at least
an attempt at the realization, of human purposes which any
one of us singly could not realize. United in community, persons can serve human goods in themselves and one another far
more adequately than isolated individuals can.

Community—common commitment—takes the form of
people actively working together on behalf of the same purposes. To be sure, real-life communities, even the best, commonly contain at least some admixture of selfishness and exploitation; and communities at their worst can be debased
caricatures of good communities, settings in which people seek
vicious ends in vicious ways. Still, the ideal of community
persists and, sometimes at least, is found embodied in real life.

In a genuine community common commitment to a common purpose or purposes exists alongside a recognized and
respected diversity of roles and functions of community members in pursuit of the purpose or purposes they all share.
Respect for the goods to which other community members are
committed along with oneself leads to appreciation for the
particular characteristics and contributions of the others, to
the extent that these foster the realization of the good. For at
the heart of any good community lies the sense that it is more
important that the good be realized than that I as an individual
realize it in myself. In such a community, too, people are

careful to delimit the shared commitment which binds them together as members of *that* community, from the other commitments which each has to other communities involving other persons. It is within such parameters as these that one can meaningfully and fruitfully speak of necessary diversity, healthy pluralism, and responsible tolerance.

As we pointed out at the very beginning of this chapter, however, there are other views of the individual and community which are in sharp contrast with this one.

There is, for example, a psychological theory of egoism which denies that genuine love of others is possible. True, we have affection for others and act toward them with spontaneous sympathy or compassion—indeed, we act this way even toward animals. But according to psychological egoism at bottom we are incapable of willing others' good for their own sake, and we never seek the good of others except when we foresee some payoff for ourselves. Those who think this way do not try to justify such egoism as an ethical stance; they merely say that this unavoidably is how people are.

In fact, if there were no real unity among persons, they would be correct. It would not be possible to love others if loving others meant we had to seek an alien good—a good foreign to us, in which we had no real part.

It is possible for us to love one another, however, if we are committed to seeking together a good or goods which we know to be our own and yet recognize as "bigger than all of us." Community in goods understood and willed as fulfilling for two or more persons really does make them one, and insofar as they are one, the good of each is found in the good of all, and the good of all is good for each.

Willing this common good, therefore, any member of the community truly wills the good for others, and wills it as good for them, not just for the sake of some selfish payoff which he or she hopes to enjoy. At the same time, in willing the good for others one is oneself fulfilled. So, for example, in truly and unselfishly caring for their children parents become good parents, and being good parents is fulfilling for them—it makes their lives in this respect truly meaningful and worth living. Whereas failing to be a good parent—for example, exploiting children for the emotional gratification one can get out of them (the classic "stage mother" who pushes her child into show business to make up for her own failure to be a star)—is bad for parents themselves, since it spoils and wastes their lives in this respect.

Where some deny the possibility of real community, still others view the individual as all but swallowed up by society, and so deny the significance of individuals and their unique responsibility. But genuine community does not come about by denying our individuality, our otherness, in a blind effort to submerge ourselves in an anthill society. Community is based instead on a shared commitment grounded in personal free choices by which each individual shoulders his or her special share of the responsibility for realizing the values which originally drew separate persons into the relationship called "community."

Up to this point we have learned something about the meaning of freedom, about the various kinds or levels of action, and in particular about the kind of action which is self-determination. We have considered fulfillment, which is closely tied to freedom of self-determination. And we have looked at the crucial role of social relationships. All this, however, has only laid the groundwork for determining what makes action morally good or bad. It is time now to begin to consider this central question. Our first step will be to examine and criticize views that would make it impossible to say for sure what is right and what is wrong.

Questions for Review and Discussion

1. One theory of society is the organic view, which sees the individual as hardly more than an abstraction from the social whole. This is sometimes called "the anthill society." Do you know of any specific theories of this sort or any historical attempts to bring into reality societies which conform to such a model?

2. Large corporations (and other organizations) spend a great deal of money on personnel offices and public relations staffs to try to

personalize their relationships with employees and customers. In what circumstances and to what extent can such efforts be genuine?

3. In a true community what unites the members into a single whole? What distinguishes them so that they do not get lost in that whole?

4. Some people fear loving and being loved because they are afraid of losing their identity in too close a relationship. Do you think such a fear can be well grounded? If so, how can the problem be overcome?

5. Analyze the Preamble to the U.S. Constitution as an example of a community-forming act. Compare this with mutually exchanged wedding vows as another example of a community-forming act.

6. Can the same society simultaneously involve aspects of genuine community, of contractual relation, and of exploitation? Why would it be important to take account of these various forms of relationship in order to understand the behavior of people in a society?

7. Compare the problem of integrating social roles faced by a person in contemporary society with the problem faced by a member of a primitive tribe.

8. Some ethical theories give a very special place to the political community, going so far as to hold that ordinary ethics does not apply to it. According to the theory presented here the political community is only one among others and not exempt from the claims of ordinary ethics. Why is this so?

9. Community is impossible among people who do not think that there is anything bigger than both (or all) of us. Does this "something bigger" necessarily imply that there is some superhuman reality, such as God?

10. In one way or another the ideal of loving others in community is often described as forgetfulness of self. Do you think that is an adequate or even a helpful way of describing it?

6. We Don't Always Know What Is Good for Us

We are free to choose what we will do. But we are not free to make whatever we choose right.

We must follow our best judgment concerning what we ought to do. But our best judgment can be mistaken.

Many people find these four propositions self-evident and unassailable, but for many others they are neither—indeed, they are flatly untrue. These propositions contradict the relativism and subjectivism which are prevalent today and which, for the beginner at least, constitute a major obstacle to serious reflection regarding ethical issues.

What do we mean by "relativism" and "subjectivism"? Even though the words do not commonly come up in conversation, the attitudes they stand for are commonplace. How often, for example, when it is a question of whether a particular action is right or wrong, does one hear it said, "It all depends on what the society you live in regards as good" or "It all depends on the kind of life you want to live"? Such remarks sum up a whole approach (at least, a conscious approach) to ethical problems: "It all depends. . . ."

Of course, in a certain sense it all *does* depend. Decisions about the right and wrong of actions depend on many different factors, including those so strongly emphasized by cultural relativism and individualistic subjectivism. As with many other approaches to ethical questions, relativism and subjectivism are not totally devoid of truth. But they have fastened upon particular truths while excluding other aspects of reality which must be taken into consideration in developing a well-rounded ethics that respects all the facts of experience. Not totally divorced from reality, they are instead distortions: they single out certain aspects of reality and ignore others.

2   Relativism and subjectivism make ethics (that is, the serious and sustained examination of one's life and society from the viewpoint of what actions should and should not be performed) a virtual impossibility. They are ethical theories which cut short the ethical enterprise. They deny in principle that moral judgments can be simply true or false.

If no moral judgment were simply true or false, the effort to examine one's life or one's society by methods of rational criticism would ultimately be pointless. The conclusion of any such examination would always be "It all depends on the kind of life you want to live" or "It all depends on what the society you live in regards as good." This marks a dead end to reasoned efforts to judge which actions are right and which are wrong and why.

The position we hold is reflected in the series of propositions at the start of this chapter: "We are free to choose what we will do. But we are not free to make whatever we choose right. We must follow our best judgment concerning what we ought to do. But our best judgment can be mistaken." It is not enough, however, simply to assert these things. And even before examining and developing them further, we need first to criticize relativism and subjectivism.

A. Cultural Relativism

Cultural relativism is an offspring of anthropology, the study of the customs and beliefs of people of diverse cultures. Although cultural relativism is rejected by many contemporary anthropologists, it continues to have an impact on popular attitudes.

Everyone has encountered cultural relativism at one time or another. The conversation at a party turns to some exotic practice—human sacrifice, say—and invariably the cultural relativist in the crowd will say something like, "Well, if those people really believed (or believe) that it was the right thing to do, I suppose it was right *for them.*" In other words: Norms of right and wrong action are totally derived from the society in which one lives; the only criterion of right and wrong is what one's own society happens to believe on the matter, since in the last analysis all moral norms are determined by social conditioning and by the circumstances and needs of particular cultures.

Upon reflection most people instinctively draw back from wholehearted acceptance of cultural relativism; they do not really care to be in the position of saying that such practices as human sacrifice or cannibalism or ritual prostitution are good and proper in a society which happens to regard than as such. There are, however, better reasons for rejecting cultural relativism than the instinctive repugnance people feel for the conclusions to which it logically leads (even though that instinctive repugnance is itself not without significance in the matter).

For one thing, as we have noted, cultural relativism is now losing support even in the professional anthropological circles where it once prevailed. It is perfectly true that there are striking differences among the ethical values of particular cultures. But these differences are to a great extent explicable in view of differences in physical conditions, beliefs, knowledge and ignorance, levels of scientific and technical progress, and other accidents of history prevailing at different times in different societies—notably including the errors, oppressive structures, and moral compromises peculiar to particular cultures. Given such factual differences, even a single set of universally valid moral principles can be expected to yield strikingly different concrete judgments. One need not, in other words, postulate cultural relativism as an ethical theory in order to account for the fact of ethical diversity among various cultures.

Moreover, contemporary anthropology has pierced beyond the surface of the differences which distinguish one culture from another and succeeded in identifying the basic points of convergence in which superficially very different cultures are in fact very much alike. Cultures have come to be seen as ways in which human beings seek to satisfy common, underlying human needs. These needs correspond, as far as the testimony of contemporary anthropology can tell us, to certain basic, universal human goods.

Consider an example. Human life is a basic good: a value respected, so far as the evidence shows, at all times in all cultures. This is not to say that all cultures have expressed their sensitivity to and respect for life in the same way. On the contrary, many cultures limit their respect for life to members of the tribe, the group, those identified, by whatever criteria, as belonging to "us."

In other cultures respect for the value of life is extended to embrace others who are not identifiably part of the small in-group, until, ideally, respect for human life is extended to all those who possess life (a point at which, possibly, no culture in history has yet truly arrived, and which is certainly beyond the moral grasp of our own contemporary culture). In spite of the extreme diversity, however, centering basically on the question of who are and are not members of the group whose lives deserve respect, the important fact is that every culture in some way manifests awareness of and respect for the value of life.

The same is true of many other basic human goods: the begetting and raising of children, which has always been recognized as a central value by every culture; intellectual knowledge; play or recreation; and so on. Clearly there has been enormous variety in the ways by which particular societies have expressed their recognition of these values, and clearly, too, there is a true relativity of duties, since these vary according to the institutions and practices of particular societies and the various roles of individuals in them (property rights, for example, vary according to the economic structure of the society). But beyond the differences, running as a permanent thread through all cultures has been the recognition that such values are important and indeed fundamental to human life. Cultural relativism represents too superficial an analysis: in emphasizing the differences among cultures it fails to take into account the basic sameness below the surface.

It is no less important, moreover, to grasp the fact that forms of behavior which seem superficially alike very often have markedly different meanings in different cultures. The relativizing which results from failure to comprehend the implications of this can lead to some very bad arguments.

Thus, for instance, someone observing that a nomadic tribe abandons its sick and elderly without moral qualms might reason that this lends support to our doing the equivalent with our aged and infirm in the United States. In our case, however, "abandoning" these persons would signify that we do not care for them and think they—and we—would be better off if they were dead. In the case of the nomadic tribe, however, behavior which looks very much the same merely reflects the fact that nomads cannot carry their sick and elderly with them without jeopardizing the whole group. The old and the ill are left behind, not so that they will die, but so that the rest of the tribe will have a chance to live.

Similarly, the lending of money has a very different meaning in a simpler economy, where there is no way to invest it, than in our complex economy. In an economy like ours it is fair and reasonable to charge and earn interest on money which is lent, since the money could otherwise be invested in some profitable enterprise. In a simpler economy, however, charging interest might be wrong because it signified extorting something from the borrower on account of his need.

Apart from these considerations cultural relativism has become increasingly irrelevant in our times for the simple reason that distinct cultures, as historically understood and studied by anthropology, are disappearing. Today perhaps no truly isolated group is left in the world—no group unaffected by the beliefs and attitudes of other groups—and if there should be such, it seems certain to vanish in the near future under the impact of communications technology.

Our world may in fact be moving toward the day, perhaps not too far off, when it will no longer be possible to speak of "cultures" but only of a single "world culture" in which remaining local variations of belief and custom will be of rather minor significance. As this state of affairs emerges, it becomes increasingly artificial to attempt to apply the concept of cultural relativism to the realities of life.

Finally, as a practical matter, if one were to be consistent in espousing cultural relativism, one would logically have to apply this theory to one's own culture, and doing so would make it impossible to criticize values of the society in which one lives. For if ethical values are endowed with validity simply by the fact that a culture accepts them, there is no ground on which a person can reasonably criticize the ethical status quo of any existing society, even if that status quo involves the policy of *apartheid* or the functioning of the Gulag Archipelago.

The effect of this is to make efforts to achieve reasoned social change impossible. Instead, social change comes to depend on the ability of individuals and groups to impose their will, their vision of how things ought to be, on other individuals and groups in society—a power struggle rather than a debate.

Thus cultural relativism must be rejected. It rests on a confusion: between social facts—what actually is required in various societies as a matter of custom and convenience—and moral norms, which delineate what *ought* to be done on principle, not merely for the sake of conformity. In every society some individuals have always found the conventional standards more or less inadequate and unacceptable and have sought a better and more firmly grounded understanding of what a morally good life entails. Cultural relativism does not help but hinders this effort.

B. Individualistic Subjectivism

Even more prevalent, perhaps, than cultural relativism is the attitude known as individualistic subjectivism. It is based on the belief that individuals spin their own moral norms out of their own interiors and that, ultimately, the only criterion for judging behavior, one's own or someone else's, is consistency. That is, the only ethical judgment possible is that persons either are or are not living according to the standards they have set for themselves. "It all depends on the kind of life you want to live."

It is true of course that different individuals have specifically different moral responsibilities arising from their different prior commitments. So, for example, a particular teacher has a particular moral responsibility which no other teacher has to prepare for *his* particular classes; an actress has a responsibility which no one else in the cast has to learn *her* lines. But this is very different from saying, "It all depends on the kind of life you want to live."

If that view of things is correct, it makes no sense to argue either for or against any moral proposition. Teachers can prepare or not prepare for class, as they prefer; performers can learn their lines or not learn them, whichever suits them best. There is no standard according to which one can maintain that, say, the dropping of the atomic bomb on the civilian population of Hiroshima was wrong—or, for that matter, that it was right. Assuming that the people who made and executed the decision were doing what they thought they should do, one can only agree that undoubtedly what they did was the right thing *for them* to do.

Yet people evidently do attempt to argue for and against such moral propositions. It is almost as if they intuitively recognize that there are moral norms which transcend the limits of individual preference and consistency and apply to many (perhaps all) people. In practice no one concedes that differences about fundamental moral issues are on the same level as differences of taste concerning such things as music and movies.

If subjectivism were correct, however, it would mean that in the end no one could ever do anything really wrong, except through lack of ingenuity. We are after all free to choose what we will do, and if that freedom can make what we choose right, who would ever choose to do anything while choosing at the same time to make it wrong?

It might be objected that in this view of things "inconsistency" (not living up to one's subjective standards of behavior) is "immorality," and that it is quite possible for a person to be inconsistent, and therefore immoral, as a result of confusion or inconstancy. But it is easy to be consistent without being constant, provided one is ingenious enough to incorporate so many qualifications and limitations into moral decisions that no particular decision is ever really binding, as a matter of consistency, in the future. All that "consistency" in this sense requires is enough sophistication to arrange things so that inconsistency becomes a practical impossibility.

In any case, a closer look at subjectivism shows that the whole theory is built on ambiguity and confusion in the use of language. Subjectivism might be neatly expressed by saying that morally responsible individuals must decide for themselves what is right and wrong, because only they can decide what they will do. Stated thus, subjectivism almost sounds self-evident. But the word "decide" is being used here to refer to two very different things: judgment and choice. We decide (judge) what is right, and this judgment is *objectively* true or false. We also decide (choose) what we will do, and our choice, which is neither true nor false, leads for good or ill to action and the *realization* of what we chose. Thus, while people can and must both decide (choose) what they will do and decide (judge) what is right, they cannot determine what is right and wrong by their judgments as they can determine their actions by their choices. Subjectivism ignores the fact that the two kinds of deciding are not the same, and so mistakenly attributes to moral judgments the irreplaceable initiative characteristic of free and self-determining choices.

It is likewise necessary to make a distinction between the rightness or wrongness of what we do and our individual guilt or innocence in choosing to do it. It is possible to commit atrocities with a good heart, just as it is possible to cause genuine benefits with evil intentions. In the first case the goodness of the intention has no effect on the badness of what is done; just as in the second the goodness of what is done has no effect on the badness of the intention. The intention and the action are and remain distinct, and each must be considered in making judgments about the morality of one's own or other people's action.

If, finally, subjectivism were correct, we could not help knowing what is morally right for us to do. At the same time that which is morally right for us, whatever it may be, must surely be what is in the moral sphere most profoundly good for us as persons. Yet our common experience tells us that we do not always know what is really good for us in other areas of life:

in matters affecting our health, for example, or our vocational choices. And if it is frequently so difficult for us to know what is best for us in other areas of life, why suppose that it should be so simple in the moral sphere—so simple, indeed, that whatever we choose is automatically the best thing for us? None of our beliefs and attitudes in other areas of life are beyond rational examination and criticism. Why suppose that it is different in the moral domain?

Part of the attraction of subjectivism arises from the support it lends to the tolerant, permissive, nonjudgmental style which is widely admired today. By contrast, those who believe they know the absolute truth about morality can seem harsh, intolerant, and fanatical. Yet this need not be the case.

On the one hand, it is possible to hold that there is moral truth but that it leaves room for diverse lifestyles, that behavior which one considers wrong often should be tolerated for the sake of goods like justice and liberty, that those with whom one profoundly disagrees on moral matters—with whom, indeed, one may be in tragic conflict—are nevertheless not vicious even if they are mistaken.

On the other hand, it is possible for committed subjectivists to hold and act upon intolerant and even fanatical views. In that case, denying that there are any objective moral standards which one should use as starting points both in self-criticism and in debating with opponents, subjectivists are particularly likely to be self-righteous and to use nonrational methods of "persuasion."

Sometimes a kind of transference occurs. Ethical subjectivism is imputed to authority, not as an aberration (which can indeed be the case) but as something inherent both in authority and in the making of ethical decisions. This view is expressed in such a challenge as, "Who makes the rules—and why should I be bound by someone else's rules?" The objection seems superficially weighty when it concerns matters where the moral norms themselves are under challenge: today, for example, in regard to sexual morality, where traditional norms are widely rejected. But it scarcely occurs to anyone to object about rules where the norms are taken for granted. If, for example, a professor gave A's to her favorites and F's to students she personally disliked, nobody would defend such behavior by saying, "If that's the way she wants to grade, she shouldn't be bound by somebody else's rules."

Essentially, however, ethics is concerned neither with making rules nor with enforcing them; it is concerned with finding standards—moral truths—which no one makes. And if, as we have argued here, it is not true to say that we make whatever we choose right by the fact of choosing, then clearly we need standards to apply in making our choices: standards by which we can determine whether the things we choose are right and also whether our reasons for choosing them are right. In the chapters that follow we shall try to show what those standards are.

Questions for Review and Discussion

1. Why are relativism and subjectivism in principle incompatible with the position that ethical judgments can be simply true or false?

2. Are white South Africans members of a different culture from that of black South Africans, from that of white Americans, from that of black Americans?

3. The truth underlying cultural relativism is that, as a matter of fact, there are wide differences between the ethical values of particular cultures. Why does this not settle the theoretical issue in favor of relativism?

4. Some cultural relativists used to criticize members of Western societies for their intolerance of the primitive ways of less civilized groups. Do you see any incompatibility between offering such criticism and holding the theory of cultural relativism?

5. Why is an affirmation of freedom of self-determination compatible with the denial of subjectivism?

6. Distinguish between subjectivism and the position which says that each person is obliged to do what he or she sincerely believes to be right (the obligation to follow one's conscience).

7. If subjectivism were correct, would it make sense to say of an individual that "He is guiltless when he does what he sincerely believes is right, even though he happens through no fault of his own to be mistaken in this belief"?

8. As a matter of fact, more people are likely to express a subjectivist attitude on questions of sexual morality than on questions of social

justice, such as racial discrimination. Again, some people who are absolutely certain that U.S. aid to anticommunist dictatorships is immoral hold a subjectivist position on such issues as the morality of the use of drugs. Do such differences necessarily mark inconsistencies? How can such differences be explained?

9. Rejecting relativism and subjectivism doesn't mean that one must hold that all people in all places at all times have exactly the same moral obligations. Can you think of reasons why—even though moral judgments are objectively true or false—different people should have different moral obligations?

7. Human Goods: Reasons for Choices

If subjectivism and cultural relativism are not adequate guides in the difficult task of directing and judging human action, our own and others', we must look elsewhere. Examining the reasons for which people act is an important step in the right direction.

Before beginning, though, we need to make a point about terminology. We speak here of human goods. In this context, however, the use of the word "good" does not mean that we have reached the stage of being able to discriminate between what is *morally* good and bad. At this point we use "good" simply to refer to a reason for third-level action, whether the action itself be morally good or bad.

Also, the goods we shall consider are very broad in scope, so broad, in fact, that it is difficult to find a single label which adequately describes any one category. The labels we use are not precise theoretical definitions but attempts to call attention to the starting points which underlie all our practical thinking.

A. Purposes

There are two quite different ways of understanding purposes. One is to view them as objects of desire, goals we pursue, things we want just insofar as we want them; purposes in this sense are plainly outside us, extrinsic to us. The other way is to see them as particular instances of human goods which we seek to serve and share in, without ever finally encompassing and exhausting them. Purposes in this sense embody aspects of human flourishing; for human goods are *not* extrinsic to us but instead are elements of what human fulfillment—the fullness of being a human person—is all about. It is purposes in this latter sense (instances of the basic human goods) that we are concerned with here.

Often of course we seek one purpose, one goal or objective, as a means to another purpose which is the end we have in view. There is nothing wrong or unusual about this. People commonly act in this way, and there is no reason to criticize workers, say, who do their jobs not exclusively or even mainly for their own sakes but in order to earn what they need to support themselves and their families.

At the same time it is possible to seek some realizations of the reasons for acting simply for their own sakes, without reference to anything else. Ordinarily a man who leaps into a river to save a drowning child is simply trying to save the child; he is *not* trying to save the child in order to be interviewed as a hero on television or receive a reward from the child's grateful parents. Unless she is unusually calculating, a girl absorbed in piecing together a jigsaw puzzle is working the puzzle simply for its own sake, not in order to please her parents or improve her mind. Unless they are unusually insensitive, people listening to a beautiful or stirring piece of music are enjoying the music for its own sake, not because they have bought concert tickets and want to show their neighbors how cultured they are.

These simple examples illustrate the fact that there are goods for whose realizations one can act for their own sake, without reference to any other purpose. They also illustrate the fact that instances of the same goods can be and sometimes are sought as means to ends beyond themselves. The emphasis here, however, is on the first characteristic of these goods: one can act for their sake and their sake alone. Or, to put it another way, we act for purposes—but purposes are particular instances of human goods, and it is the latter which make purposes interesting and worthy of choice in the first place. It is in such goods that one can participate by third-level action. Thus they serve as starting points of our choices and actions by providing us with reasons to consider some possibilities as worthy of being chosen. On closer examination it appears that human goods fall into several categories. This is significant in itself. The diversity of the human goods and their irreducibility—the fact that, as we shall see, none can be reduced to another or to some still more basic, ultrafundamental good or purpose—are neither accidents of history nor interesting but irrelevant psychological data. Rather, as aspects of the flourishing and fulfillment of the human person, these goods express the inherent complexity of human nature as it manifests itself in individuals and also in communities. In much of what follows we shall be probing the implications of this crucial fact.

B. Eight Categories of Basic Human Goods

One group of goods, corresponding to the fact that human persons are organic substances, can be lumped together under the heading "life." This category clearly includes the preservation of life: so-called "matters of life or death." But it also includes various aspects of life, such as health, safety, and the avoidance or removal of pain. Also encompassed here is procreation, the begetting of new life and the nurturing of children, for a couple can desire to have a child for no other reason than to hand on life and give this new individual a start in sharing in all the other goods which contribute to a human being's flourishing and fulfillment.

A second group of goods, reflecting the fact that human persons are rational, can be labeled "speculative knowledge." As a fundamental human good, this is knowledge which is sought for its own sake, not just for its usefulness as a means to an end. One might say that it is knowledge sought simply to satisfy curiosity. Formidable as it may sound, "speculative knowledge" should not be identified only with the activity of such apparently detached thinkers as scholars and scientists. The quest for speculative knowledge is often present in very down-to-earth situations: in the activity of a child who takes a clock apart to see how it works or of a man chatting over the back fence with a friend about the new family which has moved into the neighborhood.

Likewise corresponding to the rational character of human persons and to the impact of intelligence on human sensibility is a group of goods pertaining to "aesthetic experience," the appreciation of beauty. This includes not only such things as enjoying works of art like symphonies and paintings but also other, superficially very different experiences. The pleasure one takes from a beautiful scene in nature can be an aesthetic experience; so can the pleasure of watching a football game on television. Again, although there are obvious specific differences between football and ballet, the pleasure one takes from either can involve genuine aesthetic experience. An aesthetic experience is one which a person seeks because the experience itself is valued, not because it leads to anything beyond itself.

Unlike aesthetic experience, a fourth group of goods—corresponding to the fact that human persons are at once rational and animal—involves skillful performance by oneself, not others. Very broadly, these goods can be labeled "play." Work itself can be a form of participation in this good, which essentially involves transforming the natural world by bestowing meaning and value upon it through skilled performance. Certainly "play" includes games and sports, but it is possible for a person to be engaged in extremely taxing activity, physical or mental, and still be playing, even though a casual observer might call the activity work. While the spectators are participating in the good of aesthetic experience as they watch a ballet or a football game, the dancers and the athletes are most likely serving the good of play.

While the goods grouped in these four categories are plainly quite different from one another—and indeed, as we shall see, cannot be reduced to one another or to some common denominator underlying them all—they all do at least have this much in common: it is possible to understand them without reference to action; as reasons for acting, their meaning is independent of human action (though this is not to say that they themselves have an independent existence, as if they were Platonic Ideas).

There is, however, another group of goods which can be sought for their own sake but whose meaning inherently implies human action; self-determining action is involved in their very meaning. All have to do in one way or another with the resolving of tensions and the achieving and maintaining of harmony, either within the self or in one's relationships with others. (Although the terminology is not especially important here, the goods of the first kind can be called "substantive" and those of the second "reflexive.")

All people experience tensions within themselves. The concern with "getting it all together" points to the fact that people generally sense that they are *not* able to get it all together, at least not permanently or to the degree they wish. Different given aspects of the self seem continually at war with one another, and people struggle—more or less successfully for different persons at different times in their lives—to resolve these tensions and conflicts and achieve inner harmony. The objective sought is integration of the aspects of the self. And this reason for acting is appropriately referred to as "integrity," in its basic meaning of wholeness.

A similar tension exists between the realistic insights of individuals and their actions. It is true that an action is the act of the person performing it, yet the action is something other than the actor. Conflict is possible here, too, a conflict expressed in such comments as "I wasn't really myself when I did that" or "I feel so foolish; I knew better than to do what I did." Naturally enough, we wish not to experience this tension and to enjoy harmony between our selves and our actions. This good we call "practical reasonableness."

Looking further beyond the self, it is evident that we experience tensions in our relationships with others, and we also seek in many ways to overcome these tensions and establish harmony between ourselves and other people. The good sought is "friendship." But the word has a very broad meaning here. In popular parlance friendship describes only the relationship of persons who know and like one another. As a basic good, however, friendship encompasses much else, for example, justice and peace among individuals and groups, even the harmonious relationship between entire nations. In this extended sense one could say that, ideally, friendship is the fundamental purpose of an organization like the United Nations.

Finally, in this group of reflexive, relational goods one moves beyond relationships within and among people to consider the relationship between human beings and the more-than-human ultimate source of meaning and value. The fundamental good here is "religion."

Religion, as we are speaking of it now, does not of itself imply that God exists or require belief in his existence. The philosophical-religious quest begins in the universally shared recognition that it is necessary and desirable to find what we have called the "more-than-human ultimate source of meaning and value" and enter into a satisfactory relationship with it. But this effort has generated a variety of worldviews, not all of them theistic: Confucianism, for example, does not require belief in a personal God; Marxism denies that God exists while recognizing a dialectic of matter and history as the ultimate source of meaning, to be accepted and respected; yet Confucianism and Marxism are both religions in the sense in which we are using the word.

As a reason for acting, then, religion is the good of harmony with the more-than-human ultimate source of meaning, toward whom (or which) the philosophical-religious quest is directed. It is universally assumed that some such source exists, and this gives the effort to find it a practical orientation. That quest always aims at a right relationship between us and the source of meaning and value and is not directed merely at acquiring an idea or unmasking an illusion.

At this point the question very legitimately arises, Is this all? Does this list—life, speculative knowledge, aesthetic experience, and play; integrity, practical reasonableness, friendship, and religion—exhaust the categories of basic human goods which can be sought for their own sake? It seems so.

Anyone, of course, can identify many more reasons for acting than these—goods which to particular individuals or particular cultures seem or have seemed far more important than any of the ones listed here. Upon examination, though, such other goods are seen to be no more than aspects or combinations of aspects of these fundamental goods. The fact that they may seem more important to an individual or a group simply reflects the choices which have been made within the limits of the cultural conditioning or psychological inclination of that individual or group.

Historically, for example, particular societies have placed their major emphasis on a good such as patriotism. But "patriotism"—a word describing the relationship of mutual loyalty and support of individuals in the same country—is no more than a limited aspect of the broader category of goods we have called "friendship."

Again, an individual may say that the basic goal of his or her life, the reason which gives everything else meaning, is some such good as self-fulfillment. But, as we saw in chapter four, fulfillment, although in a very general sense that which gives meaning to human life, is also a blanket term which, while it means different things to different people, invariably takes in various aspects of the goods we have described here.

In short, these basic categories of human good seem to comprise all the fundamental reasons for human action. Any other reason either will include a bit of some or all of them or will represent a limited aspect of some of them. Wherever there is practical thinking—thinking about what to do—one or more of these basic reasons underlie it as its starting point; wherever there is a choice, one or another of these goods provides the reason for making it.

C. Human Goods: Aspects of Our Personhood

Two points about basic human goods need underlining here. One concerns their irreducibility, the fact that these goods cannot be reduced to one another or to anything else. The other has to do with their specifically human character.

These reasons for acting are basic goods, not mere means. True, their instances *can* serve as means: a student can study to pass an exam to get a degree to land a good job, and so on; a young man can attend a concert for the sake of impressing a young woman with his cultivated good taste. But basic goods can also be reasons for which a person acts without having any further reason: a student studies because he or she finds the material interesting; a young man attends a concert for the sake of the music. Our observation, then, is that the basic human goods are irreducible to one another. Each marks out its own special area of human possibility, distinct from all the others.

This is not to say that the basic goods might not be reducible, for theoretical reflection, to some ultimate source in reality. For example, religious believers in the Judeo-Christian tradition accept the idea that human goods are rooted ultimately in the goodness of God, in whose image and likeness human beings are made; and this mysterious "goodness of God," according to the same tradition, enjoys absolute simplicity, in contrast with the irreducible diversity of human goods. But even so, the complexity of human goods does remain. For divine goodness cannot be realized in human beings by their actions except insofar as they act on behalf of and realize the possibilities of their own human nature; and the various ways of realizing these possibilities are precisely the fundamental human goods which we are considering.

The second point which needs emphasizing is, as we have said, the specifically human character of the basic human goods. Against Aristotle we argued earlier that the dignity and excellence of human beings—that in us which truly deserves the name "human"—does not pertain solely to the intellect. *All* aspects of our inherently complex human nature are human; all dimensions of our personhood are personal; and all the basic human goods, which correspond to different aspects of human nature and personhood, are part of the full-being or fulfillment (some speak of "flourishing") of human beings. No part of human nature, and no basic human purpose, is subhuman or nonpersonal. So, for example, the bodily aspects of human life are quite as "human" and "personal" as the mental, psychic aspects, and goods which correspond most immediately to the former dimension—life, health, procreation and so on—are as fully human and personal as goods like knowledge and aesthetic experience.

To speak of the complexity and irreducibility of human

goods does not mean, however, that they are not related to one another. As a matter of fact, integrity, practical reasonableness, friendship, and religion are so intimately related that to the degree one fails to realize one of them, one also fails to realize them all. This is because each of these goods involves, in a different way, the quest for harmony in life: harmony with the source (or sources) of meaning and value, harmony among human communities and individuals, harmony of choice with conscience and of behavior with commitments, and harmony of feelings with one another and also with one's free choices. It is a fact of experience that when any one of these relationships is disturbed, the other relationships are also affected and to a degree undermined.

Furthermore, these relational goods are related to the substantive goods—life, play, aesthetic experience, speculative knowledge—in the sense that the latter must serve as vehicles for the former. It is impossible to act simply to achieve integrity, practical reasonableness, friendship, or religion. Inevitably it is necessary to include in one's action one of the goods from the substantive group in order to give content to the activity by which one seeks to realize a good from the reflexive group.

Consider friendship. One might say that one seeks to realize friendship by being friendly. Yet a friendly act must have some substance to it. If a young man and young woman go on a date together (a friendly act), the date has to involve some sort of specific activity: taking a walk in the park (play), going to a concert or a movie (aesthetic experience), talking (speculative knowledge, with perhaps a bit of play or aesthetic experience thrown in), or whatever.

The reverse, however, is not true. Life, play, aesthetic experience, and speculative knowledge *can* be sought by themselves, without reference to integrity, practical reasonableness, friendship, or religion. To go back to an earlier example, the man leaping into the river to save a drowning child has just one end in view: saving the child's life. It is most unlikely that he is concerned at the moment with integrity, practical reasonableness, friendship, or even religion.

Worth noting, too, is the fact that people rather often single out a particular aspect of a good and act on its behalf, while disregarding other aspects of the same good understood in its entirety; as we shall see later, this sheds light on how persons come to choose wrongly. For example, "feeling well" is a purpose which expresses part of the good of life and health, yet it is by no means unheard of for people to do things for the sake of "feeling well" which are in fact harmful to life and health viewed in a larger perspective. Similarly, "getting it together" and "feeling no pain" are aspects of the good of integrity or self-integration, but it is quite possible to do things in the name of "getting it together" which are contrary to the good of self-integration understood as harmony among all parts or elements of the self: this happens when one brings feelings and choices into accord by choosing to follow one's stronger feelings without a good reason for doing so or even against a reason for *not* doing so.

In listing and describing the fundamental human goods we do not mean to suggest that they already exist fully or even that, conceptually, they are fully determinate. The particular purposes for which we act are instances of the goods but do not exhaust them. Indeed, nobody can say definitively what is meant by life, play, integrity, friendship, and the rest, because they have never been fully realized and never can be.

Why not? Because these purposes constitute, as we have said, the outline of human possibility, the outline of what it means to be a human being. Just as we cannot help but understand them to some extent (because they are part of us, because they sum up what it means to be what we are: human beings), so we can never fully comprehend what they mean because we never in our lives exhaust the fullness of what it means to be human.

No matter how deeply we explore any or all of these fundamental human goods, there is always something beyond— some further possibility for realizing, within these categories, what human life is all about. We can gain ever deepening understanding of these goods only by dedicating ourselves to them and seeking their realization in our own lives and the lives of others.

Since the fundamental human goods sum up the possibilities of human personhood, they constitute the framework within which self-determination is possible. In some way every act of self-determination is directed to some aspect of one or more of these goods. But not every self-determining choice is *morally* good. Thus we have much further to go to establish workable criteria for determining what makes a choice good or bad in the moral sense. Next we shall consider the first and most basic criterion.

Questions for Review and Discussion

1. Why is working for money not one of the basic goods listed in this chapter?

2. Many empirical psychologists would list such things as food, drink, oxygen, and so forth as basic needs. How does the position set forth here take into account the fundamental character of activity directed toward satisfying such needs?

3. Traditionally, liberal education has been concerned with play, aesthetic experience, and speculative knowledge. But as education becomes available to a larger part of a population, it tends to become less liberal and to concentrate more on vocational preparation. Why do you think this is so?

4. Can you develop a theory explaining why an interest in play, aesthetic experience, and speculative knowledge might have developed as human beings moved from more primitive to more civilized conditions?

5. By what principle are integrity, practical reasonableness, friendship, and religion differentiated from each other?

6. Can you think of a theory in psychology, ethics, or some other field that tends to define the ideal of the good human life in terms of one (or less than all) of the goods distinguished here?

7. Acts done simply because they are morally virtuous have traditionally been considered ends in themselves. If this is correct, the moral virtues must be included in the scheme of basic goods. Where would they be included?

8. It might be argued that you cannot act for any one of the goods in the second group of four—integrity, practical reasonableness, friendship, and religion—without to some extent tending to realize all of them. Can you think of reasons for or against such a position?

9. According to our thesis, integrity, practical reasonableness, friendship, and religion require life, play, aesthetic experience, and speculative knowledge as vehicles. Illustrate this idea by the example of a quest for international justice.

10. Using examples from history, show how one of the goods—justice, for instance—can be definite enough to serve as an objective but also open-ended enough to permit the unfolding of new dimensions of meaning.

8. "Ought" Points toward Fullness of Being

Having identified the basic human goods, which are the fundamental reasons for which it is possible to act, we have made some progress toward establishing guidelines for making moral judgments about action. But we have not yet answered the central question: What makes some actions morally good and others bad?

Curiously enough, though, in everyday life people routinely and without difficulty make value judgments in areas other than morality. They spontaneously say that objects and experiences are "good" or "bad," that something is or is done as it "ought" or "ought not" to be or be done. Examining what is meant by such nonmoral judgments will not immediately tell us what moral judgments signify, but it will give us insights to help us understand moral "good," "bad," and "ought."

At the outset, though, we need to set aside one way of thinking which might seem promising at first. Not a few people suppose that the pleasure we experience as sentient beings is a great good, while sensible pain is a great evil. Does not this tell us something helpful and important about moral good and evil?

In chapter three we saw that pleasure does not satisfy the requirements of true human happiness; while in chapter seven we saw that purposes are not just things we want but the embodiments, as it were, of human goods which are reasons for deliberate action. It follows, then, that sensible pleasure, both as an experience and as a goal of action, cannot be equated with fulfillment. True, pleasure and fulfillment can and sometimes do converge, for instance, in the eating of a meal which is both tasty and nourishing. But it is also true that they are sometimes in conflict, for instance, when one suffers through a painful dental procedure—root canal work, say—for the intelligible purpose of having sound teeth. Pleasure and pain are sensible good and bad, corresponding to the sentient dimension of our human nature; but it is intelligible good and bad, corresponding to the fact that we are intelligent beings as well as sentient ones, which offer a pathway into the meaning of moral good and evil.

A. Good and Ought, Bad and Ought Not

The meanings of the words "good" and "ought" (as of the words "bad" and "ought not") are closely related. Their relationship becomes clear when one looks at areas other than morality. In doing so, however, it is important to bear in mind that we are merely trying to learn what can be learned by analogy about the meaning of these words. As we shall see, they are used in many different contexts and in diverse senses. It is important not to slip into the error of appropriating a meaning from some other context (for example, the idea that "goodness" is equivalent to "health," "evil" to "sickness") and applying it simplistically to morality. We can learn *something* about the meaning of "good" and "bad" as moral concepts from this kind of exercise in analogy, but we certainly cannot learn everything.

A good car is one which does well what a car ought to do. Of course, different people have different ideas about what a car ought to do, and thus they may disagree on whether a particular car is good or not. One driver puts the emphasis on speed and judges that any car which cannot do 120 mph is not a good one. Another driver is looking for economy and concludes that only a car which gets at least thirty-five miles to the gallon is good. Such differences, however, are beside the point here— the point being that however an individual determines what a car ought to do, a good car for that person will be one which meets his or her particular standards of oughtness.

The same fact—that "good" is closely related to "ought"—is universally observable. A good argument is one which reaches its conclusion as an argument ought to reach it. A good diet is one which provides what a diet ought to provide. A good father does what a father ought to do.

There is of course plenty of room for diverse tastes, whether in cars, diets, arguments, or fathers; yet everyone who uses the words "good" and "ought" in these and other contexts quite naturally understands that they are inseparable in meaning (as are their counterparts "bad" and "ought not"). This is not a moral judgment. It is simply a judgment that the good thing will be the thing as it ought to be.

What exactly is this judgment expressing? What do we mean by saying that the good thing is the thing which is as it ought to be? To answer that it is necessary first to take note of the fact that existing things are often incomplete. Part of their reality is still in the order of potentiality. They are *something*, certainly, but not yet everything they can be. They have not yet become all that they are capable of being.

The possibilities of actually existing things are not mere fictions. It is not a fiction to say that a child is capable of becoming an adult. The future adulthood of children is real, even though it does not exist yet. Adulthood for a child is an entirely real possibility which the child has simply not yet reached and realized.

We are not, however, leading up to the conclusion that moral goodness means realizing one's potential, while moral badness is failure to do so. The matter is considerably more complicated than that.

After all, badness is as real a possibility as goodness. The car which one purchased in the hope and expectation that it would be a good car can turn out to be a lemon, constantly laid up in the shop for repairs. The child whom one raised to be a good person can turn out to be evil, and in so doing he or she is fulfilling possibilities just as truly as if he or she were good. People who are cruel, who exploit others, who break down community, realize their potential to the extent that cruelty, exploitation, and the destruction of community were among the possibilities open to them. The mere realization of potential does not mean that a thing or a person is thereby good.

B. Being and Being More

Some theories of what it means to be morally good and morally bad say in effect that goodness is health and vice is disease. This is the explanation offered, for example, by the psychoanalyst Erich Fromm. It is not an adequate explanation, because it does not leave room for freedom of self-determination, and in ruling out this freedom it rules out the whole moral question as well.

If, after all, vice is simply a form of disease, from which one suffers but which one does not choose, then self-determination just does not enter into the picture; and activity which is not the result of self-determination is not moral action at all (that is, it is neither moral nor immoral; it is simply amoral). It is true that some people act viciously because they are diseased, but in such cases they are not acting immorally, even though they are acting viciously. Where freedom is entirely lacking, one cannot properly call action either moral or immoral.

But even though we cannot accept literally the goodness-is-health-and-badness-is-disease theory, the notion does contain the kernel of an idea worth exploring. Both "health" and "disease" describe ways in which an organism can function. How do we distinguish between them? One way of describing health is to say it is that way of functioning which is compatible with and leads to functioning further and more fully, while disease is a way of functioning that interferes with and closes off other possible functions.

In the nature of things disease makes an organism less capable of further functioning; if the disease is serious enough, it eventually makes the organism incapable of functioning at all because it ends in death. Health on the other hand is a condition in which the possibility of functioning is open, and the more healthy the organism is, the more capable of functioning it is. Thus what is good for the organism (health) is to live and live more fully, whereas what is bad (disease) is for it to live less fully and eventually not live at all.

A similar pattern exists in the area of thought and inquiry. In this field, too, we make value judgments by saying, for example, that a particular argument is "good" or "bad." This need not be a moral judgment. One can properly acknowledge a good argument for what one regards as a morally bad position, just as one may recognize a bad argument for something regarded as morally good.

Various criteria enter into the nonmoral judgment that an argument is good or bad. One thing demanded of a good argument is clarity: no one regards confusion as desirable. Another trait is certitude: it is considered desirable that an intellectual inquiry lead to a definite conclusion instead of losing itself in vague rambling. A third criterion is explanatory power: in natural science it is considered desirable that a hypothesis be able to account for additional phenomena rather than that a new hypothesis be required to explain a newly observed phenomenon. Finally, one desires consistency: a train of thought should hang together, and its components should not undercut one another.

Why are these characteristics—clarity, certitude, explanatory power, and consistency—regarded as desirable? Because when they are present, knowledge is able to continue to grow and expand, and new areas for investigation and further understanding can open up; whereas when they are absent, further growth in knowledge and understanding becomes impossible. Confusion, endless inquires, the absence of unifying principles, inability to explain things, internal inconsistency—these block thought and hamper investigation. We are impeded in our efforts to acquire further knowledge. Thus, in the area of thought and inquiry the good is that which makes possible further growth in knowledge, while the bad is that which frustrates and renders impossible further growth.

Much the same pattern is found in the fields of art and technology. Creativity in fine art refers not only to the successful exploration of the possibilities of a particular medium but to an exploration carried on in such a way as to point to the possibility of still further fruitful explorations to be carried on by artists who come after. From this perspective the most creative artists, masters like Mozart and Rembrandt, are those who significantly expand the borders of their art form. Lesser artists are those who for the most part operate within the confines of what has already been achieved in a particular genre or style; they come up to the mark, but they do not exceed it. As for artistic failures, they do not achieve even what has already been achieved. If they are innovators, their innovations prove to be dead ends. If they belong to an established artistic school or tradition, their work is mere sterile imitation, repeating the outward form of previous works without their inner spirit and tending to set art on the path of retrogression.

In technology, too, creativity means the opening up of new possibilities for further development—the sort of thing achieved by an Edison. Efficiency is also regarded as desirable in these areas, and efficiency is good because it fulfills possibilities in a way that leaves open further possibilities. By contrast, stultification sets in when the creative spirit flags and investigators are unable to go beyond what has already been achieved. Inefficiency is likewise bad because it not only fails to set new standards but is a waste of resources—because, in other words, it tends unnecessarily to limit possibilities.

In all of these areas—health, intellectual activity, art, and technology—we value or regard as good that which leads to being and being more; we judge to be bad that which cuts off further possibilities and tends toward the restriction of being.

To be sure, this is very abstract language. But the abstractness is necessary in order to sum up what one observes repeatedly in concrete circumstances in many different areas of life. The good is on the side of that which promotes being and its expansion and fullness. The bad is on the side of that which limits and contracts being and eventually terminates in nothingness or nonbeing.

C. What about Morality?

We still have not arrived at an understanding of moral good and bad, but we are getting closer. Up to now we have seen what in various fields and apart from morality is meant by such words as "good," "bad," and "ought." We have not discovered anything very surprising—only that, in very general terms, the good is that which preserves being and makes possible more being, while the bad is that which limits being and tends toward nonbeing.

It is reasonable to suppose that the same pattern is present in the area of morality, with adaptations required by its particular matter. The subject matter of morality is free, self-determined human action. If therefore what we have just said is correct, moral goodness will be found in a kind of human action which not only realizes a person's potential for free action but realizes it in a way which tends toward fuller realization. By contrast, moral evil will be a way of acting which also realizes the human potential for self-determined action but does so in a manner that closes off possibilities for further free, self-determined action.

This is a very general criterion indeed and scarcely enables us to determine whether a particular action is morally good or bad. Even at this very general level we must examine more closely what the principle we have just expressed means and why it is plausible to regard it as the principle of moral good and evil. In the next chapter, too, we shall formulate the principle more precisely than we have done here. Beyond that it will be necessary to see how the principle, assuming it is accepted as valid, can be applied to specific kinds of actions in order to make moral judgments about them.

Yet the fact remains that, tentatively at least, we now do have a very general principle for discriminating between moral good and evil. Moral good is that which fosters human *being* and *being more*, human living and living more fully. Moral evil is that which puts limits on human being and contracts human life.

Moral evil amounts to a kind of existential self-mutilation, and when it is committed by members of communities acting either together or against one another, it tends to destroy genuine community. Moral goodness amounts to ever-increasing growth in the realization of our possibilities as human persons, both in our individual lives and in the communal forms of life in which we share. But what makes such growth possible? In chapter nine we shall try to answer that question.

Questions for Review and Discussion

1. Some have argued that *good* is the more basic concept; others, that *ought* is more basic. We do not directly enter this argument. Do you see why not?

2. If someone thinks of potentiality as nothing more than a way of referring to actuality at some time in the future, he or she would not be able to make sense of the theory outlined here. Can you think of arguments for or against the position that when we say "X can," we mean something more than "X will, if certain conditions are fulfilled"?

3. Some philosophers say that values are irreducible to facts—"ought" is irreducible to "is"—while others say values are nothing but a particular set of facts. How does the position outlined here resolve this issue?

4. To what field does the concept of "health" belong? Biology? Investigate the history of the concept and current attempts to define it and compare with our analysis.

5. Good and bad in the area of thought and inquiry are in the province of logic. If you have already studied some logic, analyze what was done in your course with reference to the criteria for this area which we suggest.

6. Exemplify from the field of art and literary criticism the way in which originality is used as a criterion of quality in the fine arts and literature.

7. Compare our remarks about efficiency with definitions of it to be found in introductory works in economics.

8. Some propose self-realization or self-actualization as the moral ideal. This position is obviously related to ours. But for several reasons we avoid such a formulation. How is our formulation more complex?

9. It has been said that the most fundamental question in ethics is "Who makes the rules?" Criticize this formulation of the problem in light of the analysis proposed here.

10. In each of the fields discussed in this chapter the values involved lead to do's and don'ts, and the standards of what ought to be lead to negative evaluations of that which falls short of the standards. Does this mean that disciplines like hygiene or logic are essentially negative and restrictive? If our analysis is correct, would the same conclusion apply to ethics?

9. The First Principle of Morality

Perhaps some readers are growing impatient by now. This discussion seems to be running very long. Is it not possible to cut short the explanations, and say plainly how to tell what is morally good from what is morally bad?

We are happy to oblige. To be morally good is to be completely reasonable; to be morally bad is to be somewhat less than *completely* reasonable.

Is that all?

In a sense it is. We know very well, however, that the statement which has just been made seems on its face to be simplistic, even banal. Actually, it is far otherwise, but showing why that is so unavoidably involves further explanations. The aim in this chapter is to identify and explore the first principle of morality. But we are not being coy or misleading, for at the end we shall see that what we have said is true: To be morally good is to be completely reasonable, to be morally bad is to be somewhat less than *completely* reasonable. And we shall also see, in considerably more depth than is now the case, what this seemingly shallow statement means.

A. A Matter of Choice

The question of choice becomes of critical importance at this stage of our discussion. Analyzing the process of choosing

97

will carry us forward in the task of identifying and understanding the criterion of moral good and evil which we are seeking.

As has been seen earlier, though, there is a more fundamental reason why choice is important to the discussion of ethics. The very notion of moral good and evil involves freedom of self-determination. Where there is no free choice, morality is not in question.

At least implicitly, however, we have also seen that free, self-determining choices do not occur in a vacuum. To say a choice is "free" does *not* mean that it is purposeless or undirected. Quite the contrary. Choices are guided by basic human goods, understood not merely as things we want but as starting points for practical reasoning. All morally significant acts, all free choices, are for reasons, and the "reasons" are the basic human goods.

This is true of morally bad choices as well as morally good ones. There is a crucial sense in which immoral choices are not as reasonable as they should be, yet even bad choices are not sheerly irrational. Bad choices are made for purposes which are interesting to those who make them. But there always are reasons why purposes are interesting, and, as with good choices, the ultimate reasons are the basic human goods.

What is it, then, about a bad choice that makes it bad? If the reasons underlying both good and bad choices are basic human goods, it must be that the critical difference between good and bad does not concern what is chosen so much as the way in which the choice is made. It is true, as we shall see, that it is never morally right to choose certain things, but this is so essentially because these things cannot be chosen in a morally right manner. (There is no morally right way of choosing to rape a woman, torture a child, enslave a man, or do quite a few other deeds.)

In brief, the basic human goods, described in chapter seven, create the field within which self-determination is possible. Taken together, they sum up the possibilities of human personhood, so that there can be no act of self-determination which is not directed to some aspect of one or more of them. But moral goodness plainly consists in something else than simply choosing to pursue a fundamental human good. That happens *every* time we choose (for the prospect of sharing in a human good is what makes anything interesting and appealing to us), yet not all our choices are morally good. Moral goodness and evil, therefore, specifically concern the manner in which choices are made.

B. *Two Ways of Choosing*

In the last chapter we saw that the meaning of the word "ought," when applied to morality, parallels, with due regard for morality's proper subject matter, its meaning in other areas. "Ought" generally points toward full, fuller, and fullest being. Thus the moral "ought" points toward full and fuller freedom of self-determination and, ultimately, to the fullest possible self-determination. But because "self-determination" is only another name for realizing what it means to be a person, "ought" in the moral sphere points ultimately to an ideal of the fullest possible personhood and the richest possible community. The moral "ought" is a kind of verbal road sign directing travelers to their full humanity realized through freedom of self-determination.

The question before us now is how our choices—or, more precisely, our *way* of choosing—can foster or impede the realization of this ideal.

Basically there are limitations of two kinds on the power of our actions to realize human goods—to contribute, that is, to our own fulfillment and that of other persons. Limitations of the first kind are unavoidable and, because they cannot be avoided, have no direct connection with morality. A person can do just so much, for any individual's insight into how to be of service to human goods and his or her capacity for serving them are limited by many factors over which he or she has no control: intelligence, strength, health—even such basics as where and when he or she happens to live. Furthermore, a person can act to realize certain goods only within limits required by the nature of those goods themselves. So, for instance, if Mary marries John, she cannot also marry Henry; and the good which will be realized by her marrying John will be not-realized by her not marrying Henry. These limitations, to repeat, are unavoidable and do not constitute immorality.

However, people also sometimes limit their service to human goods in ways that are avoidable. In this case the limitations are not dictated by the inevitable limits on what a person can do or by some requirement of the goods themselves. The limitations come from somewhere else. Quite simply, they come from nonintegrated emotional factors—feelings—in the person who is making the choice; the individual chooses in a way different from the way in which he or she would choose if reason were not affected by these feelings.

Take the case of someone choosing to harm another person in response to feelings of anger and hatred. In themselves the basic human goods point one in the opposite direction, toward the benefit of human beings rather than their injury. Moreover, human goods direct one to live at peace with others and to avoid doing injury to oneself, and everyone knows that harming others is likely to have consequences contrary to either or both of these interests.

Still, it is possible to find grounds in some of the basic human goods for anticipating certain benefits from revenge. One may reason that it will discourage the other party from engaging in provocation in the future and lead to more peaceful relations in the long run ("He won't dare do *that* again") and also that failure to take revenge would be unjust ("It would be a crime to let her get away with that"). One may know very well that it is unreasonable to anticipate such benefits in this particular case and that, were it not for hostile feelings, one would not cause the harm here being contemplated. But one can set aside the first objection by reasoning, "You never know what you can accomplish until you try," and come to terms with the second by acknowledging that revenge would be sweet—that taking revenge will bring about harmony between one's feelings and one's choice *by making the choice which is in accord with one's feelings.*

So the vengeful person chooses revenge. In doing so he or she fetters reason by one of its own practical principles, one of the basic human goods: that which is concerned with the harmony of feelings among themselves and with one's judgments and choices. There is a rational element in this choice—precisely this basic human good one has in view—yet the choice is not as fully reasonable as a choice against revenge would be, because one sets aside other human goods for the sake of a stunted, partial participation in this one.

Not all immoral choices come about in just the same way, however. Sometimes what one has in view does not offend against reason, a real benefit is involved, and in other circumstances it would be possible to choose similar acts without hobbling reason.

In the public library you find a new novel which you have been wanting to read, charge it out, and bring it home, with the object of reading it and enjoying the benefit of esthetic experience. Up to this point no problem at all.

Suppose, however, that you find the novel on a reserve shelf; in order to read it at once, you will have to discard the six-month waiting list attached to the book before charging it out. In doing so you will be acting for your benefit at the expense of others. But you know that people cannot live together in harmony unless they treat one another as they themselves wish to be treated, and that community with others is required for fulfillment. Feelings aside, reason tells you not to act this way.

Still, you really do want to read the book, and as your craving gnaws at you, you think some more: the harm to others in having to wait a bit longer for the book is very small, you have not used the library much lately and you deserve your fair share of what it offers, the librarians are to blame for not providing more than one copy of a popular book, and so on—until you stuff the waiting list in your pocket and check the book out at the front desk. Quite simply, your choice to take the book home satisfies your craving to read it, and so, once again, you have achieved harmony between your feelings and your choice by suiting the choice to the feelings.

Selfish people are reasonable in anticipating a benefit to themselves, yet theirs is a reasonableness with blinders on. In setting aside the interests of others their choices fetter reason by abusing one of its practical principles to prevent the full play of others.

It is in this sense that the attitude underlying immoral choice can be called "exclusivistic." This means that, to some extent at least, realization of the ideal of integral human fulfillment—fulfillment in respect to the whole range of basic human goods—is impeded in the one choosing and, very often, in others as well.

We have just seen two examples of this, but it can happen in a number of different ways. Even though we have spoken of an attitude toward choice, it is possible to offend against integral fulfillment by omitting, out of inertia and sloth, to choose and act for *any* good (for example, a woman who has a number of projects clamoring for her attention at work but, finding the pressure disagreeable, kills the afternoon straightening up her desk). Or irrational partiality may lead one to seek the realization of the good by one party to whom one happens to feel well disposed, while neglecting its realization by others in whose well being one has reason to be equally concerned (for example, a father who exhibits favoritism toward one of his children). As we shall see later in considering what we call "modes of responsibility," there are several distinct categories of behavior by which one's willing can fall short of the ideal of integral human fulfillment.

In willing what falls short we subjectively limit the good to some instance of it which our feelings lead us to prefer, while downgrading or denying the worth of some other instance or instances of human good in ourselves or other persons. And although this has an element of reasonableness insofar as it shows some concern for a human good, still it is less than fully reasonable because it denies the worth of other instances of the same or other goods. Thus we whittle down human possibilities to fit our limitations; our capacity for realizing ourselves and for helping others to realize themselves is diminished, not only here and now but also in the future, to the extent that an exclusivistic choice guides other choices yet to be made.

What about the morally good choice? As this analysis of immoral choice implies, moral goodness consists in being guided in one's choices by one's understanding of all the relevant human goods—those, that is, which are actually at stake in each particular situation of choice—and by the opportunities for realizing them which are suggested by the facts of the situation considered in an open and unprejudiced way. Even though one must choose one alternative out of two or more, still one continues to respect the values which are present in the alternatives not chosen. Moreover, one chooses that alternative—and there is always at least one—which does not require one to adopt an exclusivistic attitude toward any principle of practical reasoning, any instance of basic human good. One's choice is fully reasonable.

Although for the sake of convenience we use the word "inclusivistic" to characterize this attitude toward choice, toward instances of human goods, and toward the sum total of human goods which comprise the ideal of integral human fulfillment, no single word really sums up the complexity of the attitude we are describing. Reverence for persons and respect for fundamental human goods are part of it, yet they suggest something too passive; concern and interest capture some of it, yet the attitude includes none of the partiality these words imply. Perhaps closer to the mark are such notions as caring for persons and appreciation of goods, understood as involving readiness to serve.

C. The First Principle of Morality

At this point, then, we are able to express the first principle of morality. It is this: *In voluntarily acting for human goods and avoiding what is opposed to them, a person should choose and otherwise will those possibilities, and only those, which it is compatible with integral human fulfillment to will.* (While it does not require lengthy discussion here, "otherwise will" in the foregoing formulation simply refers to the fact that, technically speaking, there are other kinds of volitional activity besides choice.)

Moral truth and moral goodness are a matter of taking fully into account all the principles of practical reason—all the basic human goods. Ideally, free choices would be made consistently in light of them all. Furthermore, since moral truth points to human fulfillment, freely chosen actions consistently shaped in this way by moral truth would bear fruit in the fulfillment of all persons in all the basic human goods. This ideal community is what is meant by integral human fulfillment. It is not individualistic, for what is envisaged is the flourishing of all persons and communities.

Integral human fulfillment is not something concrete, not the sum total of all conceivable instances of the human goods, and not therefore a goal to be achieved as the outcome of a master plan such as might be produced by the calculations of a giant computer programmed for social engineering. It is a guiding ideal, not an objective to be attained. Inasmuch as fundamental human goods are open-ended, it is never possible to say that any of these possibilities has finally and definitively been realized, so that no further realization of it can be imagined.

Moreover, integral human fulfillment is not some kind of supreme good, similar to but greater in magnitude than other human goods like truth and friendship. Basic human goods like these are reasons for choosing and acting; the ideal of integral human fulfillment serves to guide the interplay among these reasons, ensuring that one's choices are indeed fully reasonable and do not, in response to unintegrated feelings, express unreasonable preference for some persons or some instances of human goods over others.

Consistent respect in choice and action for the ideal of integral human fulfillment corresponds to what we suggested earlier is the core meaning of the moral "ought": the fullest possible self-realization of the human person. For it leaves us open to self-realization for ourselves and others even in directions we do not actually choose. Although here and now we choose X rather than Y and Z, we continue to acknowledge the good which made Y and Z interesting. Thus we remain fully open to the possibility of realizing that good at another time in different circumstances, as well as to its realization by others. Whereas exclusivistic choice, involving an attitude which denies the value of that which is not chosen, is not only here and now opposed to self-realization (for oneself and often for others, too) but tends to block it in the future by creating or reinforcing a mind set which denies that there is something there worth choosing.

D. *The Meaning of Immorality*

The truth of what has just been said becomes more clear when it is seen that the criterion of moral evil outlined here fits various other meanings commonly attached to the word "immorality." When we call something immoral, we are saying not only that it is unreasonable but that it is a kind of self-mutilation, that it is a violation (at least incipient) of community, and that it is a rejection of the reality sought by the religious quest.

First, self-mutilation. When we are confronted with a choice, each alternative corresponds to something within us or in other persons which is reaching out to be realized. True, in choosing at all we leave something unrealized here and now. But in exclusivistic choice, instead of preserving an attitude of respect for and openness to that which is not chosen, one in effect suppresses and irrationally denies the value of some instance of one or more fundamental human goods, aspects of one's own personhood and the personhood of others.

Second, violation of community. Obviously, community is violated by actions like cheating and stealing which do immediate, visible harm to others. But even immoral choices which apparently do no harm to anyone else undermine the foundation of community in a subtle way. The foundation of community lies in shared appreciation and service of fundamental human goods; to the extent that it repudiates some instance of one or more of these, immoral choice inevitably does injury to community.

Third, rejection of the reality sought by the religious quest. An inclusivistic approach to choice acknowledges and submits to reality, inasmuch as it takes properly into account all the human goods which are at stake here and now and all the persons involved. Thus, it is also consistent with the effort to identify the more-than-human source of meaning and value and to enter into a harmonious relationship with it. But an exclusivistic approach to choice, by setting aside the ideal of integral human fulfillment as its guiding principle, dismisses as unimportant the possibility that the meaning and value embodied in this ideal come ultimately from some more-than-human source with which it is important to be in harmony. The disharmony thus introduced into this relationship is contrary to the human purpose of religion—it is irreligious. To put this in traditional religious language: Sinners implicitly reject God's wisdom and love and so disrupt their relationship with him.

It bears noting, finally, that inclusivistic choice involves an attitude of service to, rather than domination of, the fundamental human goods. People who come at choice in this way do not impose their vision on reality; rather, they acknowledge goodness where it exists and seek to realize it to the best of their ability, even while admitting that because of their own limitations they cannot realize every possible instance of human good in their own lives. This mode of choice thus corresponds to the third level of action, which, as we have seen, basically involves the realization of human goods through participating in them.

If, however, we regard the alternatives in a choice situation in such a way that not choosing something transforms it by removing the value which it previously possessed (exclusivistic choice), from then on in regard to that good we are involved only in action at the second level. For this approach to choosing implies that a thing has goodness only insofar as it is a concrete objective and that if we choose not to seek and possess it, it ceases to have value.

This is the paradox—the irrationality in action—of exclusivistic choice, seen now from another point of view. We set out to make a free choice, to exercise self-determination; we end up pursuing a particular objective, our action now merely a matter of doing as we please. Instead of realizing one's self by remaining open to fuller personhood in one's own case and that of others, the person choosing exclusivistically makes even that aspect of the self which is fulfilled by the choice a definite and limited objective, which is now *extrinsic* to the very center of his or her personhood. In choosing exclusivistically one moves from *being a person* to *having something* one happens to want.

This is not to say that it is impossible to act immorally at the third level. Quite the contrary. For the point is precisely this: Immoral action could well be described as third-level action which consists in choosing to place oneself at the second level—and stay there. Later we shall see more of what this means. For now it is enough to say: To be morally good is to be completely reasonable; to be morally bad is to be somewhat less than *completely* reasonable.

Questions for Review and Discussion

1. One reason some people take a subjectivist position is that they are afraid of an externally imposed morality—one which would make morally good action into second-level action. Discuss the way in which the theory outlined here reconciles objectivity with freedom.

2. Is inclusivism itself exclusivistic inasmuch as it excludes its opposite?

3. In what sense can one choose to do what is morally wrong?

4. Think of examples of actions which you consider morally evil but in which you can nevertheless find the good for which the action might be done. How must a person who resists temptation proceed if he or she is to choose inclusivistically?

5. Some people argue that those who voluntarily forgo the satisfaction of some of their desires—for example, for sexual communion, personal possessions, and social status—are guilty of self-mutilation. But by their vows of chastity, poverty, and obedience, people like Saint Francis of Assisi and Mother Teresa engage in self-restraint with respect to such desires. Do you think they violate the first principle of morality as we formulate it? If not, why not?

6. What is the difference between the rationality of action demanded here and the consistency that even a subjectivist theory requires?

7. Some theories of ethics hold that the morally good is what builds up community, while the morally bad is what harms others. Distinguish the criterion of morality proposed here from such alternative theories.

8. Some religious theories of morality reduce moral goodness to obedience to divine commands. William of Ockham, a fourteenth-century theologian, went so far as to say that if God commanded us to do just the opposite of what the Ten Commandments say, we would be morally obliged to do so. How does our view of immorality considered from the point of view of religion differ from religious theories of that sort?

9. The theory proposed here rejects the idea that in choice we create or transform values. How, then, can it be said that in this theory there is room and need for creativity in moral life?

10. The Ethics of Love

By now advocates of the new morality who have been following this discussion are very likely in a highly exasperated state. "What is all this talk about levels of action, categories of goods, inclusivistic and exclusivistic choice, integral human fulfillment, and the rest? What does this have to do with morality? There is no need to make a production of moral judgment, and all your jargon merely obscures what is in reality perfectly simple. The moral criterion is love. If people act lovingly, they act morally. That's the long and the short of it."

Would that it were so simple! Several different ethical theories are embraced under the headings of the "new morality" or "situation ethics," but none provides an adequate account of human action or the standard by which moral judgments are to be made. And to say "It's all a matter of loving and acting lovingly" turns out upon examination to be no more than a source of confusion at best and, at worst, an excuse for shirking the hard work of judging and acting morally.

A. Relatives and Absolutes

In speaking of "situation ethics" and "situationism" different people mean different things. Some mean that received moral absolutes—moral norms declaring that some things ought never to be done—should be put aside, and a view substituted according to which the morality of actions is determined case by case, according to their good and bad effects.

108

This approach is more properly called "consequentialism" or "proportionalism." We deal with it in chapter twelve.

Others, however, believe that the situation itself somehow directly determines what ought to be done. This is the case, for instance, with the moral relativism of John Dewey. His is a rather pure version of the situationist ethic, which holds that there are no absolute values: all values are relative to a particular situation. The value of values, one might say, is determined by the situation, not by anything inherent in the values.

This view is founded on a false understanding of the moral situation. It assumes that, morally speaking, the situation is something given, which imposes morality on us. In reality, though, the reverse is true: the situation does not impose morality on us; we impose morality on the situation. The moral dimension becomes present according to how we perceive the facts and how we respond to them through free, self-determining choices. An example makes this clearer.

The time is sunrise. The place is a downtown street near the railroad station. Lying unconscious in the gutter is a well-dressed man of middle age. This is the physical situation. The moral situation only comes into being when someone enters on the scene and is required to choose what to do.

Let us imagine three different people confronting this physical situation and making such a choice: a woman just off from work who is running to catch the train which will take her home, a dedicated member of Alcoholics Anonymous, and a common thief. It is entirely likely that each will respond differently: the woman commuter by passing by, the Alcoholics Anonymous member by stopping to help, the thief by robbing the man. It is also entirely possible that each will feel morally justified in the course of action he or she has chosen. Even thieves—to say nothing of people who are "too busy to get involved"—are capable of rationalizing their behavior so as to justify themselves in their own eyes.

The point, however, is not that any course of action is acceptable provided one can find some subjective rationalization for it. There is little doubt that in the example given only the second course of action—stopping to help the fallen man—is, objectively speaking, the right thing to do. But that is not the point either.

The point instead is that each of these three individuals—the commuter, the Alcoholics Anonymous member,
and the thief—encounters the same physical situation but creates a different moral situation because of preexisting attitudes
and commitments. It might be said, for example, that the
thief's basic moral commitment (a highly immoral one of
course) is to self-satisfaction. But because this is so, he simply
does not see the physical facts—an unconscious person lying in
the street—as making a claim on his generosity and selfless-
ness. Rather, he perceives this physical situation as one more
opportunity for the exercise of his habit of thievery.

A situationist like Dewey goes wrong in several ways. For
one thing he fails to see that people come to a physical situation
with an understanding of basic human goods. Otherwise they
would never conclude that the situation required anything of
them. The mere data of a situation do not tell one even that a
response is demanded or appropriate; it is impossible to get an
"ought" from an "is," unless the "ought" preexists on some
other basis than the situation which brings it into play.

Situationists like Dewey also go wrong in not recognizing
that, as in our example, people come to situations with definite
moral attitudes which must be criticized, not just taken for
granted. The notion that one can find what one ought to do
simply by examining the situation only seems plausible to
people who are so insular—so isolated from the rough-
and-tumble of exposure to seriously held (and acted upon)
moral views at variance with their own—that they seem hardly
aware that there are other ways of evaluating and responding
to particular situations besides their way.

If situationism were correct, the individuals in our example
could not have responded differently to the same situation, for
the situation would have imposed a uniform response on them
all. But in fact just the opposite occurred. Individuals created
the moral situation for themselves on the basis of their prior
choices and their understanding of the facts. In saying that the
morality of a situation is given by the situation itself, situationists are only saying that previous choices often cause people to
perceive particular situations in a certain way, so that they are
no longer interested in taking another look—either at their

prior choices or at their perceptions—to determine whether they square with reality: "Don't confuse me with facts." While people do often act this way, that does not constitute the basis for a true and viable ethical theory.

B. Utilitarianism

Also embraced under the "new morality" is the theory of utilitarianism, which received its classic statement in the works of Jeremy Bentham and, especially, John Stuart Mill. Actually, utilitarianism is a form of consequentialism, which we shall treat in chapter twelve. But it has its historical importance, as well as its specific difference, which merit separate consideration here.

Utilitarianism is most easily identified by its slogan "the greatest good for the greatest number of people." Like Marxists, however, the nineteenth-century British utilitarians were interested mainly in alleviating social misery resulting from the industrial revolution, and this led them to equate "the greatest good" with pleasure or the satisfaction of desire. They were, one might say, high-minded hedonists.

Bentham began with a simplistic equating of goodness and pleasure, but this was soon seen to be a faulty explanation since it leads logically to the conclusion that, for example, a happy pig is in a more fortunate condition than Socrates. Mill improved the theory by arguing that the good involved is the greatest happiness for the greatest number of people and by further recognizing that it is not merely the quantity of pleasure which is important but its quality. In the final analysis, however, happiness still boiled down to a gratifying state of consciousness.

Utilitarianism necessarily involves a number of grave difficulties which render it unacceptable as an ethical theory. Despite the attempt to move from a quantitative to a qualitative measure of happiness, the fact remains that as long as the moral criterion is supposed to be the greatest happiness for the greatest number, morality remains at bottom a matter of quantitative measurement.

But how to do the measuring? Qualitatively diverse values are not reducible to one another, nor does the ideal of maximizing satisfaction for a group constitute a further and more fundamental purpose by which all other objectives can be measured. Furthermore, as we have already seen, human goods are not goals which we seek to reach and encompass by particular courses of action; rather, they are reasons for choosing and aspects of human personhood which we seek to realize through choice. They are, then, essentially open-ended, and it is impossible to devise a master plan either for individual or social life according to which one could at some point say that friendship had been "achieved" once and for all or that speculative knowledge had been "accomplished" definitively and there was no more learning to do. Yet in the absence of some such workable master plan, complete with quantified targets and goals, the whole idea of the "greatest good for the greatest number" becomes meaningless.

Again, in telling us to act in a way that will bring about the most good for the largest number of people, utilitarianism offers little guidance as to which people it has in view. Does this apply only to people who have been born? It makes a considerable difference: for example, in determining the morality of abortion (where most utilitarian advocates of the new morality would exclude the unborn from consideration) or in judging the morality of proposals for building possibly accident-prone nuclear energy plants (where many of the same supporters of the new morality, adverting to the danger of genetic damage from radiation, would reverse direction and include unborn future generations in their moral calculation).

It should of course be noted that, within limits, a calculation of the net pleasure and pain resulting from a course of action, as envisioned by utilitarianism, *is* possible, but only at the second level of action, where one acts to achieve limited, concrete goals. Once again we emphasize that this way of calculating and acting is an altogether necessary and proper part of life. But morality, as we have also emphasized, is basically concerned with self-realization, one's own and others', through third-level action: action by which one determines one's self by the attitude one adopts toward human goods.

Calculation of the kind presupposed by utilitarianism is impossible at this level, because the values involved are not embodied in a set of specific external objectives to be achieved but are instead aspects of human personhood to be realized through free, self-determining actions.

In their democratic and subjectivist way utilitarians often equate value with what people want and disvalue with what they do not want. But it is out of the question to weigh and measure all the positive and negative objects of even one individual's diverse and frequently conflicting feelings, and if it is impossible in the case of a single individual, how much more so in the case of the vastly more numerous—and still more conflicting—wants and aversions of large groups of people, classes, communities, nations!

Nor does utilitarianism offer any support for making commitments and remaining faithful to them. A commitment, as we have seen, is a large, overarching choice to participate in a good, requiring a whole series of further implementing choices for its carrying-out. There is no way of knowing what these later choices will involve nor what fidelity to the commitment will entail. Sometimes it may entail pain. At this point the utilitarian approach would encourage one to give up on the commitment, quit, and try something else which seems to promise more "happiness."

Other objections can easily be added to the list of criticisms of utilitarianism/new morality/situation ethics. What really is the situation in question? Situationists typically include in their analysis only as much of a particular situation as happens to suit their purpose. They take into consideration those with whom they are immediately dealing or for whom they feel particular concern, while ignoring others whose claims are equally great but whom they find it convenient to ignore.

Consider the "situation" involved in dropping atomic bombs on Hiroshima and Nagasaki. The usual defense of this action—a utilitarian argument—is that it saved lives by hastening Japan's surrender. If the situation is considered in this very narrow framework, the conclusion seems correct. But this is only because the "situation" *is* so arbitrarily limited in this analysis. Those who opted to drop the A-bomb on Hiroshima and Nagasaki considered only short-term effects, not the implications for the long-term future after the war. Alternative ways of hastening the war's end—imposing a blockade or abandoning the demand for "unconditional surrender"—were excluded. And the suffering of the victims seemed not so bad because they were Japanese, against whom there was a great deal of wartime prejudice and hostility. The point is that those who made the choice defined the "situation" to suit the choice they wished to make. In situationism the one who defines the situation also and automatically determines the moral verdict.

C. Love Is/Isn't Everything

Despite its contradictions and inconsistencies the new morality has a powerful appeal today, particularly when it employs the attractive slogan that "love alone is the standard of morality." Who can be against love?

Yet those who argue that love is all do not sufficiently consider the enormous ambiguities involved in the use of the word. Just which love are we speaking of here? In one sense all people love themselves and others and always act out of love. The difference between a moral and an immoral disposition does not concern whether one loves and acts on the basis of love; it concerns *how* one loves. Presumably people love those with whom they engage in sexual intercourse, but it makes a great difference if someone, aware of being infected with AIDS, does or does not inform an unsuspecting partner. In another sense love is a sentiment, a feeling. Happily it is a feeling which almost everyone experiences at some time or other in life and perhaps at many times. But the experience of being in love has nothing directly to do with morality, even though it can well prove the point of departure for moral goodness.

When we look into our own loves, we find not one love but many. Each makes a more or less plausible claim to get its way by controlling our choices and actions, but in fact our diverse loves are more or less in conflict. People love their country, and they also love their own lives. Are they, therefore, acting morally or immorally in risking their well-loved lives to defend their well-loved country?

This conflict of loves within us is the beginning of the moral problem. If we had only one, dominant love, we would never have to ask ourselves the question "What is my true responsibility?" But because conflicting loves make conflicting claims, we must wrestle with moral problems. We are forced to seek a standard for making moral judgments, and this seeking is the beginning of ethics. To say "Follow love" is not an ethics at all but a refusal to take ethical problems seriously.

The love-ethic is nevertheless attractive because it assumes as real an ideal which is unquestionably appealing. If we were perfectly good—if, that is, we loved in a fully open way all the goods that together comprise the flourishing of human persons, if we therefore cared generously not only about our own fulfillment but everyone's, if our whole personality were integrated in harmony with this attitude, and if, further, we lived among other people who were just like us in this—then (and only then) we would not need any criterion of morality beyond our own inclinations.

"Follow love" would then make perfect sense, because our love would be a perfectly reliable moral guide. Confronted with alternatives, we would always make the morally right choice because nothing wrong (disordered, unbalanced, exaggerated) would have made any inroad in us. We would in fact "sense" what was right, much as healthy people sense without reflection the appropriate movements and responses necessary to keep their balance. This, in sum, is the meaning of St. Augustine's often quoted and almost as often misunderstood words "Love God and then do what you will."

Unfortunately, none of us seems yet to have arrived at such a state of perfection. Some are closer to it, some further away, but none is there yet. For those whose love is more or less imperfect the advice to follow love only amounts to saying "Do what you please." Many rationalizations, not infrequently couched in idealistic terms, can be found for doing what one pleases. But in the end to do what one pleases is to do what one pleases. It is not an ethical position; it is ethical nonsense and moral chaos.

To do what is morally right we need moral guidelines. Thought is admittedly a weak instrument in this area, but it is the only one we have. Without falling into the trap of supposing that our love is perfect, we must ask ourselves what we would do if our love *were* perfect. This is the ethical question, the answers to which will make it possible to develop sound ethical rules for living our lives. Next we shall examine the question and its answers in some detail.

Questions for Review and Discussion

1. John Dewey says situations present problems: felt evils to be dealt with. What is presupposed by the perception of a set of facts as evil?

2. Utilitarianism is based on the application of a technical model to human action: it amounts to thinking of all human action as if it were second-level action. How does this sort of theory have a legitimate application?

3. Why do you suppose such a theory as utilitarianism became so popular in the last century and this one?

4. Using situation ethics, think of opposite decisions that might be made on the morality of important current issues. Show how either decision, once made, can be given a plausible utilitarian justification.

5. Is it possible for the same person consistently to hold to subjectivism and utilitarianism in ethics?

6. Distinguish and exemplify as many different senses of "love" as you can.

7. Explain what is involved in the ideal case of perfect love. Do you think anyone ever approaches or has ever approached this ideal? Are there instances in your own experience in which your love of the good was sufficient to make you see the right thing to do, and do it, without even asking yourself what was the "right" thing?

8. Authors who advocate situation ethics often use examples involving sexual morality. Can you think of any reason why they should concentrate on examples from this field?

9. Some advocates of situation ethics claim that it is Christian morality and that for Christians the only moral absolute is the demand to do what love requires. How does this square with your reading of the New Testament?

11. Guidelines for Love

Moral rules do not enjoy an especially good reputation today. The preceding chapter suggests why. A state of affairs in which moral rules are necessary is less than ideal, and many people wish to make a dramatic leap into the ideal. Yet human beings seem to be something other than ideal—which is why moral rules are necessary. People with 20/20 vision do not need eyeglasses, but those with imperfect vision find them a necessity. Morally speaking, we all have imperfect vision. Moral rules help us see more clearly what we ought to *do*.

To see more clearly in this case means to know with some degree of exactness what our concrete moral responsibilities are. Although in what follows we are not attempting to provide a moral handbook, a summary of common moral responsibilities, we do seek to offer assistance to individuals who wish to think through their own lives and come to a better understanding of their responsibilities. As we have seen, the basic principle of morality is that one's will be in line with integral human fulfillment—an ideal of a perfect community of all people richly fulfilled in all the human goods. The question is: How does this basic principle take shape in each individual person's unique body of moral responsibilities?

The moral guidelines we shall discuss might be described as general principles from which each person can develop his or her own detailed moral code; they are also principles by which any existing or possible moral code can be evaluated. Since these principles shape and control moral responsibilities, we call them "modes of responsibility." We shall deal with seven in

117

this chapter; an eighth, of particular difficulty, will be treated in the chapter that follows. The first three are directly concerned with other people, the next four with one's ambivalent attitudes toward goods, the eighth with unreasonable partiality among goods.

The modes of responsibility are rooted in the basic human goods; they specify the ways of choosing and acting which are incompatible with respect for and service of the goods. They are not external rules, but part of the intrinsic structure of moral life, not something apart from or over against human beings, but prerequisites of human fulfillment.

Each mode of responsibility has a social as well as an individual dimension. As moral principles the modes apply not only to individuals but to communities and their common action. Much of the time, perhaps most of the time, we act not alone but with others. The need for moral guidelines is no less where the number of those involved in an action is greater. Still, for simplicity's sake, in what follows we generally use examples of individuals acting alone.

The need for principles like these is evident. The first principle of morality is too general to offer specific guidance about what one should do here and now; for to say that one ought always to act in a way that will be in line with the ideal of integral human fulfillment does not settle the question of whether *this* particular choice is consistent with integral fulfillment. Hence the need for intermediate principles—the modes of responsibility—by which to make this determination.

Since they rule out ways of choosing and acting which are against integral human fulfillment, the modes are best expressed negatively. This does not mean that morality is essentially negative, a set of "thou shalt nots." In excluding ways of choosing and acting which are against reason's direction toward the basic goods, the modes exclude what is incompatible with human fulfillment; they render a negative service to a positive ideal.

Moral philosophers have sometimes mistaken one or another of the modes for the first principle of morality itself. That is not surprising, since the modes are specifications of the first principle. But the first principle is broader and more basic than the modes; to observe the first principle consistently, we must take into account all these intermediate principles and choose in a manner consistent with them all.

Very often the same immoral act violates two or more of the modes simultaneously. When that happens, one can tell that the act is wrong by noticing that it violates just one of the modes, but one will only appreciate all the reasons why it should be avoided by considering how it violates other modes as well.

Now let us see what the modes of responsibility are. Elsewhere we have listed them in a different order. Here we begin with three which concern our attitudes toward other persons; then we shall consider several which concern our ambivalent attitudes toward human goods.

A. The Golden Rule

The best known of the modes of responsibility is the familiar Golden Rule: Do unto others. . . . We express it this way: *Do not, in response to feelings, act or refrain from acting toward someone on the basis of a preference, unless the preference is required by human goods.* Do not play favorites.

How does this specify the first principle of morality? Although the first principle enjoins openness toward people and goods, everyone in fact narrows the range of persons and goods which he or she actively cares about. Sometimes this is reasonable and necessary, as when an individual chooses one person to marry rather than any other. But sometimes the narrowing is not reasonable: one acts on the basis of feelings which, although motives for behavior, are not *rational* motives, because they fail to express the requisite openness to everyone's potential for sharing in the relevant human goods.

The Golden Rule tells us not to be governed by certain of these emotions: feelings of preference for ourselves and those to whom we are attached. That is not to say that in certain circumstances one should not put one's family (or one's friends or school or country) first; actually, a person often has real, special obligations of this sort. Instead, this mode of responsibility says something else: one should act upon emotional preferences (for family, friends, school, and so forth) only if these reflect what is rationally required by human goods and the possible ways in which they can be realized; one should *not* simply be ruled by the preferences themselves.

For instance, a man gets angry whenever he hears that other people have been gossiping about him and his family, but he gossips about other people without giving it a second thought. An attorney devotes careful attention to the affairs of clients who are his friends or social acquaintances, but he deals in a perfunctory manner with clients whom he does not know or judges to be his social inferiors. A woman readily asks other people to do her favors, but she always finds excuses for begging off when others ask favors of her.

The virtuous disposition corresponding to this mode of responsibility is fairness; people who observe this principle are called disinterested, impartial, and so forth. Unfairness is the common theme of violations, and violators are said to be selfish, prejudiced, playing favorites, and so on.

People oriented toward the ideal of integral human fulfillment as their first moral principle will at all times take into account all the human goods, not only as they apply to themselves and those who are near and dear but as they apply to all other human beings. Such people do not regard themselves, family, and friends as special cases, demanding concessions they are unwilling to grant to others. They regularly ask themselves, "How would I like it if someone did this to me?"

The Golden Rule also embodies what has been called the principle of universalizability: One should act toward one person or group of persons just as one would, all rational considerations being the same, toward any other person or group. From one's way of conducting oneself here and now it should be possible to derive a universal norm applicable to every case involving no rational consideration other than those involved in this case.

B. Patience and Readiness to Forgive

A second mode of responsibility is this: *Do not act out of hostility to the detriment of any basic human good.* It is easy to see how violations conflict with the ideal of integral human fulfillment. In destroying, damaging, or impeding some instance of the human good in response to feelings of hatred, anger, hostility, and so forth, one reduces the possibility of human fulfillment without any real reason for doing so.

This mode does not rule out every expression of anger. Sometimes hatred of evil reasonably moves one to act to protect good or to resist the evil. Sometimes, too, a person can work off hostile feelings by doing things like tearing up an old telephone directory, say, that are useless in themselves but harmless. What this mode rules out is destructive, including self-destructive, behavior engaged in out of anger.

Vengeful behavior is a typical violation. The son of a Mafia boss is killed by a rival gang member; the boss contracts with a hit man to liquidate both the rival gang member and one of the children of the boss of that gang. Students outvoted by their classmates in planning a class social stay away from the event out of spite. A man whose wife snapped at him over breakfast gets back at her by treating her coldly over dinner. In such cases hostile feelings lead people to act against the human good for no good reason.

Violators are typically said to be vengeful, resentful, bearers of grudges, and so forth. The virtuous disposition corresponding to the mode is described by words like patient, forgiving, forbearing, long-suffering, gentle, and so on.

C. Sharing and Cooperation

A third mode of responsibility can be expressed this way: *Do not be an individualist in acting for the sake of the good in response to feelings of enthusiasm or impatience.* Unnecessary individualism cannot be squared with the ideal of integral human fulfillment, because the latter requires a fellowship of persons sharing in human goods.

Sometimes, of course, one has to act alone, either because the nature of the activity requires it (sonnets are not written by committees) or because nobody else is willing to join one in standing up for what is right (the solitary martyr for a just cause). But this mode envisages individualistic behavior arising not from sound reasons but from impatience and eagerness for results.

Few people have much sympathy for the hotshot basketball player who, scornful of his teammates' lesser skills, insists on shooting rather than passing. But violations sometimes also take forms which appear praiseworthy on the surface but are not really so. In groups of many kinds the more active members frequently take on tasks and responsibilities which *could* have been shared with the rest. They may be regarded as generous and self-sacrificing; almost certainly they will think of themselves that way. But they discourage others from making the contributions they could make and so prevent them from sharing in the common fulfillment as they might. Moreover, if such behavior is carried too far, such people end up spread too thin and unable to do all they have signed up for, while the group itself suffers. This is the fault of leaders who, unable to delegate, insist on doing everything themselves.

The virtuous disposition corresponding to this mode goes under such names as "team spirit" or, when it is a question of having a well integrated set of commitments leading to an orderly and productive life, "having it all together." The corresponding vice is indicated by expressions like "going it alone" and "being overcommitted."

D. Readiness to Act

Turning now to those modes of responsibility which concern our ambivalent attitudes toward human goods, we begin with one which can be expressed this way: *Do not let feelings of inertia keep you from acting for the good.* Doing nothing when doing something is called for violates the first principle of morality, which requires appropriate and timely action to achieve the benefits one can in accord with the ideal of integral human fulfillment.

Not that one always has to be doing something, *anything*, rather than keeping still. There are times when everybody needs a rest; there are also times when it is reasonable *not* to tackle a job which is too big and too taxing. But this mode has in view situations in which a person thinks of something worthwhile to do, sees no reason not to do it, yet refrains from acting simply because of feelings of sluggishness and inertia. For example: a man in good health who planned to devote Saturday morning to needed household chores but stays in bed until late morning simply out of laziness.

No doubt such behavior sometimes arises from depression or some other debilitating emotional condition over which an individual has little or no control. Ethics does not deny the existence of pathological emotional states which give rise to behavior contrary to human goods. But this mode of responsibility is concerned with behavior which, although it may resemble the sluggishness of a depressed individual, arises not from psychological illness, but from lethargic feelings one could override if one wanted to.

The vice opposed to this mode goes by names like laziness, sluggishness, slothfulness, dilatoriness, and so on. The corresponding virtuous disposition has various aspects and is generally named by reference to various sorts of activity—"ambitious," "enthusiastic," "energetic," "diligent," and so forth.

E. Fortitude

A fifth mode of responsibility can be expressed this way: *Do not act on the basis of feelings of aversion except to avoid some real evil other than the tension of enduring those feelings.* It is easy to see how this mode is grounded in the first principle's concern for integral fulfillment, for it rules out holding back from acting, or changing one's course of action, out of fear and repugnance unrelated to intelligible good and evil.

Not that one should act in a foolhardy manner, ignore dangers and risks, charge ahead with one's eyes closed, or play the role of Pollyanna. An individual who reasonably anticipates that something which *need not* be done is likely to have bad consequences—going mountain climbing under hazardous conditions, say—is under no obligation to engage in the activity and may be obliged to refrain from it.

But this mode of responsibility has something else in view: the situation in which, seeing that acting in a certain way will serve a real good, a person nevertheless chooses not to act because of feelings like fear of pain, disgust, and repugnance, the wish to avoid being criticized, anxiety in the face of obstacles, and so on. The feelings are genuine, but they are not rooted in intelligible good and evil.

Violations are often committed by people who abandon vocational commitments because perseverance would be hard: for example, the married person who leaves a spouse who has come down with a serious mental illness. Or people may postpone or fail entirely to adopt a reasonable health regimen of diet and exercise because it involves some discomfort. Or fear of failure may lead an artist to abandon serious work in favor of a steady output of easy, popular successes.

Fortitude, courage, perseverance, guts, tenacity—these words express aspects of the virtuous disposition corresponding to this mode. Cowardice, squeamishness, being a quitter, express the vice.

F. Self-control

A sixth mode of responsibility can be expressed this way: *Do not seek to satisfy emotional desires for their own sake but only as part of the pursuit or attainment of some intelligible good.* One might say: Do not settle for emotional satisfaction at the expense of integral fulfillment.

People often do settle for emotional satisfaction. Feeling some inner tension, they act in response to impulse, habit, or fixation in order to relieve it. But in acting for emotional satisfaction rather than for an intelligible good, they act contrary to the ideal of integral fulfillment. True, inner harmony is a human good; what this mode has in view, however, is not all action directed to the good of inner harmony, but action which contributes to inner harmony solely by reducing tension as one gives in to emotional demands for gratification.

For example, a man sees no good reason for having another drink or taking another helping of rich food or killing an evening watching TV, but he does it anyway because he feels the urge; a woman whose children have grown up and moved away insists on following the same schedule and household routine as when they were young and at home, not because there is any good reason for doing so—her time, in fact, could now be better spent in other ways—but because the routine itself gives her a sense of security; a man works harder and harder, longer and longer hours, not because he needs the money or will put it to good use, but because doing so relieves his anxiety and makes him feel important.

There is nothing wrong in and of itself with relieving tension; the problem is with action to relieve tension which is unrelated to any intelligible good. Spontaneous behavior has its place, and morally mature people regularly act spontaneously within the framework of their preexisting commitments (for instance, good parents who spontaneously act for their children's well-being). But spontaneous behavior on behalf of infantile goals—urges, cravings, wants, and so forth—is a different story, and it is such behavior which this mode rules out.

Self-control best describes the virtuous disposition corresponding to the mode, but we can also speak here of "discipline," provided it refers to a freely chosen way of behaving rather than to an externally imposed set of rules. Temperance, modesty, chastity, and a simple lifestyle are particular aspects of this disposition. The vice is expressed in lustfulness, greed, gluttony, jealousy, impetuosity, and so on.

G. Reality vs. Illusion

A seventh mode of responsibility can be stated this way: *Do not choose and act for the sake of the experience of participating in a*

good in preference to the reality of doing so. In seeking the illusory
in preference to reality one acts against the ideal of integral
human fulfillment rooted in real participation in human
goods.

Violations abound. Instead of undergoing effective but un-
pleasant treatment for his illness, a sick man settles for a quack
cure which lets him feel that he is doing something construc-
tive to get well. Instead of settling down to study for an important examination, a student spends time reorganizing her
notes, putting her desk in order, sharpening pencils, talking
with her roommate about the exam—doing a lot of things
which make her feel like she is preparing but which really do
not prepare her at all. Instead of telling the members of his
wealthy congregation that corrupt business practices, over-
charging clients, cheating on taxes, and similar activities are
evil, a clergyman confines his sermons to assurances that God
is kind and that charitable giving earns them merit in God's
eyes.

The virtuous disposition corresponding to this mode has no
one name. Practical wisdom, seriousness, clearheadedness,
"having a sound set of values," and other expressions describe
aspects of it. The vice is signified by expressions like superfi-
ciality, self-deception, "kidding yourself," frivolity, childish-
ness, and "lacking a sense of values."

H. In General . . .

Various ethical theorists, as well as many ordinary people,
have made the mistake of seizing upon one (or several) of these
modes of responsibility in isolation from the rest and attempting to make it (or them) the sole measure of morality. This
mistake is particularly common in the case of the Golden Rule,
fairness. How often has one heard it said that the Golden Rule
or some variation of it "is the only moral rule anyone needs"?
But this is not so. Although the Golden Rule is a mode of
responsibility, a very important one, it is not the only one.
Morality requires that all the modes be observed, precisely
because all are derived from the first principle of morality—to

will in line with integral human fulfillment—and stand as intermediate principles between it and specific moral norms (perform this action, do not perform that one).

Not that all modes of responsibility are equally important. For example, in and of itself the obligation to be fair is weightier than, say, the obligation to resist sluggishness and inertia (the fourth mode above). Still, the obligation to which that mode calls attention is also real: laziness *is* morally wrong, even though it is usually less wrong than taking revenge or treating someone else unfairly.

Moral goodness does not lie in respecting one mode of responsibility only, any more than it lies in respecting only one basic human good. Moral goodness means service of all the human goods and observance of all the modes, which specify various ways of acting against human goods. In this chapter we have discussed seven modes. We shall consider an eighth in the chapter that follows.

Questions for Review and Discussion

1. Kant, who bases his ethics on the mode of responsibility we have listed first, rejects as too narrow the formulation "Do unto others as you would have them do unto you." He offers the formulation "Act so that the maxim of your action can at the same time serve as a universal law." Compare these formulations with each other and with the formulation offered in the text.

2. The mode of responsibility which we have listed second (patience, readiness to forgive) seems to leave those who observe it open to being victimized by others. Do you see ways, consistent with this and the other modes, in which people can protect themselves against this eventuality?

3. Similarly, the third mode (sharing, cooperation) seems to require that one put up with inefficiency, poor performance, and even collective failure for the sake of involving others in group enterprises. What ways do you see of coping with the problem?

4. Think of some striking examples in history, everyday life, or literature in which the fourth mode (what we have called "readiness to act") is violated in serious ways.

5. As we have formulated the fifth mode (fortitude), it centers on "feelings of aversion" and how we handle them. Do you think there is a positive role in the moral life for such feelings? What might it be?

6. Do you think there is a danger that rigorous observance of the sixth mode of responsibility (self-control) can make a person cold and calculating? Give some examples of truly spontaneous behavior by a person who is fully observing this mode.

7. The mode of responsibility we have listed seventh tells us not to prefer the illusion of participating in a good to the reality of doing so. Why do people so often have trouble telling the two things apart?

8. Can you think of reasons for the tendency to build an entire ethics around one or two modes of responsibility and neglect the others?

9. When the standards of conduct someone takes for granted are called into question, they can be defended rationally only by appealing to one of the modes of responsibility. Find some examples of moral argumentation—in real life or in fiction—which exemplify such an effort to reduce a previously assumed standard to one or more of the modes of responsibility.

12. Persons, Means, and Ends

Are there ethical absolutes? Are there moral norms which should never be violated and therefore things which should never be done regardless of the circumstances and the consequences? In other words, is there anything about which it is true to say "It is *always* wrong to do *that,* no matter what"?

Almost instinctively most people would answer Yes, and then would go on to cite some action which they feel should never be performed: purposely to torture a small child, for instance. Yet for many ethical theorists the answer is No. For them there are no ethical absolutes and therefore no actions which can flatly be ruled out as beyond the pale of acceptable human behavior.

This is not to suggest that such theorists are themselves vicious or immoral. People who do not believe in ethical absolutes may indeed be high-minded and right-living, in particular cases more so perhaps than those who hold that there are some actions which ought never to be performed.

The issue here, however, is not whose private life and personal conduct are more upstanding and blameless. The question is, rather, Whose ethical position is true? Is any action whatsoever allowable, at least in certain circumstances? Or are there actions which it is never morally right to perform?

What is at issue here is far removed from idle speculation. This is one of the most burning ethical questions of our times, a matter of far-reaching practical ramifications for individual and social life.

Most, and perhaps all, of the modes of responsibility yield ethical absolutes, and people generally have no difficulty accepting them as true. Few, for example, would suggest that revenge, as contrary to the mode which excludes acting against an instance of human good in order to vent one's wrath, sometimes is morally acceptable behavior. While destructive feelings are not within our direct control, we nevertheless have a responsibility to control such impulses in indirect ways and to refrain from harming ourselves or others to satisfy hostility. No matter how difficult it is to fulfill, no decent person doubts that this is a serious responsibility. Decent people do of course differ in their views of what constitutes "revenge," and some would argue—wrongly in our view—that some acts of a retaliatory nature are permitted or even required by, say, justice. The point, though, is that, even if they consider certain retaliatory acts acceptable, decent people always consider it wrong to harm anyone simply to satisfy hostility.

The case, however, is often very different with regard to ethical absolutes generated by the eighth mode of responsibility. It can be expressed this way: *Do not let the attraction exercised by one instance of a basic human good lead you, in pursuing it, to act against another instance of a basic human good.* It is never right to act directly against some instance of a human good for the sake of another—to treat one as a mere means, as if it were not an aspect of the person, and the other as the end. To do so is clearly contrary to the first principle of morality and the ideal of integral human fulfillment, which enjoins consistent openness to the whole spectrum of human goods.

"To act directly against an instance of a human good" means to make and carry out a choice to destroy, damage, or impede that good in one or more instances. Critics of our position have sometimes seized on such expressions to undermine it. How is it possible to destroy, damage, or impede a basic human good? But notice that we are speaking of particular instances of a human good, the good as it is realized or realizable in some human being or human beings. Obviously, one cannot literally destroy, damage, or impede a basic human good as a reason for acting, but one can do enormous harm to human beings. Even the Nazis could not destroy the basic good of human life in itself, but they did kill millions of people.

A. *Respecting Human Goods*

Openness to human goods is the basis of a right moral attitude. In acting directly against an instance of any basic good for the sake of another instance (either of the same or a different good) we treat that against which we act as if it were nothing but a means to an end. But the goods that comprise the elements of our personhood are themselves the reasons and the ends of human action; as such they cannot reasonably be treated as mere means. The minimum requirement for a morally correct attitude—simultaneous respect for all the basic goods—in practice means refusing to do injury to one instance as a means of achieving another.

What does this notion of acting directly against one instance of the fundamental goods for the sake of some other really entail? In practice something like the following. A person who is about to violate this mode of responsibility is about to adopt a proposal which involves detriment or injury to a human good in a particular instance. He or she is inclined to do this because it contributes to the realization of another instance of a good. Clearly, such an individual already has made or is about to make a determination that the good which will be realized in the second instance outweighs the good which will suffer injury in the first. In adopting such a proposal an individual simply cannot remain open to the good which will suffer detriment, for this good is being violated. In adopting the proposal he or she also necessarily wills this violation and in doing so adopts, at least implicitly, a narrowed and restricted view of the purposes which go to make up human personhood, that is, of personhood itself.

But, the objection goes, the way of proceeding which we have just described is reasonable—indeed, it is the morally right way to act in many cases—if the quantity of good in the instance preferred outweighs the quantity in the instance treated as a means to the end. Is it not rational and ethically correct to choose the way of acting which promises to bring about the greater good?

This is the line of reasoning recommended by those who

subscribe to the ethical system known as "consequentialism" or "proportionalism." But their recommendation is mistaken. Instances of basic human goods are incommensurable: they cannot be measured against one another as the proportionalist calculus requires.

There is a twofold incommensurability. First, it is impossible to measure different categories of human good against one another, since the basic human goods are not reducible to one another or to some ultrabasic category of good underlying all the rest. Comparing categories of good is rather like dividing apples by oranges. Choices, though, are not between or among categories of goods, but instances of goods, so this incommensurability is not precisely what renders the calculus impossible. (In earlier editions of this book we suggested that it was, but we have revised our thinking on this.)

Second, however, it is no less impossible to measure different instances of the same good against one another and determine that one instance outweighs the others. Each instance, each real possibility for choice, has some appeal not found in its competitors. Where shall I go on vacation, the mountains or the seashore? I find both possibilities appealing, but in somewhat different ways, and that is precisely why I must *choose* between them; if the seashore had all the appeal of the mountains and its own besides, there would be no choice to make—I would simply tumble spontaneously and without choice for the clearly superior alternative.

Consequentialism would work if choices were between possibilities which differed from one another *only* in the quantity of good they promised. If, for instance, one had a pure case of bringing about the deaths of more people or fewer people, and nothing else of human importance were involved, one would surely prefer to kill fewer. The greater good/lesser evil would be so clear that no choice would be required or even possible.

An example helps make this clearer. You are at the controls of a runaway trolley car approaching an intersection where the tracks divide. To the right a crowd of people is crossing the street, to the left only two or three. You clang the bell and steer left. But where one does hesitate and deliberate it is because the problem is more complicated than bringing about the deaths of more or fewer people. Something else is involved. Suppose that, as you career down the hill on your trolley, you actually know something about the people in the two intersections: the crowd to the right is made up of a gang of toughs crossing against the traffic light because they habitually ignore the rules of society; the handful of people to the left are decent citizens—a mother with a baby in a stroller, an elderly rabbi—crossing the street on a green light. And you ask yourself: Shouldn't I avoid killing those few people who have the right of way, even though that will mean killing those many people who are not respecting others' right of way?

Artificial as the example is, it makes the crucial point that whenever we have a real choice to make, it is because we are confronted with various possibilities, each embodying a diverse mix of human goods. Consequentialism or proportionalism requires that one weigh and measure the good as represented in the various possibilities and opt for the instance promising more good. But each of the several possibilities comprises, not merely so much (on an imaginary scale) of a certain human good, but a unique "package" of instances of various goods whose very uniqueness makes it impossible to measure it against other, similarly unique "packages" competing to be chosen.

Many proportionalists recognize the difficulty with their system and have tried to correct it. However, it cannot be corrected. Their system requires that two incompatible conditions be met: first, that a morally significant choice be made; second, that the option offering the greater quantity of good be known. Now, where a morally significant choice is made, one has the option of choosing the morally wrong alternative while knowing the morally right one. But if one alternative really did embody the greater good and if that were known, it would be impossible in such a case to choose the inferior alternative, for people are incapable of preferring less good to more. All that proportionalists or consequentialists really are saying is that it is wrong to choose that which practical judgment, according to their understanding of it, makes it impossible to choose. Their approach is not just false but utterly unworkable, and thus it is meaningless as practical guidance.

B. Are There Inalienable Rights?

It is essential to bear in mind that human goods are what human life and action are all about. The language we use here is unavoidably abstract. But the goods themselves are not abstractions, existing "out there" beyond us and other people. Rather, they are aspects of human beings, ourselves or others—aspects which either already exist in actuality or have the potential of being realized. To act directly against one of the fundamental goods is therefore to violate an actual or possible aspect of the personhood of a real person or persons: to violate "life" means violating *somebody's* life—for instance, means killing or mutilating someone. This amounts to using a human person as a mere means to an end.

Critics of the view that there are ethical absolutes nevertheless sometimes refer to them disparagingly as "legalistic absolutes." Rhetoric aside, the implication is that this position exalts law (legalism) at the expense of the person. But the defense of ethical absolutes, properly understood, does not mean assigning primacy to bloodless law over flesh and blood persons. On the contrary, it constitutes a defense of persons and their inalienable rights.

If there are no absolute responsibilities, there are no inalienable rights. If it were true that any action, no matter what, is permitted in certain circumstances, then no good intrinsic to the person would be safe from invasion and suppression, provided the justifying circumstances existed. This is true even in regard to ethical theories which propose the existence of virtual absolutes: norms which proponents of such theories say they can hardly conceive as being in practice subject to violation and actions whose justifying circumstances they can scarcely envision as ever arising. While the proponents of such theories may not be able to envision such circumstances, others less idealistic are quite able to imagine, and find, just the circumstances in which people can be sacrificed to the attainment of ulterior ends.

If there are no ethical absolutes, human persons, rather than being the norm and source from which other things receive their value, become simply items or commodities with a relative value—inviolable only up to the point at which it is expedient to violate them in order to achieve an objective. It would then make no sense at all to speak of the immeasurable value of the human person. Far from being immeasurable—that is, beyond calculation—the value of a person would be quite specific and quantifiable, something to be weighed in the balance against other values.

As a matter of fact, it is often assumed that just this sort of weighing of human goods and human persons is possible. The assumption enters in, tacitly in many instances, as a result of confusion between fundamental goods constitutive of the person, each of which shares in the immeasurability of the still unfolding mystery of the person, and a specific objective which is never completely identical with the person.

Typically, an individual with such an attitude will think along the following lines: Two lives are better than one; therefore, if two innocent lives can be saved by sacrificing one innocent life, it is entirely right to sacrifice the one life in order to save the two.

An example dramatizes this attitude. In wartime a military commander is confronted with a group of prisoners who possess important information about the enemy's plans. He needs the information in order to prevent loss of life among his own troops, but the prisoners will not tell him what he wants to know. In order to compel the prisoners to talk, he has one of them executed as an example to the others and thereby frightens the survivors into divulging the desired information. By taking one life he has saved other lives, and according to the principle that two lives are better than one (or twenty better than two, or two thousand better than twenty, and so on) his action seems not only expedient but morally right.

As we have seen, this way of reasoning would make good sense if the only issue were whether to cause more deaths or fewer. But that is not so. For example: the military commander *chooses* to kill the prisoner, whereas the deaths he hopes to prevent are not ones which he would choose but—if he were to act differently—would only accept; moreover, he breaks faith with the prisoner, since it is commonly understood that military prisoners who behave themselves will not be executed; furthermore, he leads the other prisoners to betray their comrades, something repugnant to soldiers which the commander would not wish to happen to his own men. A *lot* more than causing more deaths or fewer is at stake.

One arrives at a different judgment of how one ought to proceed in such circumstances if human life is regarded, not as one of the things of relative value which a person *has,* but as an intrinsic component of the person, and so as a value which shares in the *dignity* of the person. In denying that we can choose to kill one person for the sake of two, we really are denying that two persons are "worth" twice as much as some other real person. On this view it is simply not possible to make the sort of calculation which weighs persons against each other (my life is more valuable than John's life, John's life is more valuable than Mary's and Tom's combined, or vice versa) and thus to determine whose life shall be respected and whose sacrificed. The value of each human person is incalculable, not in any merely poetic sense, but simply because it is not susceptible to calculation, measurement, weighing, and balancing.

Traditionally this point has been expressed by the statement that the end does not justify the means. This is a way of saying that the direct violation of any good intrinsic to the person cannot be justified by the good result which such a violation may bring about. What is extrinsic to human persons may be used for the good of persons, but what is intrinsic to persons has a kind of sacredness and may not be violated.

Returning to our earlier analysis of human action, it should be apparent that the attitude which regards goods intrinsic to the person as inviolable is inclusivistic: one remains open to all the goods even though one cannot always act to realize each of them. On the other hand, the attitude that any instance of any basic good can, at least in principle, be violated if that is what it takes to achieve some other, "greater" instance is exclusivistic: the good not chosen becomes, by that fact, worth less—worth so much less, indeed, that one can act directly to its detriment.

C. Ethical Absolutes and Consequentialist Solutions

Ultimately, of course, the conviction that the end does justify the means and that, in consequence, there is no action which could not in some circumstances, however remote, be morally justifiable represents a consequentialist/proportional-ist approach to the entire question of ethics and action. In concluding this chapter it may be worth speculating on why this attitude has become so common in our times and society, and, in particular, why it is so evident in regard to the fundamental human good of life. There are, it seems, several reasons.

First, of course, people naturally tend to think in second-level, means-ends terms; children learn this kind of action first. At this level the reasonableness of what one does depends on its effectiveness in getting what one wants. And whenever anyone, child or adult, disregards moral requirements in order to get what he or she wants, the behavior has at least this much reasonableness—it makes sense in that narrow frame of reference. Hence those doing what is morally wrong can console themselves with the thought "I'm acting reasonably." From this it is only a short step to saying that moral goodness means acting efficiently to get what one wants, especially when one's objective is morally acceptable and the only question concerns the means of getting it.

Second, as we have seen, there is a legitimate place for calculating the costs and benefits of various means and choosing one over another on that basis. We do this whenever we have a second-level objective in view, and the differences among the various means of reaching it appear morally insignificant.

In modern times, however, this way of thinking has come to bulk larger and larger because of the rise of technology, accounting, cost analysis, and similar techniques. Because this approach is so reasonable and effective in its place, there is a tendency to extend it to areas where it does not belong—specifically, to the settling of moral issues. The situation is exacerbated when, as commonly happens, in wartime or war-related circumstances leaders adopts this approach, disregarding moral constraints and considering alternatives simply for their effectiveness in forcing the enemy to surrender.

This points to yet another possible element to explain the prevalence of the attitude we are describing: the nuclear deterrent strategy of the United States and other countries.

It is a central element of this strategy that, if pressed to the wall in war, the United States and other nuclear nations would rain down nuclear bombs on enemy cities. Leaving aside the question whether such a course of action would make sense (although it would in fact be senseless), the strategy is built on the presumption that the United States and the other nations involved would really do what they say they are prepared to do. Otherwise the deterrent would not be credible.

For years, then, Americans and the people of other nations which have nuclear deterrents have been living with the knowledge and intention that this is how their countries would, in certain circumstances, act. In subtle but real ways this fact—of nuclear deterrent strategy and all it implies—has helped to undermine the foundations of moral perception and moral thought in our society. This is a broad statement, and one whose truth it is impossible to demonstrate. Yet it stands to reason that this appalling fact has, like a sort of moral disease, infected national life, deadened ethical sensitivity, and poisoned many aspects of our society. It has accustomed us to the idea that it is morally right to will evil for the sake of good.

We do not propose a solution. We only suggest that the nuclear deterrent strategy represents a frighteningly logical application of the principle that the end *does* justify the means. Having willingly although regretfully accepted this principle in one critical area of national life, we can hardly expect to be immune from its influence in many others.

It is of course true that acceptance of the principle that there are ethical absolutes—that the end does not justify the means—implies willingness to accept or tolerate some finite damage rather than act directly against an instance of fundamental human good. A nation unwilling to act unjustly in war, for example, may have to accept defeat; an individual unwilling to act dishonestly in a competitive situation may have to accept some financial or other loss.

Those who argue that the end justifies the means will frequently argue as well that this readiness to suffer damage is unreasonable. But to one who is determined not to limit the meaning of human life to the quantifiable, who is determined instead to preserve the inviolability of the person against threats and infringements, it will be the most reasonable thing in the world.

We have now considered all eight modes of responsibility. They do indeed give us moral guidelines; yet we are obliged to recognize that applying them is by no means a cut and dried matter. Doing so can in fact be excruciatingly difficult in the case of action which is or seems to be ambiguous. In the next chapter we shall examine this problem and see how it can be resolved.

Questions for Review and Discussion

1. If moral absolutes flow from several or all the modes of responsibility, why do you think so many people seem to have such difficulty accepting the absolutes generated by the eighth mode in particular?

2. Some who reject moral absolutes argue against them as legalism and say law is made for human beings, not human beings for the law. How can this challenge be answered within the framework of the present approach to ethics?

3. Does the negative form of the moral rules yielded by this and other modes of responsibility point to a theoretical priority of evil over good?

4. There is a sense in which good ends do justify the means necessary to achieve them, provided these means are not in some way morally objectionable in themselves. With this in mind clarify the saying "The end doesn't justify the means."

5. We mention in this chapter some military-political examples of the doctrine that the end does justify the means. Think of examples involving each of the categories of fundamental human purposes in which someone might be tempted to go directly against the good for the sake of an ulterior purpose.

6. One who holds a consequentialist or proportionalist point of view often will argue against the eighth mode of responsibility by proposing examples in which there seems to be a huge disproportion between the damage done if one refuses to act directly against an instance of human good and the damage done if one does so act. Can you suggest a strategy to be used in dealing with such examples?

7. There was an ancient Stoic maxim "Let right be done, though the heavens fall." Is this a fair statement of the philosophy involved in the eighth mode of responsibility?

8. To what extent do you think it might be possible to accept the rest of the ethical theory outlined in this book while rejecting the eighth mode of responsibility? In other words, how much can be salvaged by someone who likes the approach in general but is unable to agree with this last mode of responsibility?

13. When Action Is Ambiguous

Seldom is life as simple as one might wish. In ethics this truism is amply illustrated by the problems posed by actions which have more than one aspect. Looked at in one way, such an action seems to promote the realization of a human good and therefore to be itself ethically good. Looked at in another way, it is seen to be detrimental to a human good and therefore appears ethically evil.

How evaluate an action with such intrinsic ambiguity? Does one properly emphasize the positive and, concentrating on the good aspect, judge the act to be morally good? Or is it ethically correct to place the emphasis on the evil aspect and judge the act morally wrong? As a practical matter, may one or may one not perform such an action?

This is not a decision to be made casually, on the basis of a hasty judgment. Confronted with an apparent dilemma of this sort, one must look closely at the action in question in order to determine its structure and its relationship to the diverse benefits and harms one must anticipate from doing it. Only on the basis of a clearsighted analysis of the action is it possible to determine whether it is right or wrong to perform it.

A. Not Either/Or but Both/And

At this point it is important to recall something said earlier: Morality is not a matter only of external behavior, nor is it a matter only of internal intention. Both are important and both are inseparable in human action. To determine the morality of

140

an action one must always answer two questions: "What am I doing? Why am I doing it?" It is not enough to answer only one of these questions. The point is important. Some are tempted to solve the problem of ambiguous action by saying that a good intention is sufficient to make such an action morally good. This is the position taken, for example, by those who attempt to resolve what they sometimes call the "agonizing dilemma" involved in an abortion decision by referring exclusively to the intentions of the individual or individuals involved. Thus: "It is certainly repugnant to me that the unborn child should die, but that is not really my intention. I am only interested in sparing this woman avoidable pain and suffering."

It is, however, not really that easy. As far as morality is concerned, the what and why of action are inseparable. In the case of abortion the *what* is the killing of an unborn human individual; it is not possible for any *why*—that is, good intention—to change this. It is still necessary to confront the question of whether, in these circumstances, it is or is not morally correct to perform this action which will result in the death of an unborn life.

If, then, one cannot solve the problem of ambiguous action simply by relying on good intentions, it is necessary to find another approach. The key lies in closely examining the action involved to determine its real structure. There is, to begin with, a significant difference between what one brings about as a means to one's end and what one brings about as a side effect, accepted but not directly willed, of carrying out one's choice. If, then, an action directly realizes a human good, and if one performs the act for the sake of the good in which it allows one to participate or to help another to participate, then one need not be wrongly disposed toward the good which is simultaneously damaged. Provided one is not so disposed, one's action might possibly be morally upright.

If, on the other hand, one's intention does include detriment to the good which is damaged—if one's will is set against this instance of the good—then one is acting wrongly in performing the action. If, furthermore, analysis of the action shows that its two aspects are related to each other as means and end (the good one seeks is only attained through choosing to bring about the bad, which then leads to that good), then one must attend to the principle that the end does not justify the means and conclude that it is immoral to perform the action.

These sentences are packed with meaning and deal with complex matters. For the rest of this chapter we shall be attempting to explain what they say and why they say it.

B. Two Kinds of Ambiguity

As has just been suggested, the ambiguity of ambiguous action can be of two kinds. In one type the destructive aspect of the action is the means by which the positive aspect is realized. In the second the two aspects are inseparably linked in the one action: the positive aspect does not produce the destructive, nor does the destructive produce the positive; one act encompasses both results directly.

The difference between these two kinds of ambiguity may be clarified if one considers actions insofar as they carry out proposals. Whenever one acts deliberately, one has confronted two or more options for acting, considered the pros and cons of each, and settled the indeterminacy of the situation by making a free choice. The open options about which one deliberates are proposals, very like motions on the floor of a deliberative body. Proposals point to opportunities to achieve some good or avoid something bad and include a plan for bringing about the desired outcome. In adopting a proposal by one's free choice one determines oneself to live by the values it promises and to execute its plan.

The ambiguity of an ambiguous action is of the first type if the proposal one adopts is or includes the destruction, damaging, or impeding of an instance of some basic human good, even though the reason why one adopts the proposal does not lie in the action's destructive aspect but in some benefit which one anticipates will come about through carrying out the proposal. The ambiguity of an ambiguous action is of the second type if (1) the proposal one adopts neither is nor includes the destruction, damaging, or impeding of any instance of any of the basic human goods and if (2) the reason why one adopts the proposal is not in the destructive aspect of the action. Here one only foresees and accepts that carrying out the proposal not only will achieve the benefit one anticipates but also will result in harm to one or more instances of one or more basic human goods.

An example will help make this clearer. There was a time when boys with beautiful soprano voices were castrated so that their voices would not change and they could continue to sing in a choir. The action had two aspects: it was a mutilation of the body, an attack upon an aspect of the basic good of life; it was also a *means* to facilitate the beautiful music which was desired to give glory to God. Clearly, however, the mutilation was one action and the production of the music a quite distinct action. The proposal carried out by the castrating operation was, precisely, to mutilate, although the reason for adopting this proposal was the beautiful singing it made possible. Thus, the two meanings of the initial act were not intrinsic to it; rather, the mutilation was an extrinsic means to the ultimately desired end, the beauty of the church service.

In this way of acting, instances of one fundamental human good (bodily integrity, which is part of the good of life itself) were subordinated to other goods (aesthetic and religious). But it is immoral to subordinate instances of basic goods to each other in this way, since all are aspects of the human person, and each is good in its own special and irreplaceable way. Thus, the castration of the choir boys was not morally justifiable. This is so even though the interest of those who did this was presumably focused not on the destructive aspect of the action but on its positive effect. And we may add that this is so even though the boys and their parents were entirely willing that the castration be performed, since *castrati* made a much better living by their singing than they could have made otherwise.

The structure of an action is what it is. It does not change simply because one's primary concern is directed toward one aspect rather than another. Even though, in emotional terms, someone may not feel that he or she wants the destructive aspect of an action, the person inescapably *intends* it inasmuch as it is required as the way to reach the goal toward which his or her feelings are directed.

Let us suppose, however, that a young boy is found to have a cancerous growth involving his testicles. Stopping the disease requires that the boy be castrated. Here the act also has two aspects, but it is ambiguous in a way different from the previous example. On the one hand, the integrity of the body is damaged; part of the reality of a human life is literally cut off. But, on the other hand, in the very same act the boy's life is protected so far as possible from the destructive attack of the disease. Here the proposal is, not to cut off part of the reality of the boy's life, but to cut away the disease which is threatening his life, although the carrying out of this proposal at the same time damages his bodily integrity.

In this case an instance of one fundamental good, or aspect of a good, is not being sacrificed for another: the relationship between the two aspects is not that of means and end. Although the damage done by the operation is foreseen and fully understood, there is a real sense in which it is inseparable from the good to which this very act makes its own immediate contribution. The operation is not castration done as a means to an ulterior end, but cancer-removing surgery which makes an immediate contribution to the good of life and which incidentally and unfortunately also is permanently mutilating. The operation is morally justifiable.

It is necessary now to relate this analysis of the structure of ambiguous action to the person performing such action.

People are responsible primarily for their choices. What people do is, speaking most strictly, that which carries out the proposals which they adopt in making choices. Thus, what people do constitutes them in a real sense: it directly shapes their character. But secondarily people are responsible for more than what they "do" in this strict sense; they are also responsible for the effects which come about as a result of their actions. The effects are results of actions but not strictly part of them.

If the effects are foreseen, they are voluntary; they are accepted by the person performing the action which produces the effects. But there is a significant difference between the voluntarily accepted effects of one's action and the chosen means to one's end. The means to ends are included in the proposals one adopts: one identifies with them. And a means which is incompatible with or detrimental to an instance of a basic human good cannot be adopted by an individual who understands what he or she is doing without involving the person in immorality.

By contrast, effects which are only accepted, not intended, by the person performing the action have no real bearing on his or her attitude toward the basic human goods. In themselves they neither express the individual's intent to realize a good nor do they express his or her intent to act to the detriment of the good. Thus we see how, hypothetically at least, an action which produces effects harmful to an instance of a good can be performed by an individual without involving him or her in immorality. It is possible to perform such an action without violating the eighth mode of responsibility.

It is important, however, to see this matter in its full complexity. The anticipated but unintended effects of one's behavior can have an impact—and often have an extremely important one—on oneself or other people. Thus, although it may be possible in some cases to perform actions which are detrimental to an instance of a human good without violating the eighth mode of responsibility, one may be acting in violation of some other mode.

For example, if one's will is truly oriented toward the ideal of integral human fulfillment, one will not show partiality or favoritism to some people at the expense of others in performing actions which have harmful (as well as beneficial) effects. Nor will one tolerate effects which one has a duty to avoid according to some other mode of responsibility. We are not responsible for the effects we accept in exactly the same way we are responsible for our actions, but our responsibility for accepting bad side effects can nevertheless be just as serious as our responsibility for the actions. Managers of businesses which sell defective products which they know will lead to the death of a certain number of customers need not violate the eighth mode, for they do not choose to kill anyone. But if such executives were honest with themselves, they would have to admit that they are not treating others as they want others to treat them and those they love. And so, not acting fairly, they are guilty of the deaths they foresee.

At the same time it is perfectly true that we can be so confused in our thinking or our feelings that we are not fully aware of the real structure of our actions. Under pressure we can confuse the two kinds of ambiguous action and imagine our action to be justified without adopting the maxim that the end justifies the means—while, as a matter of fact, only that maxim would rationalize what we do.

In particular cases such confusion can reduce or even entirely remove personal guilt for wrong acts. Yet a person who wants to act—or at least to judge—rationally, and therefore morally, will strive to overcome intellectual and emotional confusion in order to analyze ambiguous actions carefully and make correct moral judgments about them.

C. Killing the Unborn

Many other cases illustrate the difference between the two kinds of ambiguous action. There is, for example, an important distinction to be made concerning operations performed on pregnant women which result in the death of the unborn: some kill the unborn individual as a means to an ulterior end; other operations directly result in a benefit to the mother's health and only incidentally kill the unborn.

Since abortion is such a pressing and controversial issue, it is worth remarking that it does not really matter whether or not one wishes to call the fetus a person. It is alive; it is human; it is an individual. No one can prove that it is not a person, and it need only be let alone for a while in order to prove to everyone that it is. Moreover, quite apart from whether one does or does not call the fetus a person, willingness to destroy the unborn is willingness to destroy human life. It is only because some wish to kill the fetus that anyone denies this is personal life. People typically find subtle grounds for questioning the personhood of those whom they wish to destroy. It happened before in this country with blacks and native Americans; it is happening now with the unborn.

If a woman does not want a baby because it would interfere with her career or stretch her family budget too far or cause her embarrassment or for any other reason at all, and if she has an operation or does anything else to get rid of the unwanted pregnancy, then this killing is a means to an end. Although she has an ulterior reason, which may be entirely legitimate, her proposal is to get rid of the unwanted new life. Such action goes directly against the basic good of human life as it is embodied in the unborn, and it is wrong for that reason.

Still, there are cases in which it can be permissible to perform a procedure which results in the death of the unborn child, even when this outcome is known in advance. For instance, sometimes the embryo lodges in the tube leading to the uterus, and it is necessary to remove the tube and embryo, long before the tiny individual is old enough to survive outside the womb, to protect the mother from loss of blood which occurs when the embryo becomes too big and the tube ruptures. But this operation is not properly called abortion, nor need it be regarded as morally wrong. Here the death of the unborn is not the *means* of benefiting the mother. It is only an unavoidable *side effect*, incidental to the lifesaving operation.

The structure of this action, unlike the act of abortion, does not require that one intend the death of the child, and so there is no turning against the child's life, even though the destruction of life inevitably occurs. (If, of course, those involved in such a procedure really do propose to bring about the death of the unborn child as well as to save the mother's life, then the situation is radically different from the point of view of ethics, and the action is morally wrong.)

D. Other Examples

A man is walking down a dark street at night when a deranged-looking individual leaps out of the bushes, knife in hand, and attacks him. May he use force to resist such an attack? May he even kill the attacker? The answer: it depends.

According to the principle we have been examining, the man is certainly justified in acting to preserve his life: in the situation described this is the good which he has preeminently in view. Although he anticipates that his self-defensive act will harm the attacker, that harm is no part of the proposal he adopts. Since that is so, he can take action to preserve life which also results in some harm to his attacker, provided there is no alternative open to him.

But is another course of action besides the use of force feasible? If such a practical course of action (for example, flight or evasion) does exist, then one who does not propose harm to the attacker will prefer it.

Supposing, though, that the only thing possible in the circumstances is to resist force with force, then the man should choose a form of resistance which involves no more force than necessary. Suppose the individual who has been attacked is a policeman. He should, if possible, stun his attacker with his billy club instead of shooting him with his revolver; if it is necessary for him to use the revolver, he should shoot to wound his assailant, not kill; he should kill only if he has no nondeadly way of resisting the attack.

Granted the artificiality of the example (few people, policemen or not, would be in a position in such circumstances to make the nice determinations and judgments just outlined), we are using it to clarify a principle, not to describe the mental processes of an actual person in an actual situation. And the principle is this: If it is possible to realize the good one has in view without engaging in an ambiguous action which involves simultaneous harm to another instance of human good, one should do so; if such an ambiguous action is truly unavoidable, one should act in a way that involves no avoidable detriment to the good.

It may be objected that in this case the good which suffers detriment is actually subordinated to the other good which is realized as a means to an end: the policeman clubs or shoots his assailant precisely in order to preserve his own life. Again, we can only say: it all depends. If the proposal the policeman adopts is or includes harm to his assailant, then he is subordinating the latter's life to his own, as means to end. But it is not necessary for him to propose his action in this manner. He can correctly view injury to his assailant simply as the unavoidable consequence of doing what he must to repel force and protect his life. Precisely how he regards the situation and his response is a question which only he, and perhaps not even he, can answer with certainty.

This, however, is not the same thing as saying that the morality of the action is determined by how the individual happens to regard it, as if one could make an intrinsically wrong act right simply by choosing to think of it as right. The point, rather, is that the structure of the action just described is such that it can legitimately and without doing violence to reality be seen as an act whose destructive aspect is not really a means to another good but rather an unavoidable consequence of the same act in which another good is realized.

The situation is quite different, however, in a not dissimilar case: capital punishment. Some, of course, argue that in cases where a life has been taken, the one who has taken it must be killed to balance the scales of justice. But, even if one agrees that justice requires that crime be punished, it does not follow that killing those who kill is necessary to restore the balance of justice. What is necessary is that criminals' unjust self-assertion be counteracted, and that is accomplished by depriving them of their freedom to live their lives as they please. The claim that only the death penalty satisfies the demands of justice really comes down to little more than the morality of "an eye for an eye and a tooth for a tooth." Thus, it seems clear that the only compelling consideration in favor of capital punishment is that it serves as a deterrent to would-be criminals.

There is some evidence that capital punishment actually does not deter crime. But supposing that the deterrent argument is factually valid, it still fails to constitute an ethical justification for capital punishment. Analysis of the action of capital punishment can only lead to the conclusion that life is being taken precisely as a means to a remote good end: the deterrence of crime. Even if the reason for choosing capital punishment is a good one, the proposal carried out when a criminal is executed precisely is to kill—for example, the criminal is sentenced to "be hung by the neck *until dead.*" (The same thing would apply to the argument that a particular person must be executed in order to prevent *him* from committing additional crimes in the future.) Since this is so, one must conclude that there is no ethical justification for capital punishment.

The same principles come into play in addressing another set of cases and questions which today are widely debated: whether one does or does not have an obligation to seek to prolong the life of a gravely handicapped newborn or a terminally ill patient. Partly the answer depends on whether the proposed course of action would carry out a choice to kill.

Suppose the question arises in the case of a newborn with Down's Syndrome who, in order to survive, needs a fairly simple operation to correct some other condition. If the parents, not wanting a handicapped child and believing the child would be better off dead, refuse the operation with that purpose—the child's death—in view, they have made a choice to kill. Sympathy for their plight should not blind one to the fact that their choice is morally wrong.

But suppose that a man is in an irreversible coma and suffering from a condition which can only end, sooner or later, in death. Suppose also that his life can be prolonged only by rather expensive care in a hospital or nursing home. Knowing that he will surely die without ever recovering consciousness in any case, his family might discontinue the treatment to save its expense without adopting a proposal to kill and so without violating the eighth mode (though one would still have to examine the particular circumstances closely to determine whether or not some other mode, such as that requiring fairness, were being violated).

E. War

Finally, it may be helpful to apply what has been said to the difficult and controversial question of warfare—not in order to pronounce on the morality of any particular war but in order to illustrate the process by which an individual might make a judgment regarding participation in war.

A great many requirements must be met before it is possible

even to conclude that a military action has the quality of ambiguity discussed here. First, a military action cannot be morally acceptable if it is itself carrying out an unjust policy or intention. Second, it cannot be justified if there are alternative ways, short of war, for protecting or realizing the goods which are at stake. Third, there must be solid reasons for believing that the military act has a chance of being effective, of realizing the goods at which it is directed; useless killing is always immoral. Fourth, inasmuch as war is a social act, it cannot be undertaken merely on the whim or private decision of any person—even the highest public officials—but only in accord with the procedure authorized in a given society.

Still, assuming that these conditions are satisfactorily met (a very large assumption, since they seldom are), there remains the question of how an individual soldier on the battlefield should behave and how he is to judge his action. May he or may he not kill an enemy soldier?

He can look on this action—the act of killing a member of the opposing military force in time of war—in either of two ways. He can propose to kill another human being as a means to an end: saving his own life, promoting the cause for which he is fighting, or whatever; or he can propose only to reduce by a certain amount the unjustly used force of the opposing side.

In the latter case he is not choosing to kill for the sake of some other, presumably good end. Rather, he is performing an action directed at resisting and reducing unjust force, an action which unavoidably results in the injury or death of another person. His intention does not include a detriment to the fundamental good of life, even though an instance of this good—the life of an enemy soldier—is snuffed out as one consequence of his action. As in the case of the policeman outlined above, it is not suggested that the soldier's feelings will necessarily correspond with this analysis of action. The issue is, however, not his feelings but the proposal he adopts and the will with which he engages in the act.

We are not making a defense of war. First, as we have said, the conditions which might justify a particular war are rarely satisfied in fact. Second, the requirements for an individual's participation in war, even assuming the war is not unjust as a whole, are not easily satisfied and are in fact generally ignored. But it is at least possible for an individual serving on the just side in a just war to carry out certain military duties in a morally right manner.

It is clear now why the problem of ambiguous action is, from an ethical point of view, such a difficult one. Many different factors enter into the question: behavior, intention, close analysis of the total action in order to grasp its true structure. In real-life situations moral evaluation of such an action can be difficult, even painful. But the task is one which no one concerned with judging and living in a morally responsible manner can avoid. Furthermore, it is relevant and important even in regard to emergency situations—those in which one clearly has no time for such a process of reflection and analysis. Many of the problems which arise in emergency situations can be anticipated, at least in a general way, and in some cases are even recurrent; hence, moral analysis of ambiguous action with reference to the kinds of problems that may arise in such situations is an important preparation for actually facing the problems when they do arise.

The ethical approach which we have just been elaborating applies not only to individuals but to communities. We have made this point in a number of different contexts and have sought to illustrate it with a variety of examples. The matter comes to the fore, however, in regard to the subject—duties—which we shall examine in the next chapter.

Questions for Review and Discussion

1. Does the discussion in the present chapter amount to a limitation or restriction of the eighth mode of responsibility?

2. Some people think the argument presented here gives up too much—that it leads to a position indistinguishable from proportionalism or consequentialism. What is your opinion?

3. What difference does it make whether the detrimental effects of an action are or are not included in the proposal one adopts by choice?

4. Can you think of examples of ambiguous acts which escape being wrong under the eighth mode of responsibility because of their ambiguity but which nevertheless would be wrong under some other mode?

5. Through the examples in this chapter an attempt is made to outline a consistent ethical position with regard to acts which threaten or destroy human life. Do you think the position is really consistent?

6. Some have argued that people necessarily intend all the aspects and results of their actions which they certainly foresee. Can you think of counterexamples to this contention?

7. At a number of points in the Bible, especially the Old Testament, God seems to be commanding someone to do something immoral. Assuming for the sake of argument that one takes these examples at their face value, is it possible to deal with the moral issue by using the theory of ambiguous action explained in this chapter?

8. Some argue that if war can ever be justified, the nuclear deterrent strategy intended to prevent war also can be justified. Do you agree?

9. If persons who do their best to do what they think is right avoid moral guilt anyway, why bother to make a close analysis of ambiguous actions? Why not instead simply tell people to follow their consciences?

14. Duties: Responsibilities in Community

In many people's minds duty and morality are virtually synonymous, so that "doing your duty" seems to be the sum and substance of moral goodness. Although there is a great deal more to morality than that, duties do constitute a very important, and complex, part of the moral life.

Duties are essentially social: they arise from relationships between and among people. As *moral* obligations they are grounded in one or more of the modes of responsibility. One has duties not to kill or hurt others based on the second and eighth modes, duties not to treat others unfairly arising from the Golden Rule and its equivalents, and indeed a duty to form community (arising from the mode excluding individualism in pursuit of the good) so that others will have opportunities to seek and share in human goods. Looked at this way, it is clear that duties and rights are facets of the same reality: you have a right to that which I have a duty to give or allow you.

The concept of duty, as we shall see at greater length below, applies not only to individuals but to communities; and a community can have duties toward individuals and also toward other communities. But for all that there are basically only two kinds of duty.

A. *Contractual Duty*

One might be called contractual duty. As the name suggests, it arises on the basis of a contract or agreement. An individual wants to achieve a certain objective and needs someone else's help; in order to get the help, he or she agrees to do something for the other person in return. It is not necessary that a contractual duty involve a formal, written document. Very often, for instance, there is no written agreement setting out a person's terms of employment, yet the arrangement between the employer and employee is precisely a contractual one involving contractual duties. Here is a simple example of a contract: a man wants his house painted and agrees to pay the painter to do the job. In such a situation each party to the bargain has a duty to fulfill his or her part in it.

There will of course be exceptions. For example, one is not obliged to carry out an agreement to do something morally wrong. A hired gunman has no real duty to kill the person he is paid to assassinate. Again, responsibility under a contract disappears when circumstances change in such a way that it would be disastrous for one of the parties to fulfill the agreement. A circus tightrope walker is not obliged to go up on the high wire when feeling dizzy, even to meet the terms of a contract with the circus management.

In order to see why one should generally keep one's agreements—and also why one should sometimes not keep them—it is enough to consider that this is how one would want others to treat oneself (the mode of responsibility enjoining fairness). Workable contracts and agreements are impossible unless those who make them are governed by the moral principle "Do unto others as you would have them do unto you." For if this principle does not govern the mutual conduct of the parties, they must assume that agreements will be broken whenever it is advantageous to break them, and so they will be forced to try to construct them in such a way that it will never be advantageous to break them, no matter how circumstances may change.

Generally speaking, contracts and agreements similar to them represent the coordination of people's behavior at the second level of action. In fulfilling a contract one performs actions which are specific means to specific objectives. Contracts are immensely important—indeed, essential—to everyday life, but, morally speaking, they do not raise many special problems and they are not very interesting. Far more difficult and significant, in ethical terms, is the question of duty as it relates to social relationships involving and based upon third-level action.

B. Communities and Duties

We all have a variety of social roles arising from membership in various communities, and each of these social roles carries with it a variety of duties. But why, normally, are these duties real *moral* responsibilities? Why do they concern good and evil and involve our self-determination? To answer that question, we need to bear in mind what constitutes a genuine community.

A crowd brought together by something extrinsic to the members of the group, such as accident or force, is not a community. Neither is a group whose members recognize no more than contractual responsibilities toward one another. Instead, a community is constituted by a kind of third-level act in which two or more people engage together, so that it becomes in a real way their action in common. A community is characterized by shared commitment on its members' part to the realization of some fundamental human good or goods, and by structures and activity appropriate to bringing this about. Our very membership in communities is grounded in moral responsibilities. The first principle of morality and the modes of responsibility require that we make commitments and cooperate with others in various structured and continuing ways in pursuit of human goods, since generally they can be achieved in no other way. One might say that one's first duty is to be a community member.

A good family is in many respects a model of community. Its members are joined by ties of mutual dependence, to be sure, but also by a joint commitment to common purposes of a very basic and intimate sort. Husband and wife are one flesh, and the children are offspring of their parents' bodies. The family members learn together, growing in knowledge by conversation in which they share experiences and insights. Similarly, they participate together in recreation and in religious acts. They serve and care for one another. They share the same property. Each contributes to the community according to ability and receives according to need. By contrast, where commitment to such basic goods is lacking, the members of a family may coexist as a socioeconomic unit—as a convenient and perhaps even congenial arrangement—but it is not a genuine community as the word is understood and used here.

Definite structures and activity are required for the realization of the purposes which constitute a community. Institutions are necessary to articulate the purposes to which the community members are committed. This in turn gives rise to various roles—what might be called "job descriptions"—for the different community members. So, within a family, "father" refers to one role, "mother" to another, "eldest daughter" to a third, and so on. In saying this we are not encouraging stereotyping. Within certain limits job descriptions in a particular community, whether it be a family or any other, can and do change, and it is proper to reexamine them periodically to insure that they are just and workable. Our point is only that within any community various roles and tasks are assigned to its members according to some more or less clear pattern.

The fulfillment of these roles will require that people act in certain ways. These required ways of acting are duties, and a duty of this sort may be defined as something one has a responsibility for doing or not doing by virtue of one's role in a particular community. Just as we have many social roles, so we have many duties: as citizens, as family members, as students, as employers or employees, and so on.

Here, however, we need to make a distinction. There are two kinds of community, and the grounds for carrying out one's duties are somewhat different in each.

One kind of community might be called nonvoluntary (though not in any pejorative sense). Authority and the obligation to obey are not based on consent or any common commitment by all; rather, the community arises from an antecedent obligation that the members cooperate, even though not all are capable of deciding what to do. Fairness then requires that those who *are* able to take the lead do so, while the others carry out the leaders' directions. Once again a family, parents and children, provides a model.

The other kind of community is founded on common commitment: a social club, a political party, a college, a religious order, a friendship, even, to some extent, a nation. In some communities of this kind authority and decision-making are shared by the members; in others this is not practical, and authority is vested in some designated member or members. In either situation the obligation to obey has three bases: first, in the first principle of morality itself, which directs one toward fulfillment in human goods in community; second, in the mode of responsibility which rules out individualistic action in pursuit of human goods; and third, in fairness—for the sake of the others one should do one's share in a community, since this is how one wants others to behave toward oneself and toward those one loves.

This point needs emphasizing. Although a community cannot function efficiently if its members do not live up to their roles and fulfill their duties, that is not sufficient to make the duties genuine moral responsibilities. Moral responsibility enters the picture because the members of the community are engaged in joint third-level action seeking the realization of human goods.

Community members who do not fulfill their roles and live up to their duties are in effect seeking to enjoy participation in the common good for which the community is organized without putting into it what is required of them if the community is to continue to realize the good for which it exists. They are trying to get something for nothing, to enjoy a free ride at the expense of other community members. Moreover, they are undermining the community at its roots by refusing to do their part to realize its purposes. If enough members behave in this way, the result, sooner or later, will be the collapse of the community and the end of the possibility that *this* community will realize its constituting purposes.

When one reflects upon the attitude of community members who neglect or refuse to carry out their duties, it is clear that they care less about the good upon which the community is grounded than about their own enjoyment of it. They are in the community for what they can get out of it, not for what they can contribute to joint realization of the community's shared commitment. Their attitude toward other members of the community is basically exploitative: they seek to use others in order to realize their self-interest, instead of working with and for others so that all together may participate more fully in the purpose which brought them together. This exploitative attitude is fundamentally inimical to and destructive of community.

This point also can be explained in terms of the levels of action. A community is constituted by a shared commitment which is at the third level of action. Members who do not do their duty transform their own actions from third-level participation in the common good to actions at the second level, directed now to the limited objective of getting out of the situation what can be gotten for themselves. Such people naturally hope that other members of the community will continue to fulfill their duties in a dedicated way. (It should not be supposed that this explanation means that such persons have *no* third-level purpose in view. They do, but it is not the common good. Rather it is some good or goods of particular interest and concern to themselves, perhaps some aspect of their own self-integration or "self-fulfillment.")

Having said this, however, it is necessary to add two important qualifications. First, our duties as community members are real moral responsibilities only if the community itself is oriented to the realization of goods in a proper way—is not, in other words, a manipulative, exploitative arrangement masquerading as community but actually designed for the benefit and gratification of a few. Second, when duties conflict with one another, as they sometimes do, our moral responsibility is limited to fulfilling only one of the conflicting duties, but deciding which one is not at all easy. Both points deserve close examination, but before turning to them, we need to spend some time examining more closely yet another question of particular interest to communities: authority.

C. Authority

In recent years authority has become, at least in our culture, a somewhat sensitive question. Those who lack authority challenge those who possess it; those who possess it sometimes seem uncertain how, or even whether, to use it.

There are two different senses of authority. One is the capacity or competence to make judgments which persons of lesser competence will, if they are reasonable, accept as true; in this sense the dictionary is the "authoritative" source for the correct spelling of words. Authority in the second sense refers to the authority of law—the capacity in a social setting to give directions which others have a real, though not absolute, moral duty to obey. Here we are concerned with authority in this second sense.

In second-level relationships (situations involving specific means to well defined objectives) "authority" is virtually synonymous with "control." One person sets down requirements and obliges others to fulfill them; he or she is exercising managerial control. And despite the fact that "authority" and "control" are looked at askance these days, this state of affairs is necessary and entirely correct in many circumstances.

The situation is, however, quite different in cases of true community, where a third-level social act (a commitment to a shared value or values and to actions expressive of this value system) is involved. As we have seen, in nonvoluntary communities of this kind (for example, the community of parents with children) the moral obligations associated with authority and obedience are grounded in the antecedent obligation which persons of differing abilities have in order to live together in community and engage in common action. In societies based on common commitment, authority and obedience are grounded, first, in the obligation to make commitments in pursuit of human goods and then, having entered into a community, in fairness (since I want others to do their share, I should do mine).

Plainly, authority in such a community is not a bad thing but a necessity. Part of the responsibility of those in authority is to keep in mind the social act constituting the community and, when appropriate, to make its content and implications explicit. Authority also plans the organization of behavior by members of the community so that their common purposes will be realized. Evidently, then, authority can and should be a form of service to the community rather than a method of exploitative control.

In real life, though, authority often does become a problem, in part at least because of the mixed nature of many societies. Neither wholly third level nor wholly second level, they are something of both. As a result, the role of authority is similarly mixed: a combination of service to others and control over them. This also is neither bad nor good; it is just a fact of life. But it does open the door to abuses.

One of these, on the side of authority, is to make exploitative use of control over others and sometimes, in doing so, to pretend that it is service. This is the typical style of dictators and tyrants, both large and small, who present themselves as "protectors of the common good" and "servants of the people" while pursuing their own interests at the expense of those whom they profess to serve.

But problems are not all on the side of authority. The other members of the community can also abuse the relationship. This is the case with individuals who seek a free ride, taking advantage of the benefits which come from membership in the community while shirking the contribution to community required of their social role. Not infrequently such people attack authority as arrogant, arbitrary, exploitative, uncollegial, and so forth. Authority's alleged failings ostensibly justify the freeloaders' failure to help make the community work.

D. In Search of Community

A pure community with no elements of injustice and exploitation is a rare thing, so rare that it is doubtful whether such a phenomenon ever does exist in our imperfect world. Certainly the large-scale societies of which we are all members are not pure communities. They have aspects of genuine community, but they have less attractive aspects as well. Our duties as members of such societies are true moral responsibilities only when they arise from their community aspect rather than from their unjust and exploitative aspects.

Nations, including the United States, are such societies: partly community and partly a highly complex structure to facilitate self-interest and exploitation. To say this is not to engage in breast-beating or viewing-with-alarm; it is simply to state the evident fact of the matter.

As a community, the United States is many millions of people joined in a commitment to realize a number of noble purposes which find verbal expression in such formulations as the Preamble of the Constitution. This, more or less, is the reality implementing the notion of government by the consent of the governed.

It is important to note, however, that the consent envisioned here has a special meaning. It is not merely a mutual agreement among individuals that some measure of government is necessary to protect their individual security and welfare, as well as the security and welfare of those for whom they are concerned. This is part of it, but a further part of the consent in question is shared concern for goods recognized as possessing an inherent goodness which appeals to reasonable persons. The consent of the governed is consent founded in recognition of basic human goods. (It will be apparent from this description, by the way, that the legitimacy of a political society rests not on the consent of all its members but only on that of certain ones: those who are competent to consent, who are ready to regard a just government as authoritative, and who have an opportunity to consent to a constitutional plan which deserves their consent.)

While this kind of joint commitment is certainly an aspect of the nation, it is not the total picture. The United States Constitution itself, with its system of checks and balances, realistically takes into account that for many people political society is little more than an arrangement for mediating the power struggle of groups, each of which selfishly seeks the maximum satisfaction of its own narrow interests. Thus, besides the genuine joint commitment which one sometimes observes, one finds ample evidence that some individuals and groups receive preferred treatment.

Loopholes in tax laws, for example, allow some wealthy individuals to shelter a good deal of their income from taxation while other citizens must pay taxes on everything they earn. Even today, long after the civil-rights conflicts of the 1950s and 60s, the simple fact of being born with a white skin instead of black or brown tends to insure white-skinned people of prerogatives which black- and brown-skinned people seldom enjoy and then only with great difficulty. So to some extent does the fact of being born a man rather than a woman. And so in certain circumstances does the fact of being an adult human being in pursuit of self-interest rather than an unborn human being lacking means of either pursuing or protecting self-interest.

Quite simply, one can take it for granted that any large society will be only an approximation of true community. At its worst it will be a system for exploitation. Between its best and its worst it will be a system for more or less fair deals and arrangements in which community can degenerate under the eroding force of exploitation.

As a standard for evaluating social structures and policies the concept of the "common good" is often applied to societies of the kind we are describing, especially political societies. Sometimes it is used to refer to instrumental goods like natural resources and public facilities, but although these things can pertain to the common good, they are not principles of morality. When one speaks of the common good as a moral principle, one is speaking, from a communal perspective, of the basic human goods, while the social morality flowing from this source depends on the modes of responsibility viewed and applied in a social context.

All the basic human goods can be reasons for both individual and communal acts, and all involve individual and communal dimensions in their realization. That being so, the common good of a society comprises the basic human goods insofar as the members of the society are jointly committed to them and pursue them together by common action. Fairness is central to the organization and functioning of such a society and is the principle most commonly invoked in defense of the common good against various interest groups.

Viewed in this way, there are two senses in which the common good can be said to be superior to the good of individuals. First, the intelligible human goods are superior to the good as it is experienced by any one person: it is more important that the good be respected and realized than that I get my little share of it. Second, the fulfillment of the group by cooperative action takes priority over unfair individual satisfaction. The latter principle, however, should not be misinterpreted or misapplied to justify trampling individuals in order to benefit the group.

E. The Moral Limits of Duties

What does all this imply for our duties as members of such societies? Simply that such duties are real moral responsibilities only to the extent that they flow from our roles in institutions which articulate the fundamental commitment of the society as community. On the other hand, to the extent that duties arise from some form of institutionalized exploitation they are not moral responsibilities, and in some cases one may even be obliged to refuse to carry out such a duty.

An example makes this clearer. Slavery is an extreme form of institutionalized exploitation, yet slavery has been accepted in many societies throughout history. Even the United States, which articulated its belief in and commitment to essential human equality at the time of its founding, simultaneously recognized the institution of slavery and sanctioned it in law.

Slaves, as members of such a society, have a legal duty to submit to their enslavement, and this duty will be embodied in laws which provide, among other things, for their punishment if they are bad slaves. But no one today seriously supposes that this duty carries with it any real moral responsibility. In short, in a society which accepts slavery as a social institution some people may have a social duty to be slaves, but they can have no moral responsibility arising from this role, and it is not immoral of them to refuse their duty. (Of course, this does not mean that a slave has no moral responsibilities at all. At times a slave might be required by other responsibilities to endure with patience even the injustice of the condition of slavery.)

Slavery is a case in which societies have given institutional expression of an extreme variety to exploitation, and the consequent social duties are not moral responsibilities. But there are also other cases in which social duty does not carry any moral responsibility. It sometimes happens, for example, that there is a change in the purposes of a society which one joined voluntarily. In such a case one has a moral responsibility only in regard to duties which reflect the purposes of the society at the time one accepted membership; one has no responsibility to fulfill duties which reflect new purposes to which one does not subscribe.

If, for instance, one joins a recreational club, and the club later begins to change its orientation to some form of political activism, the mere fact that one is a member of the club does not impose any moral responsibility to join in its political activities if one has not subscribed to this new orientation.

Something similar happens when changing circumstances bring about a change in the fairness of the division of labor within a society. Perhaps over a period of time the amount of effort required in one area diminishes while that involved in another area increases greatly, so that after a while some members of the group find themselves doing very little work and others doing a great deal. In such a case something like exploitation has crept into the society without anyone's really intending it. When this happens, it is time for the society to take a fresh look at the situation and redivide the duties. And if the beneficiaries of the imbalance refuse to do so, as sometimes happens, the victims have no moral responsibility to continue to carry out their duties.

Even this abbreviated discussion makes it apparent that this is a very complicated subject. While it is easy enough to say in the abstract that duties which arise from bad laws and other exploitative social institutions are not moral responsibilities, in reality it may be irresponsible not to tolerate a certain amount of injustice in society. The tax laws, for instance, may not be altogether just, but if all citizens stopped paying their taxes for this reason or felt free to cheat on their tax returns, the result would more likely be chaos than reform. Similarly, when more or less well to do people who think they have good reason for not paying taxes begin concealing income, the result is to shift the tax burden unfairly onto the shoulders of those who are less well off.

Achieving and constantly maintaining perfect balance and perfect justice in the ever-changing conditions of a society are simply not possible. Knowing when to comply with duties that lack the force of moral responsibilities and when to refuse to comply often requires a subtle discernment which cannot be programmed in advance. To refer again to the example of taxes, it may in practice be quite difficult to balance one's recognition of the general obligation to pay one's fair share against one's moral repugnance at paying to help support policies and practices which are clearly immoral. At least, though, it should be clear that not every social duty is also a moral responsibility and that people may at times rightly refuse to carry out some duties. In fact, if carrying out a particular duty would be immoral on other grounds, one's moral responsibility is to refuse to carry it out. This is the principle of conscientious objection.

F. When Duties Conflict

No less complicated is the situation of an individual whose duties as a member of different communities come into conflict with one another. Sometimes, of course, people speak of "conflicts" when all they mean is that they fear the consequences of doing their duty, but other times the conflicts are real. A businessman is scheduled to make an important out-of-town trip for his company; the day before he is to leave, his wife comes down with a bad case of the flu. If he does not make the trip, a deal on which the company has been counting is likely to fall through; if he does make the trip, his wife will have to go on taking care of the children and the house when she ought properly to be in bed. What should he do—go or stay?

There is no a priori answer to that question. Taken individually, each duty would be a moral responsibility. But the duties are now in head-on conflict. The answer will be different for different individuals; the most we can do here is point to certain guidelines which are applicable to any such case.

One fundamental principle is that there is no true conflict of duties between obligations arising from a social role and obligations generated by a moral absolute. Where, for example, a woman's job requires her to offer sexual favors in order to close business deals, real duties are not in conflict—she simply may not do it.

Often, though, this is not the case, and it is necessary to bring other considerations into play. For one thing, if it is not really impossible to fulfill both duties, one has a moral responsibility to do so; but if it is really impossible, one does not have such a responsibility. We are never morally responsible for doing the impossible. Furthermore, since either of the conflicting duties would be a moral responsibility if it were not for the other, one has a definite moral responsibility to fulfill one or the other of them. The businessman-husband of our example is morally obliged either to make the trip or to stay home with his wife; he may not take the day off and go golfing.

The fulfillment of different duties often is a more or less serious responsibility depending on the harm that others will suffer by their nonfulfillment. The diverse harms (and benefits) promised by various options for choice cannot rationally be measured against one another, as consequentialists/proportionalists suggest, in order to settle which is objectively best. However, we can compare the diverse prospects on the subjective scale of our own feelings and previous commitments and then, applying the *moral* principle of fairness, resolve not to do what we would least want done to ourselves.

Likewise, having assessed the situation, we can sometimes reasonably conclude that of the conflicting duties before us one is very grave in the context of its community, while another is rather light in its context. In our example it may be that if the businessman does not make his trip, there is a real risk that his company will fail, whereas if he does, his wife will most likely recover eventually, even if her case of flu is most severe. Or the balance may tilt the other way—if, for instance, his wife's illness is accompanied by suicidal depression, while the loss to his company if he stays home probably will not be disastrous.

It may be of course that, having examined the situation, one finds no circumstances like these to indicate where the weight of obligation lies. Then, but only then, a metaphorical or literal coin toss is in order. Since both (or all) the duties are serious ones, a person will be doing the morally right thing if he or she does either (or any)—provided, of course, that it is done in the right way and for the right reasons.

But what are the right way and the right reasons? To begin with, it is reasonable to doubt an individual's honesty if, whenever conflicts arise, he or she always opts for one set of duties against the other. In the example given, it may be that the businessman consistently puts his job before his family. If so, and if in this situation, too, he chooses the job-related duty over the family-related one, his choice probably expresses a selfish bias rather than an honest judgment of moral responsibility.

In addition, people faced with conflicting duties should take practical steps to try to resolve their quandary. Perhaps, if he tried, the businessman could postpone his trip after all; or perhaps he could make arrangements for a relative or friend to care for his wife and children while he is out of town.

People in such situations should also try to discuss their problem with the other party or parties involved in order to obtain their suggestions and to determine as far as possible who will be most hurt by the nonfulfillment of duty. Perhaps the businessman will discover that his colleagues do not consider the trip as important as he does or that his wife is not really so very sick and does not object to his leaving.

The fact that duties can and sometimes do conflict underlines the need to exercise great care in making commitments and accepting membership in different communities. It is rash to take on a variety of social roles carrying duties which one might with forethought have known would come into conflict. In practice, this means that people should attempt to organize their lives so that as far as possible their various roles and duties complement and support one another instead of conflicting.

It reflects not only good planning but a morally correct attitude when a person's family life, career, civic, and church responsibilities, and other social roles mesh in a harmonious and consistent manner. To be sure, no one can be so foresighted as to eliminate conflicts of duty entirely from his or her life, and in our society it is more difficult for some people than for others: for example, more difficult for some women who must try to combine work outside the home with maternal responsibilities than for many men. Still, it is not only sensible but morally required that one try to prevent conflicts as much as possible and, when conflicts do inevitably arise, act with a combination of honesty and practicality in attempting to resolve them.

Up to this point we have been elaborating an approach to ethics which makes it possible to tell whether an action is morally good or bad. But having an approach to ethics is hardly the same thing as incorporating it into one's life or helping others to incorporate it into theirs. In the chapters that follow we shall consider ways of doing that.

Questions for Review and Discussion

1. If moral responsibility is limited to duty, what sort of theory is likely to result?

2. If duties were the only mode of responsibility, would cultural relativism (or relativity of morals to each society) be true?

3. Contractual duties are fairly obvious forms of responsibility, and sometimes the effort is made to ground all duties in a "social contract." What do such attempts imply concerning the theory of the individual and society?

4. Some people say that laws are nothing else than orders (given by people in control in a society) backed up by force (sufficient to make most people submit). How does this conception of law differ from that implied by the idea of authority in a genuine community?

5. Our section entitled "In Search of Community" suggests, but does not spell out, a theory of social justice. Can you articulate this theory more clearly? Compare it with classic theories such as the following: (1) that each individual should receive from society according to merit (Aristotle); (2) that each should contribute according to ability and receive according to need (Marx); and (3) that each should promote as far as possible the equality of all members (liberal democracy).

6. Some ethical theories suppose there can be a conflict of moral responsibilities. How does our position on conflict of duties differ?

7. In case of conflict of duties, how might it help to invoke the modes of responsibility, such as the second (fairness)?

8. Think of actual or fictional examples of conflict of duties and discuss the manner in which they are resolved.

9. Sartre suggests as typical of the situation of moral choice a case in which a young man during World War II must decide either to stay with his aged mother, who needs his care, or join his friends in the French underground. Pointing out that the young man's commitment alone will determine which is right, Sartre concludes that all moral responsibility is subjective. Criticize this line of argument in light of what we have learned about moral responsibilities in general and about duties in particular.

15. Our Development As Persons Depends on Us

Shifting responsibility is a game everyone sometimes feels tempted to play. People confronted with difficult jobs look about to see if they can find others to do the work for them. People confronting the disastrous results of jobs they have botched look for somebody or something else to blame.

This built-in reluctance to accept responsibility is so much a part of fallible human nature that it is not surprising to find it at work in regard to the fundamental task of every human being: determining what sort of persons we shall be. We are all responsible for our own development as persons, yet we are all tempted to shift the responsibility elsewhere and blame our failures on factors over which we have no control.

Not that grounds for doing so are altogether lacking, since in many respects our development as human beings does depend on factors beyond our control. These factors are of many different kinds, but basically they come down to only two: heredity and environment—the inbred characteristics transmitted to individuals by their parents and previous generations of forebears, and the circumstances of their lives and the world in which they live. Beyond doubt, influences from these sources do have a powerful impact in shaping and determining a human being. Beyond doubt, too, they are largely outside the control of the individual, although in the case of environment this is not always totally so.

Having said this, however, one has only stated the obvious, without touching at all on the subject matter of ethics, the issue of freedom and its use. Granted, there are factors beyond our control which powerfully influence our development as human beings, but what of those factors which are *within* our power to control? There is the focal point of the challenge of freedom. And it is within this context that each one of us must work out his or her development, not merely as a rational animal but as a free, self-determining person.

A. *Freedom's Power and Limits*

Our development as persons depends strictly on how we use our freedom. Heredity and environment are not at issue here, for they are factors beyond our control, while the use of freedom by definition concerns what *is* within our power to control.

True, for some the exercise of freedom is drastically limited. In practice people can only choose the options they perceive, and their choices are guided by the reasons they see in favor of each option. The poor and oppressed simply do not have the options available to the affluent, while people who lack information and imaginative stimulation do not have the option of choosing what they have never heard of (for example, in the religious context, those who have never heard the gospel cannot opt for faith) or what seems hopelessly ambitious (for example, those who have never learned to appreciate their gifts cannot opt for the education needed to develop them). Moreover, circumstances may make a morally bad option appear far more appealing than a morally good one. For example, an individual with little education, an unhappy family situation, and a low-paying, dead-end job may see little reason for *not* making heavy use of drugs and alcohol—an option which is likely to have considerably less appeal to a well educated, happily married person with a stimulating job.

But having said all this, one has not said a great deal as far as our subject—the use of freedom—is concerned. Whatever degree of freedom, great or small, individuals possess, their development as persons depends on its use.

If John is "very free" (has and is fully aware of many appeal-

ing possibilities), he has a corresponding opportunity to develop as a person on a wide front. If Jane is "hardly free at all,"
her opportunity to develop as a person is correspondingly
limited. But to whatever extent John and Jane and the rest of
us enjoy freedom, to precisely that extent each of us is responsible for our individual development according to the manner
in which we use the freedom we have.

Ethics is not concerned with psychopathology or environmental limitations or with their consequences in human action
except insofar as these are challenges to be met by appropriate
action. True, psychopathology and environmental limitations
are facts of human life. But so is human freedom, and it is with
freedom and its use that ethics is concerned.

People trying to live morally good lives may indeed sometimes find that they literally cannot do what they wish they
could do. But their development as persons does not depend
on what they are truly unable to do (or, for that matter, unable
to avoid doing) but upon that which they are able to do (or
avoid doing).

Ordinarily, when people say it is impossible to do the morally right thing, they are not speaking of real impossibility but of
something different. They may simply mean that doing what is
morally right conflicts with a prior commitment to do what is
morally wrong: in this sense a businessman in competition with
dishonest competitors might say that it was "impossible" for
him to be honest. Or they may mean that they have actually
tried to do the morally right thing and failed, as a person with a
violent temper or a drinking problem might say it was "impossible" to be even-tempered or consistently sober after his or her
latest eruption of volcanic wrath or bout of heavy drinking. In
such cases, however, if the individual could and should have
chosen available means to achieve self-control and has not
done so, what is morally correct is not literally impossible; it is
merely difficult.

Not even repeated failure demonstrates the impossibility of
what one has in view. Although repeated failure may drama-
tize the fact that what one is attempting is very difficult,
self-control is not impossible except for those whose behavior
is so pathologically determined that they literally have no

choice about behaving as they do. Thus, it is in the very process
of achieving self-control (or failing to achieve it) that self-
determination comes into play and one shapes oneself as a
person.

Also, it is necessary to recognize the reality of conversion
(not necessarily in a religious sense, but certainly that, too): a
radical change in the orientation of one's life. It is quite possible for conversion to occur as a consequence of a long, although perhaps not fully conscious, process of striving for
what is good, whereby the good which had previously seemed
impossible of realization now becomes a realistic possibility. In
short, what is morally very difficult is not impossible, unless
one *freely* makes it so by failing to do all one can to achieve
self-control.

B. Moral Ideals

Different people take different attitudes toward morality at
different stages of their lives. This truism needs examining.

Moral standards are first presented to us in childhood—by
parents, teachers, peers, a host of other persons and influences. Typically, children accept moral standards on the basis
of authority. Their morality is a morality of obedience: to be
obedient is to be morally good. With time and maturity, however, individuals outgrow the simple equating of morality with
obedience. Then they must take the stance which will govern
their attitude toward moral ideals. Ordinarily, though, this is
not done in the abstract or all at once. It comes about, rather,
over a period of time as an individual grapples with moral
questions in a variety of real-life contexts.

In general terms two attitudes toward moral ideals are possible. Aware perhaps that the moral standards which they
learned as children have imperfections and limitations (may,
in fact, be simply wrong), individuals can nevertheless adopt
an attitude of willingness to submit themselves and their lives
to more adequate moral standards—standards which may be
refined and perfected in comparison with those of childhood
but which still call for submission. Or, on the contrary, indi-

viduals can regard moral standards—any possible standards, not just those of childhood—merely as facts with which they must contend as they go about the business of getting what they want out of life. They can, in other words, approach moral standards either as the fundamental principles according to which they will strive to shape their lives and themselves, or as external factors, no more important than many others, to be manipulated according to their own preferences and inclinations.

Those who take the second attitude reject the task of developing as persons in favor of some more specific and perhaps more immediately attractive goal or combination of goals. They equivalently elect not to shape their lives by participating in fundamental goods constitutive of the human person; instead they choose lives radically limited to the pursuit of specific objectives.

In doing so they also necessarily reject genuine community, in which mutual acceptance and respect are based on the commitments to pursue fundamental goods together with other persons. They opt instead for what is at best a form of fragile coexistence with others, which threatens to break down whenever they find themselves thwarted in the pursuit of their objectives by the others' pursuit of *their* goals.

By contrast, those who regularly choose to submit themselves to moral ideals commit themselves to accept the responsibility of freedom. They acknowledge that it is up to them to determine the persons they will be and that this will come about by the use they make of their freedom. In doing so they do not automatically become complete persons. But they orient themselves in the direction—the only direction—which makes this possible.

Abstract presentations necessarily fail to capture living realities, and the foregoing paragraphs are no exception, suggesting as they do that the process by which individuals arrive at their stance toward moral ideals is a mechanical, cut-and-dried business. In fact, it is quite otherwise. Growing children do not face the question of moral standards as such and abstractly. They encounter it, as we said above, in the concrete situations of daily life.

Faced with inner conflict—between the moral ideals with which they have been presented and the inclinations which tug at them to judge and act contrary to these standards—children gradually become aware that several quite different options are open to them. They may adhere to the standards they have received; they may seek standards which are, perhaps, similar but at the same time sounder; or else they may act simply on the basis of their own desires and inclinations, without deference to any principle standing over against them in judgment.

Similarly, adolescents (including persons who are morally adolescent but may, chronologically, be well beyond adolescence) frame the problem for themselves, not in terms of self-commitment and self-constitution, but in terms of authority, obedience, and a clash between the two. Typically, the tension in their lives is between doing as they please and doing as they have to do; they are tempted to think that what they "ought" to do is no more than one part—often a large and onerous part—of what they have to do.

Many of us never leave moral adolescence, and perhaps all of us feel the tug to return there occasionally. Many individuals at this stage do not entirely reject moral norms or reduce them to mere facts to contend with, but neither do they make any kind of fundamental commitment involving a comprehensive moral outlook by which they mean to try to live. Accepting the force of some moral requirements—most often fairness, though only in selected contexts—they reject other moral requirements which would interfere with self-indulgence.

Such people organize their lives in a mixed way: pleasure-seeking, goal-seeking, a few weak and not very well integrated commitments. One sees this in the case of workers or students who put in a reasonably conscientious performance from Monday through Friday (because they want to keep their jobs in order to support their families, aim to pass their courses in order to get good jobs, and so on), but, as the weekend rolls around, gear up for partying, drinking, sexual self-indulgence, and whatever else makes them "feel good."

Many other individuals in our consumerist society settle in their own ways for rather impoverished and complacent lifestyles in which consistent commitments have little or no part.

"Decent" people, assailed by anxiety and depression, they seek to escape into immediate satisfactions, desire to have things which fulfill their dreams, pursue status as a crutch for insecurity and a source of self-worth. While generally not wanting to "hurt anybody else," they often do act in ways which hurt others: for example, marrying for self-satisfaction (though no doubt with emotional affection for the other party), which makes the partner essentially a mere means, to be discarded when someone else comes along who promises more satisfaction; or taking jobs which offer high pay and prestige, with no concern (except for the superficial minimum required to get ahead) to give either employers or the public their money's worth.

Among still others one finds egoism which is less gross but no less real. For example, in many good families in our society the members avoid the more dramatic forms of indulgence and have real commitments to one another. Yet the family is wrapped up in itself, concerned with its own possessions and advancement, its own comfort and convenience, and quite unconcerned about anybody else. Religion, the state, and society as a whole are regarded as sources of services for the members' well being. There is no getting closely involved with others, no sense of service even to neighbors in need, no notion of spreading the faith or working for justice.

Conventional morality in our culture complements and supports such attitudes. Those who wish to take a serious view of morality and moral standards, both in principle and in the concrete circumstances of their own lives, need to take a hard look at this conventional morality, bearing in mind what Socrates said centuries ago: The unexamined life is not worth living.

Moral maturity is not something that happens all at once. Only gradually do people become able to remove the element of conflict and confrontation from their moral lives and achieve for themselves a stable reconciliation between those two poles: "What I want to do" and "What I have to do." Once an individual has reached this point, he or she has in effect reached moral maturity.

Even so, "moral maturity" does not necessarily mean the same thing as moral goodness. Morally mature people who are bad take account of what they have to do but live insofar as possible according to what they want to do. Morally mature persons who are good see that moral standards represent the possibilities of human life, the goods with which they can identify: they perceive that in acting for such goods (and never acting against them) they are engaging in true self-determination or self-constitution.

C. Overcoming Obstacles to Freedom

Yet not even morally mature good persons have solved all their problems or reached a point at which the exercise of freedom of self-determination is easy and effortless. Human freedom always faces many obstacles—ignorance, weakness, the unsatisfactory character of concrete circumstances—and we must contend with these if we wish to become morally better than we are.

There is no magic formula for dealing with the factors which obstruct the exercise of freedom. The best counsel is common-sense advice—for example, that ignorance can be reduced by reflection and study concerning the factors which bear upon one's life, by seeking and listening to the advice and counsel of others, and by periodic self-examination.

Priority in this matter of practical means to overcome obstacles to the use of freedom goes, however, to what has traditionally been called "formation of conscience." There are many confused notions about what conscience means—a kind of moral intuition; a mysterious voice telling one what to do; or the neurotic, guilt-ridden urgings of Freudian superego. But we mean something which is part of everyday experience: the capacity for making a judgment that here and now it would be morally right to do X and morally wrong to do Y.

Ignorance and error can cloud this judgment. It is important to follow conscience, yet "following conscience" is not enough; we must also try to be sure that our consciences are correct. To do this one must know and apply moral norms, but one also must see at least one morally right alternative in order to be able to choose it (and at least one morally right alternative is always available: that of not doing anything at all if every option to do something is morally excluded). Hence the need for conscience formation in three distinct areas: the norms which distinguish right from wrong, the practical possibilities actually present in a given situation, and the relationship between the norms and the possibilities. To say this only begins to suggest the complexity of conscience formation; here we simply observe that the process—a lifelong task for those who take it seriously—is essential to anyone who aspires to moral maturity.

Continuing in this commonsense vein, we note that where the issue is how to deal with feelings and desires, the first thing to do is to be honest about them. A man feeling murderous rage will not cope well with his emotions if he keeps telling himself, "I'm not really that upset—really, I'm a loving, gentle person." This suggests, too, why it is important to exercise control over thoughts and phantasies; we can hardly expect to master our emotions while at the same time daydreaming about acting them out.

Having achieved a certain insight into emotions, it is possible to take steps to deal with them constructively. Weakness can be lessened by learning to control one's emotions—not suppressing inclination but using it to shape itself. If, for instance, fear of the consequences inclines one not to do something that should be done, one may find that attention to the good aspects of the matter—including the gratification of doing what one considers right even though it is difficult—can stir up sufficient hope to overcome the fear.

Although the situations in which we find ourselves may often be beyond our power to control or change significantly, at other times we may have within our power at least some degree of control over situations, while still more often we may be able to control the way in which we expose ourselves to them. For example, a person struggling to cope with the fact of his or her alcoholism might at least be able to refrain from accompanying heavy-drinking friends on an evening of bar-hopping.

In short, while the exercise of such qualities as honesty, objectivity, and prudence will not remove everything that stands in the way of the exercise of freedom, it can do away with at least some obstacles and help to render others more or less manageable. Ultimately, our responsibility as free persons is very simple and also very difficult. Simple to state, and difficult, although immensely rewarding, to carry out. It comes down to this: to do the best we can to know what is right and the best we can to do it, refusing to give up in the face of setbacks and failures, no matter how serious and frequent they may be. We shall return to this subject—the practicalities of self-determination through the use of freedom—in chapter twenty, which deals with commitments and their role in the moral life.

Up to this point we have been concerned with laying out the basic structure of an approach to ethics. Having sketched its outlines in the preceding chapters, we have begun in this chapter to suggest how it might be applied in concrete circumstances. The balance of this book will carry this effort further, applying things already said to such matters as education, social reform and revolution, theories of individual and social progress, and the relationship of religion to morality.

Questions for Review and Discussion

1. This chapter begins a new section of the book. Can you summarize what has been completed up to this point and indicate what is now being undertaken?

2. We assume that heredity and environment can limit the possible exercise of freedom of self-determination. Identify some other ways in which limitations on freedom are sometimes formulated and expressed.

3. To what extent do you think you are free in comparison with others of your own class and generation? . . . in comparison with members of a primitive tribe? . . . in comparison with the poorest classes of our own society?

4. When a person says it is impossible to do what is morally right, what are some of the things he or she might mean by that statement? Do you think there are circumstances in which the statement is literally true?

5. In this chapter we present a rather strong indictment of the lifestyles of many persons in our society who remain at the stage of moral adolescence. Within the framework of the view of morality developed throughout this book can you think of anything positive to be said on their behalf?

6. It is frequently difficult for an adolescent to distinguish between the freedom of doing as one pleases and the freedom of self-determination. Why is this so?

7. We state that persons who generally accept and will to live by moral standards must still contend with ignorance, weakness, and unsatisfactory situations if they are to become morally better. Illustrate concretely what these obstacles are in some actual cases and discuss ways in which they might be overcome.

8. To what extent and in what ways do you think ignorance, weakness, and unfavorable situations can limit or even eliminate moral guilt?

9. Discuss the logic of the person who argues as follows: "Nobody's perfect anyway, so it isn't so bad if now and then I do something I admit to be immoral."

10. Is it possible for someone to be a subjectivist in ethical theory and still hold moral ideals and seek to live by them?

16. Shaping the Future

Bent on changing the world for the sake of a cause, social reformers almost always turn their sights eventually on children. The young are the hope of the future. Not yet corrupted, not yet morally evil, they represent the opportunity to make a fresh start.

The receptiveness of children to external influences supports this view. Unlike adults, who seem relatively set in their ways, children can be shaped and changed, both intellectually and morally. One seems to glimpse in them the chance of creating a world from which the failings and blemishes of the present have been eradicated. Thus the education of children is seen as the key to the future.

This view is by no means entirely wrong. Education, broadly considered, can indeed play a powerful role in the formation of the young, including their moral development. But we must not overstate the case. The potential—of the child on the one hand and of the educational system on the other—is limited.

Moreover, no system of formation or education can *make* children morally good, since moral goodness or badness is a matter of *self*-determination. An educational system can make it easier or more difficult for children to be morally good. It can create conditions under which children, now and in the future, are somewhat more likely to choose rightly. But that is all. There is no failure-proof formula for raising children in a way guaranteeing that they will be morally good adults. Given the reality of what it means to be morally good, there can be none.

A. *What Education Cannot Do*

Some ideas about education are based on the contrary assumption: that it is possible to make children morally good. In general, such theories involve mistaken notions about morality itself. It is worth examining some of these theories briefly, both to see where they go wrong and also as a prelude to considering what can be accomplished through the education of children.

Commonplace at present, as it has been at times in the past, is the idea that children are naturally good and need only to be allowed to do as they please in order to grow up as morally good persons. Immorality is seen as something which comes to them from outside. If they are permitted to follow their own instincts, they will spontaneously do what is morally right.

Not even the young of other primates, however, grow simply by "following their own instincts." Of course, they do follow instinct; so do human beings. But among the instincts of all higher animals are some which make them susceptible to social conditioning. The young are trained by older members of the group; they learn by imitating. If this is so among animals, it is evident that education, including moral education, is a vastly more complex affair among human beings. Permissiveness in itself does nothing to prepare a child for self-determination, which lies at the heart of adult morality. On the contrary, it is likely to leave the child singularly ill-equipped to function in an authentically self-determining manner in later life.

Another approach holds that moral evil is at bottom a matter of ignorance. If children are well informed, if they know the facts, they will act intelligently and thus morally.

One can agree that there is no value in having people misinformed and that it is desirable for them to be well informed. But being well informed is just not the same thing as being morally good. While ignorance is not a virtue, neither is knowledge. People who are well informed can put their knowledge to morally good uses or morally bad ones. A master criminal is not a morally good person simply because of high intelligence and the command of a wide range of information. Drug dealers generally know a good deal about drugs, including their addictive features and their harmful effects, but that does not keep them from recruiting new users for the sake of profit to themselves. The Faust legend dramatizes the obvious fact that knowledge is one thing and moral goodness something else again.

Another theory holds that evil arises in society—from other people—and that children can therefore be protected from evil by being isolated from its carriers. There is certainly more than a grain of truth in this: there are vicious people, and no sensible person wants to expose children to their influence.

At the same time, however, this view goes wrong when, as often happens, evil is identified obsessively and almost exclusively with one group (the "Communists" or the "capitalists," the "blacks" or the "whites," and so forth), and it is assumed that segregating the child from the group thus identified as evil will make the child morally good. In reality, none of us is perfect; each of us makes some small contribution to corrupting the young. Moreover, while it is reasonable to keep children from people who are really evil, this does not offer any ironclad assurance that the children will exercise their own power of self-determination in a morally good way.

A fourth theory suggests that if people are compelled to act in morally good ways when they are young, they will go on doing what is good when they are adults. But everything we have seen about moral maturity up to now underlines the fact that the moral goodness of an adult is a matter not of habit and routine but of correct, free, self-determining choice.

Good habits are unquestionably desirable, for both children and adults, and we may be morally responsible for our bad habits. But good habits are not identical with good morality; indeed, an action performed simply out of habit, if there ever is such a thing, has of itself no particular moral quality, good or bad, at all. The moral quality resides in our efforts to keep or alter our habits. (In chapter twenty, dealing with character, we shall take up the question of virtue and vice. These also can be called "habits," but in a special sense, involving the exercise of freedom, and so are not to be considered "habits" as we are using the word here.)

Each of these educational/formational theories goes wrong

in overlooking the fact that moral goodness and moral evil result from self-determination. Moral goodness cannot be guaranteed or moral evil eradicated by education. Human beings retain a power to dispose of their own lives, for good or ill, regardless of the educational system to which they have been exposed. And to the extent that education might deprive an individual of the capacity for self-determination, it would also drain his or her life of moral quality.

Even if the science fiction dream of some determinists were realized—a system of education which would condition individuals always to do what is right—the result would be far removed from a situation in which everyone was, in the genuine sense of the words, "morally good." In such circumstances people's actions would have no more moral quality, good or bad, than the behavior of obedient animals or well-programmed machines. The recalcitrant persistence of human freedom suggests, however, that no such system is likely soon to become reality.

B. *What Education Can Do*

More important than what education cannot accomplish, as far as morality is concerned, is the question of what it can do. We approach this matter, nevertheless, with a constant awareness, assumed in all that follows, of the limits imposed by heredity and environment. About heredity education can do nothing. About environment it can do something, perhaps a good deal; yet as a practical matter no conceivable system of education can hope to control the vast multitude of factors which go to make up a child's environment, and most systems are in practice capable of touching only a highly restricted segment of the child's total environment.

But if education cannot guarantee morally good behavior in either the child or the adult, it can at least do some things which will tend to make it easier for the child and the adult to choose and do what is morally right.

Yet education must recognize in dealing with children that in regard to morality and much else they *are* children, not miniature adults. It is a mistake to suppose that they are capable of self-determination in the same way as morally mature adults. Yet much that they do is important for their moral development. Very early they begin to perceive objectives and, spontaneously and without choosing, to act intelligently for them. Thus they have the experience of working for goals (second-level action), they effect some integration of their rational and motivational processes (knowing and wanting), and they learn to appreciate and enjoy certain goods. Rather than being fed a steady diet of television "entertainment" to keep them pacified, they should have a rich environment providing opportunities and incentives for them to do many different things.

Somewhat later, perhaps around the age of six or seven, children begin to have the experience of hesitation, deliberation, and choice. At first freedom of choice does not pertain to many areas of their lives, but gradually they come to see that more and more of their activity is, at least potentially, within their own reflective control.

Among their earliest experiences of choosing is the choice whether or not to do what parents say—to be obedient and limit themselves by a rule or to be disobedient and follow inclination. To the extent that this is really a free choice, it involves self-determination.

At first, nevertheless, children seem to be choosing only between different instances of their own self-integration: whether to follow desire and suffer guilt (and possible punishment) as a result or to obey and suffer the frustration of desire. The experience of making *disobedient* choices can be quite instructive. Children often suffer natural bad consequences (for example, the stomachache after eating the forbidden sweets) and thus learn that following reasonable rules is a way of acting for or protecting substantive goods (life, knowledge, and so on). Obedience and disobedience also have an obvious bearing on the parent-child relationship, and learning that disobedience "hurts" or "offends" parents, children begin to learn something about the good of harmony with them.

C. *Rules for Children*

Against this background we can begin to appreciate why, from the perspective of moral development, it is important to formulate and enforce sound rules governing the behavior of children. Such rules must meet various criteria. They must be consistent, since otherwise they embody some irrationality and cannot really be followed. Like any good system of law, the rules should also be clear, since otherwise children cannot tell what is expected of them (and cannot in fairness be punished for failing to do it). The rules should be oriented toward purposes and goals which make sense—and whose sense whenever possible is pointed out and explained to the children in terms they are able to understand.

The rules should be nonexploitative. Too many rule systems for children are, in fact, designed for the benefit of adults—parents or teachers—and are not really in the best interests of children at all. Ideally, a set of nonexploitative rules for children will be made up of those which they would set for themselves if they were able—if, that is, they were fully self-determining and bent on doing what is morally right.

If the rule system is developed in this way, it will be possible for individuals, as they mature, to incorporate essentially the same rules—though in many cases more sophisticated versions—into their lives. Thus, instead of having to make a sharp transition from childhood morality to adult morality, they will experience their moral lives as a continuum in which they achieve deeper insight into moral principles rather than abandoning old principles in favor of new ones.

If, however, rules for children are not really in their best interests but merely serve the selfish interests of parents and other adults, it will be very difficult for the children ever to get beyond the stage at which morality is cast almost exclusively in terms of obedience/disobedience and the only real choice lies between the guilt that comes from disobeying and the frustration of desire that comes from obeying. Under these conditions children will be adequately motivated to be "good" only by imposed rewards and punishments, and so they will learn to consider moral goodness a mere means, necessary in certain second-level acts, to getting something else they want. The residue of this morally stunted mentality underlies two complementary moral attitudes which are widespread today, legalism and rebellious libertarianism. In both cases morality ultimately means simply "playing the game (to the extent one must) by somebody else's rules."

While providing moral rules for children, an educational system must take care not to overorganize their lives. It is a mistake for parents and teachers to rigidly plan and organize all of children's time for them, even though adults may be tempted to do this "for the children's own good." Rather, there should be free areas dispersed throughout the day in which, acting within the general framework of the rules, children are at liberty to investigate and experiment in making choices among various goods. Free, spontaneous activity, within a system of rules, is extremely important to their moral development.

Some free areas should be shared with adults. On these occasions it is possible to introduce children noncoercively to goods to which it is worthwhile to commit themselves. This is done by giving them the opportunity of sharing in the committed activity of adults doing something which is valuable for its own sake.

This is not simply a matter of togetherness or even of adults giving good example to children. The point, rather, is that children learn what commitment to human goods means by seeing adults performing actions which express their commitment and by having an opportunity to share in such activity—without, however, being pressured to do so. In this way a simple family outing, during which the parents genuinely relax and enjoy themselves and the children are invited to share in the enjoyment, can teach children much more than any number of words what "participation in the good of play" is all about. Similarly, children learn what neighborliness means when they are allowed to help their parents care for neighbors in a time of need.

Equally important are the free areas which a child shares

with other children, which in our society are generally grouped under the label of "playing." To an adult a child's play may seem more or less meaningless activity, but it has a crucial role in the child's development as a whole, and not least in moral development. In play situations with other children the child develops a sense of fairness and justice and comes to appreciate the need for authority within relationships which are nonexploitative and nonpaternalistic.

Finally, children need free areas by themselves: periods in which they have opportunities to reflect, dream, and seek themselves in forms of activity in which they engage simply because they enjoy and value them. At such times they prepare for and rehearse the acts of self-determination by which they will constitute themselves as persons.

One much-debated question about the raising of children is whether and when to use force. While force must sometimes be employed to prevent children from doing what is wrong, forcing them to do what is right is meaningless as a contribution to moral maturity. Here only the good which one elects to do, not the good which one is compelled to do, has value.

Indeed, forcing a child to do good things can actually have negative results in the long run. The child who is coerced to spend half an hour a day practicing the piano may very well grow up with an aversion to music; it is much more likely that a child who has been encouraged but not compelled to take pleasure in music will grow up capable of freely appreciating the good of which music is an expression.

In short, moral rules and their enforcement should be mainly negative: directed at preventing children from doing what is wrong rather than compelling them to do what is right. Good done under compulsion at best provides a shaky foundation for later virtue.

The moral education of children also requires that their emotions be educated. It is extremely important to help them develop hope: an attitude based on the belief that things which are hard but worthwhile can be accomplished.

This can be done by encouraging them to undertake tasks which are difficult but possible. If things are always too easy, children have no need to hope, and they will be unprepared for later challenges which are not easy at all. But if things are too difficult and children are consistently frustrated by failing at the tasks which are set for them, they may very well conclude that no amount of effort is ever likely to produce good results and so adopt an attitude of despair.

Furthermore, it is wise to encourage children to strive for goals in areas in which they are interested (sports, hobbies, and so forth) even if these seem frivolous and trivial to some adults. So far as moral development is concerned, what is at stake is the maturing of a particular attitude rather than the acquisition of useful skills or social graces. Moreover, in their striving for goals children should be encouraged to pursue excellence by being praised for surpassing their own previous attainments, not simply encouraged to compete by being praised for doing better (and scolded for doing less well) than others.

The child should be helped to develop self-control. This is not done by threats and punishment but in the first place by example and then by proposing a self-ideal: "Isn't this what you really want to do and to be? Then in order to accomplish it, this is what you must do." Success in living up to the self-ideal proposed is praised and rewarded. Thus the child is given support and encouragement in overcoming emotional barriers and fitting actions to the self-ideal.

As children's ability to understand grows, they must, as we have said, be given reasons for the moral rules which have been set for them. The reasons given should be the real ones—framed, of course, in concepts and language they are able to grasp. Children also should be included in the process by which important family decisions are reached. The making of the decisions should not be turned over to them, but they should be exposed to the deliberative activity by which adults arrive maturely at important decisions and should be allowed, to the extent of their growing competence, to contribute to it.

It is also important that children have companions who share the same moral framework and outlook on life. This does not imply some sort of invidious segregation—racial, religious, economic, or whatever—which would in fact be highly undesirable even if it were hypothetically possible in a particular case. The point, rather, is that children should have the opportunity to be part of a community of children whose value system is the same and who, within the framework of that value system, can proceed autonomously to develop their own rules and structures.

Providing such a setting is, generally, not too difficult in large families, where brothers and sisters tend spontaneously to create a community whose members share the same values and moral framework. Today, however, this can be a much more difficult thing. Families are smaller, and schools and neighborhoods usually are quite heterogeneous. It may take special effort and ingenuity on the part of parents to see to it that children have the opportunity of associating with other children who share the same moral standards. But the effort is well worth making because of the importance of this factor in moral development.

D. Religious Training

Finally, a word about religious training. It is a mistake to try to make children good by making them religious, for this degrades religion by turning it into an instrument of morality—for example, the attitude of parents who say, "We send Johnny to Sunday school to be sure he gets some moral training." The worst situation of all is that in which legalism is carried over into the religious formation of children, with distorting effects for both morality and religion.

Religion should be presented to children as something which is valuable and important in itself, not as an adjunct of good moral behavior. True, most religious systems do demand a moral commitment on the part of the individual adherent. But in this case the adherents want, presumably, to behave in a morally correct manner because of their religious beliefs: they seek to be moral because they desire to be holy rather than the other way around.

The ideal of sanctity, as a function of religion, can indeed be a powerful inducement to moral behavior on the part of one who accepts the ideal. But neither holiness nor ethical goodness is likely to be served by confusing the two things and attempting to use religion or religious training as a means to induce good behavior on the part of the child.

This is not to deny that religion has powerful ethical implications. It reinforces and validates the willingness of individuals to submit themselves to values and standards beyond themselves. It can help show why and how to live a good life in the world as it is. In one way or another the principle of meaning and value with which religion is concerned sheds light on and provides additional backing for human goods. Moreover, at least some religions supply grounds for hope that living a morally good life, difficult and unappealing as it may sometimes be, will prove in the end to be not only a reasonable but a rewarding thing to do. But this view of religion is hardly likely to come across to the child in a setting in which religion is reduced to the role of a handmaid of good moral behavior.

We cannot end this part of our exposition without pointing out that our suggestions, like those of others, do not guarantee the moral progress of individuals and society as a whole. There can be no such guarantee as long as human freedom remains a reality. In the chapter which follows we examine in greater detail what this means.

Questions for Review and Discussion

1. Think of examples from your experience of educational practices which seemed to be based on the various theories of education mentioned near the beginning of this chapter. In your opinion how did these practices work out?

2. Can you think of reasons why so many approaches to education seem to be based on a denial, at least in practice, of freedom of self-determination?

3. The theories of education which we reject are not normally presented as alternatives to a philosophy of education based on freedom of self-determination. Research educational theory a bit and see how such theories are presented.

4. As long as substantive human goods are actually realized, does it really make any difference whether or not action is done by freedom of self-determination? If so, what difference?

5. Think of examples of rules made by adults to govern the behavior of children. Criticize the examples according to the criteria suggested.

6. In what sense of "freedom" are the free areas of a child's life free?

7. Do you think the lives of most children today are overorganized? What do you think of the fact that many children spend a great part of their free time watching television?

8. What subtle forms of force do adults often employ to try to compel children to do what is good?

9. Gather information about institutions for delinquent children. To what extent are such institutions likely to cultivate an attitude of hope? How could they do so?

10. How does the proposal that children be assured companions who share the same value framework differ from a proposal to practice segregation?

11. If you have experienced religious education, discuss the extent to which it may have confused the religious with the ethical.

12. Show how the theory of education proposed in the present chapter is based on considerations in chapter fifteen.

17. Progress in Perspective

Back in the 1920s a popular charlatan encouraged people to get their psychic juices flowing by repeating regularly "Every day in every way I'm getting better and better." Foolish as that sounds now, it epitomizes an enduring phenomenon: the notion that human progress is continuous and inevitable.

Belief in the inevitability of progress has been expressed in many different ways throughout history. Two of these are important in the contemporary world: Marxism and a vulgarized version of evolutionary theory.

Adopting a pseudoscientific approach, the dialectical view of history espoused by orthodox Marxists offers an account of history, very optimistic for the long run, reducing all of humankind's past problems to economic scarcity, which technology can now overcome. However, the Marxist theory of history is oversimplified; it does not account for all the facts, and predictions based on it, not having come true, have only served to undermine it further. This point has been discussed at length by critics of Marxism, and there is no need to repeat here what has been said elsewhere. It is simply a fact that history has not gone along as it should according to the dialectic of Marx and Engels.

As for evolutionary theory, it is necessary to distinguish between biological evolutionism and evolution loosely conceived as an optimistic philosophy of progress. As a biological hypothesis accounting for the variety of types of organic life, evolutionary theory does not pretend to guarantee inevitable progress. The process of selection merely determines that some kinds of life will survive and others will die off, not that

194

this will necessarily represent qualitative advancement. One can easily imagine a state of affairs in which human beings could no longer survive on earth while insects continued to flourish. The cockroach, in that case, could be the "highest" form of life.

Some philosophers, notably Herbert Spencer in the nineteenth century, nevertheless attempted to translate evolutionism into a comprehensive theory of progress. Hailed in his day as a great thinker, Spencer does not get much attention any more. The reason is obvious. The First and Second World Wars, the Great Depression, Auschwitz, the Stalinist terror, Hiroshima and Nagasaki, Vietnam—these and other vast calamities of the twentieth century have made it all but impossible to swallow the idea that the progress of the human race in history is in any way guaranteed.

Other theorists of inevitable progress offer variations on the basic themes of Marx and Spencer. For instance, Pierre Teilhard de Chardin transposes dialectical materialism and evolutionism from their original naturalistic mode into the spiritualistic mode of a sort of neo-gnosticism or theosophy. All, however, are alike in their optimism. Yet the overriding fact of contemporary history is that the human race, far from having moved steadily forward, now confronts the appalling possibility of wiping itself off the face of the earth. This is not what most people mean by progress.

A. Is Progress Possible?

Humanity has indeed made real progress in many fields over the centuries. Progress is apparent in such areas as theoretical knowledge, including the natural sciences, and technology. In fact, it is only in virtue of the progress in these areas—a progress yielding many benefits—that the human race now has the capability of destroying itself.

Scientific and technological progress occurs by accumulation. In mathematics, for example, a reasonably apt student can now accomplish things far beyond what Euclid was capable of. Mathematicians now know more than Euclid did and therefore can do more than he could. This truly is progress of a sort. The same pattern, progress by accumulation, is present in the "soft" behavioral sciences, like psychology and sociology, and in scholarly disciplines like history.

Progress exists in philosophy, too. Not that the basic philosophical problems have been finally resolved or are likely to be. Rather, over the course of centuries certain solutions have come to be recognized as unacceptable. At least the philosopher now knows that some answers to some questions—answers which at one time seemed plausible to reasonable people—are simply invalid and untenable. This also represents progress.

Technological progress is an overwhelming fact of life today. There was, after all, a time in the history of the human race when people did not know the use of the wheel and of fire. Now people travel to the moon and split the atom as a source of energy.

Similarly, although one would hardly wish to say that Picasso is a greater painter than Botticelli, or Stravinsky a finer composer than Bach, there is a kind of progress in the fine arts. Perhaps the greatest steps forward in the arts occur on those rare occasions when a whole new art form—for example, the modern novel—is elaborated and becomes available to artists for the practice of their art. But progress also occurs through the development and refinement of techniques.

The painter today commands certain techniques—methods of pigmentation and perspective, for instance—which were unknown to painters a thousand years ago; thanks to the development of modern instruments and electronic devices, today's musicians have at their disposal a far wider range of sounds than Renaissance composers did. As a result of improved technique, today's painter and composer can *do* things which painters and composers of earlier centuries could not do. Moreover, apart from accidental losses, the creative accomplishments of previous ages remain available for us to admire and, if we wish, to imitate, while our artists go on in the attempt to set new standards of creativity. While much of what they do will fall away, some of it will become part of the cultural heritage of later generations.

This list can be extended. Men and women today, at least in many parts of the world, are physically larger and stronger than their ancestors, enjoy better health, and live longer. They have more leisure and also have greater access to resources for play, aesthetic experience, and intellectual pursuits. All this, too, represents progress.

B. Progress vs. Freedom

But all these kinds of progress are quite one-sided. People are able to do more to realize certain substantive human goods more fully. To that extent the progress in question has a real bearing on human fulfillment—it enables far more people to participate more fully in human goods—and this is a desirable thing and a cause for joy. But it does not make people morally good, as would progress bearing upon the reflexive goods, involving harmony and relationships. The accumulation of skills and techniques, of tools and technologies, makes it possible for people to contribute more to human well being; it also makes it just as possible for them to bring about greater human misery.

In short, the kind of progress achieved by the human race up to now offers no grounds for assuming the inevitability of moral progress. It only means that over the centuries there has been an expansion of human ability to do both good and evil.

This has not always been clear to modern thinkers and is not clear to all of them today. More than fifty years ago, John Dewey, noting the fact of technological progress, complained that the social sciences had lagged behind the natural sciences and suggested that something could and should be done about this. Dewey believed that the moral dimension of human life should be susceptible to external control, more or less as technology had been brought to bear in the solution of physical problems. For example, supposing we fully understood the causes of crime, it ought to be possible to devise and apply techniques to eradicate or at least effectively control the criminal propensities in people.

This view fails to recognize the radical difference between

human action and technique. Techniques aim to achieve specific, concrete objectives; they fail only by error or accident. Human action as such—that is, action which is free—aims at open-ended ideals and fails precisely because of a failure of choice: people choose to settle for limited goals and thus close themselves off from other possibilities whose realization would make them more fully human.

It may be of course that a good deal of crime and deviant behavior is not morally significant in the first place because it is not really an expression of freedom of choice. Perhaps methods of social control have been or may yet be devised which are effective in dealing with such behavior. If so, we readily acknowledge that these methods represent progress in social control paralleling the progress in other techniques and technologies. Our point is that such progress, supposing it has occurred or may yet occur, is not concerned with freedom and so does not represent *moral* progress.

Suppose for a moment the hypothetical possibility of devising a psychosocial technology which would indeed somehow make it impossible to make morally evil choices. Denied the opportunity of choosing wrongly, we would in fact be denied the opportunity of choosing freely. And in the absence of freedom human life would no longer have any moral quality. Because action was no longer free, it would be neither morally good nor morally bad.

Some kind of psychic conditioning or brainwashing might—again hypothetically—eliminate moral evil from human life, but it would do so at the cost of simultaneously eliminating moral goodness. It would achieve its end by reducing the person to the status of an object, to be manipulated by "experts," persons of presumably superior and virtually superhuman wisdom and moral rectitude.

The only conclusion from all this is that as far as morality is concerned, there is no such thing as necessary and inevitable progress. As long as human beings are free, and to the extent that they are free, they retain a dual capacity for moral good and moral evil. They are able to choose well or badly. Only by eliminating freedom could one eliminate the possibility of evil choices; in the process one would also eliminate the possibility of morally good choices. Thus, in respect to the reflexive human goods, those bearing upon harmony and relationships, there is no accumulation; every human being makes a fresh start. Their realization or failure to be realized depends upon the free choices each of us makes. Individuals can make individual moral progress, but the freedom of people in each generation to be good or bad blocks any cumulative moral progress or decline.

This is not a pessimistic view. It does not say that life goes around in circles or that each generation is condemned to repeat the mistakes of its predecessors. But neither does it say that the course of history is necessarily forward and upward (or, for that matter, backward and downward). Rather, the pattern of history presents a broken front: some progress in some areas at some times, together with regression in other areas at the same time. Such a view is neither optimistic nor pessimistic; it is simply realistic.

It may be objected that in our times there are signs that the human race is indeed capable not simply of spotty and uncertain moral progress but of genuine moral breakthroughs. The weakening of nationalism, cause of so much conflict and suffering in history, is cited as one example. So is the disappearance in many places of slavery.

It is very doubtful that, as a matter of fact, nationalism has declined worldwide, though it may have ebbed in some countries. But supposing for the sake of argument that nationalism *has* declined generally, this can be seen as a mere by-product of improvements in communications techniques and the development of new technology drawing people more closely together. As for the virtual disappearance of slavery, it can be attributed to the fact that slavery is only economically practical in agricultural societies, whereas modern societies are increasingly industrialized. Furthermore, the rise of urban-industrial society has created conditions of oppression, exploitation, and misery quite as bad for many people as the conditions under which slaves typically lived and labored. The features of poverty and injustice have changed; poverty and injustice themselves remain.

In short, these and other developments in our times do not

reflect steadily evolving moral progress but only point to the fact that archaic practices and abuses are generally discontinued as they become less useful. Furthermore, without belaboring the point, it is difficult to make a compelling argument for steady and inevitable moral progress in the age of starvation amidst agricultural surpluses, widespread terrorism and guerrilla warfare, the protracted balance of terror, and virtually worldwide abortion-on-request.

C. The Search for Panaceas

Recognizing that a realistic view of history and the human condition gives no ground for optimism about the inevitability of moral progress, people at various times have come up with panaceas aimed at removing the obstacles to such progress and insuring it in the future. We shall take note of four here: the psychoanalytic panacea, the new morality panacea, the panacea of new institutions and new communities, and the religious panacea.

The psychoanalytic panacea, a complex of psychological and sociological notions based loosely on the theories of Freud and others, reduces evil to illness. People have hang-ups —mental and emotional quirks—which cause them to act badly. If they can be cured of these, and if techniques of child-raising and education can be devised which prevent their recurrence in future generations, the source of evil will be eliminated and human beings will be good.

Emotional illness is a reality, and some emotional illnesses can be cured or at least alleviated by therapy. But it is not true that if people are released from their psychic hang-ups, they will then necessarily do what is right. If therapy really makes a person more free, his or her capacity for free choice of evil as well as good is thereby increased. Curing people of neuroses may make them healthy, but it does not guarantee that they will be morally good.

The new-morality panacea argues that the old morality kept people in bondage and made them hypocrites. But human beings have come of age. Now we are to enjoy a morality of freedom. We shall henceforth act maturely and responsibly. The treatment, in the preceding chapters, of the responsibilities of freedom indicates the extent to which there is something valid in the claims of the new morality, but it also underlines the fact that freedom to do as one pleases is not the same as freedom of self-determination. Moreover, unfortunately for the high hopes entertained by some in regard to the new morality, new moralities have come along with depressing regularity over the centuries, always making the same claims to liberate humanity and usher in a new age. It has not happened yet, and, on the evidence, there is no reason to suppose it will happen in the future.

The panacea of institutional reform attributes evil to institutions, which are said to distort and corrupt human relationships. Change—or perhaps do away with—institutions, create new communities, adopt new patterns of human relationships, and people will cease to do evil and become universally good and loving and generous. As we have seen, large societies always are a mixture of community and exploitation; perhaps small communes based on immediate interpersonal relationship will do better.

While it is true that many institutions are corrupt and all are imperfect, the evidence of history shows, once again, that it is naive to expect much in this direction. Movements of institutional reform (or revolution) have recurred repeatedly and, just as repeatedly, have failed to usher in the promised golden age. Indeed, the evidence suggests that it is generally wiser to attempt to build on the basis of whatever community exists within present institutions instead of tearing down existing institutions and communities in the hope that what comes after will be better than what went before.

The religious panacea comes in several forms. One is a Christian theology (whose orthodoxy it is not our business to judge) which holds that since fallen humankind cannot attain holiness without God's help and mercy ("grace"), once that help and mercy are given in Christ, sin becomes virtually impossible and moral progress inevitable. Another is that the religion or religions we have had up to now have failed us, but a new religion will succeed. Another is that our old religion needs only updating and liberalizing in order to be fulfilling for all and burdensome to none. Still another is that all religion is a snare and a delusion which distracts people from their proper area of concern in this world and subjugates them to myths and a priestly caste bent on their perpetuation—so religion need only be done away with in order to liberate human beings from superstition and free them to pursue their proper destiny.

Each of these false solutions to the problem of human happiness and goodness has enjoyed popularity at various moments in history, and all currently enjoy a certain vogue. Yet none has contributed anything very tangible to the improvement of human life, and taken together, they cancel one another out. Partisans of religion, whether old, new, or updated, may be convinced that some kind of religion surely will bring about heavenly peace and fulfillment on this earth, but they do not account very well for a religious history that includes the Inquisition and the wars of religion, for the scandal of continuing (and in some ways even increasing) divisions among theistic believers, or, for that matter, for the violence-prone religious fanaticism abroad in many parts of the world today; partisans of modern secularism may bask in the glow of "enlightenment," conveniently forgetting that totalitarian ideologies have replaced ancient theologies and that the earthly paradise of unlimited consumption has brought the world's wealthiest nation to the point where it is smothering under its own nuclear, chemical, and organic wastes, even as poverty persists among its underclasses, the family structure collapses at all levels of society, anxiety and depression are pandemic, alcohol and substance abuse are at unprecedented levels, and future generations are being saddled with the burden of a huge governmental debt reflecting the unwillingness of the present to pay its own way.

At bottom all these panaceas are based on the conviction that human beings are not really free; the source of moral goodness and moral evil lies outside their self-determination. Yet the thrust of everything we have said comes down to this: Human beings are free, human beings are self-determining, and human beings make themselves good or evil according to their own free choice. If that is so, there is and can be no such thing as inevitable moral progress on the part of the human race. Progress is possible for us individually and together if we choose it. But to say we can make moral progress is not at all the same as saying we inevitably will. We are free to choose well, to make choices by which we realize more fully what it means to be human. But because we are free, we can also choose badly, opting for growing depersonalization and inhumanity. There is no inevitability here. In a true and profound sense it is up to us to make of ourselves, individually and together, what we choose to be.

Questions for Review and Discussion

1. We deal here only in passing with Marxism. Investigate other aspects of this philosophy as a theory of progress. Consider other criticisms proposed against the philosophy and also other aspects of Marxism which make it as attractive as it obviously is to many people.

2. In what sense does biological evolution guarantee the "survival of the fittest"? To what extent does the concept of evolution change as it is applied in other areas of the natural sciences, for example, the evolution of the physical universe? And in the social sciences, for example, to cultural evolution?

3. Has progress in science and technology been constant throughout history? How can it be accounted for?

4. To what extent would a morally good person be intent upon furthering progress in the areas in which progress is possible?

5. Explain the relationship between Dewey's attitude toward progress and his theory of situationism, discussed in chapter ten.

6. Do you know of any theories in psychology that propose to produce good people by a process of human engineering?

7. List present-day phenomena that might be used to argue either for or against the occurrence of moral progress. Apart from the theoretical consideration that human beings have freedom of self-determination, do you see any strong reasons for arguing either for or against the proposition that moral progress occurs?

8. Do you know of—or can you find examples of—the positions on progress we regard here as panaceas? What is there about each of these positions which makes it plausible to intelligent people?

9. Any theory which holds moral progress to be inevitable excludes freedom of self-determination. But proponents of such theories often argue that the end of progress will be precisely freedom, or increasing freedom. "Freedom" in what sense or senses?

18. Revolution and Reform

Both in natural communities like that of parents and children and in communities formed by common consent people experience much suffering. Some, not generated by human deeds, can be neither anticipated nor prevented (for example, the suffering which accompanies a natural calamity like an earthquake or flood); we are not concerned with that here. But some suffering arises, immediately or remotely, from human actions. Whether consciously or unawares, people often do things which hurt others terribly. The chances of this happening without the perpetrators fully realizing it are particularly great when the wrongs are part of an established system.

The suffering which has its source in human actions is our concern here—that and the following question: What are the proper roles of revolution and reform, respectively, in making human society more just and more virtuous? The issue is particularly pressing today, when revolution is frequently invoked as not only a solution but the *sole* solution to evil and injustice in society. And it is closely linked to the whole question of whether and how moral progress is possible.

A. Realistic Limits

The problem is a complicated one. There are three quite different kinds of relationships among people—exploitative, contractual, and communitarian—and they are generally found not merely side by side but intertwined in any large and complex society. Since the relationships are different, the remedies to abuses will also be different; yet because the relation-

205

ships coexist in the same society, an approach to correcting an abuse which may be right from one perspective may, considered in the light of a different form of relationship, be inappropriate and even harmful.

Thus, while violent revolution may be urged as the proper solution to abuses of an exploitative nature, we must also recognize that revolution is likely to destroy such elements of community as do exist within a society. In such circumstances it is not easy to know how to proceed in order to remedy the situation.

As in the case of an individual evil, so also in the case of evil in society, a number of false or at best partial solutions are proposed. On the analogy that society is an organism, social evil is explained as a sort of disease, a form of social pathology. Or evil is ascribed to a lack of communication; presumably, if people and groups communicate more freely and fully with one another, social evils will disappear. Another theory attributes the evil in society to a particular class or group: the capitalists or the Communists, the blacks or the whites, the rebellious young or the hypocritical middle-aged, and so forth. In still another view social evil is the fruit of bad institutions, institutions which are too large and impersonal; salvation is seen to lie in various types of small groups, which are regarded as more conducive to community.

Each of these explanations locates the cause of evil in society elsewhere than in self-determination. But, as we have stressed repeatedly, *moral* evil is precisely the result of defective self-determination. Unquestionably, societies do suffer from other ills than those which can be described as moral ones, and to the extent that various problems and abuses arising from different sorts of causes exist in a given society, each of the explanations noted above may have validity. But to the extent that the evil in society is really moral evil, no explanation or solution which ignores the fact that moral evil is rooted in self-determination can be considered realistic. Explanations which are unrealistic in this matter are unlikely to contribute to the eradication of social evil even to the extent that such evil may be due to factors other than the moral one.

Viewing the ills of the world, a determinist with an interest in politics is likely to come up with a deterministic diagnosis of social evil and a corresponding remedy. That is what Marx did. To the extent that his diagnosis seems correct (and it has a good deal to recommend it), his entire package will be appealing both to those who live in miserable conditions and to those who have compassion for them.

Not being determinists, we have nothing to offer which can compete in grandiosity and utopian promise. But because it is shaped in great part by free choices, reality is more complicated than determinists suppose. The advantage of our approach, as against that of Marxism and anything similar, is clear when one considers that deterministic schemes for changing the world *are* unrealistic. Leaving freedom out of account, they cannot deliver what they promise; they waste people's lives and ultimately lead to disillusionment. Whereas an approach which takes freedom fully into account and calls for its responsible use can contribute a great deal to overcoming particular evils, improving particular situations, and so helping people lead better lives, while also building up community among them. Even so, conscientious men and women can ultimately do only what is humanly possible, and that is quite limited.

The only remedy for the abuse of human freedom is the proper use of freedom. This immediately suggests that there are social evils to which there is no social solution: objectively bad situations which, realistically speaking, cannot be rectified by any means, or at least by any legitimate means, accessible to society as such. Failure to acknowledge that freedom exists or that it is sometimes abused leads either to a dead-end street or to the adoption of coercive and very likely unfruitful measures for correcting moral evil—in society as well as in the individual. In saying this we are not writing off the possibility of individual and social reform; we are only stating a necessary and important caution with regard to means and expectations.

B. Social Relationships

The problems which arise in each of the three kinds of social relationship are different, as also are their remedies. We shall look briefly at each in order to see what avenues of redress are open to those who suffer injury as a result of someone else's misuse of freedom.

If the relationship is exploitative, the obvious solution for those who are exploited is to gain enough power to change the relationship to a contractual one, in which both sides (or all sides) derive roughly equal benefits. If the exploitation exists within a larger society where there is a common authority, the exploited can appeal to that authority to correct the abuse and right the balance. (In the United States, for instance, through court decisions, legislation, and other means the federal government was able to do a great deal to right many of the legally enforced wrongs from which black people suffered well into the middle years of the twentieth century.) Finally, as a last resort the exploited individual or group can employ physical force in an effort to halt the exploitation. Realistically, however, there is a good chance that a resort to force will not succeed if the exploiters have made an accurate calculation of the relative power available to themselves on the one hand and the exploited on the other.

When in political society extralegal means of righting a wrong seem justified, preference should be given to civil disobedience, the open refusal to obey public authority in order to call attention to an injustice. Several things are required of those who would adopt civil disobedience in hopes of correcting injustice in society. They must avoid doing harm to others; they must accept the lawful penalty for their behavior in order to show that fundamentally they uphold the rule of law; and they must not use bad means to a good end—a point which Gandhi always emphasized, though he did not always perfectly observe it.

If physical violence is used, it is equivalent to warfare, and the same stringent limitations on the use of force in war which were noted earlier must be observed. Rebellion can only be justified as warfare is; one is not permitted to do something immoral to rectify injustice. Since among the restraints on the use of force is the moral norm that one not harm the innocent as a means to a good end, morally upright people are always at a significant disadvantage in a contest with morally unscrupulous persons in power. But if this constraint—against harming the innocent—is not respected, the revolutionary process itself corrupts the revolutionaries (and the *counter*revolutionary process equally corrupts the *counter*revolutionaries), so that the outcome even of "success" is not genuine liberation but the replacement of one gang of despots and exploiters by another.

It should be clear that revolution as we are speaking realistically of it here is not "revolution" in the same sense in which that word is often used at the present time. Contemporary prophets of revolution give the term an almost mystical meaning, using it to describe some sort of fundamental transformation in human beings and human relationships. But revolution—the use of physical force—intended simply to end an exploitative relationship does not involve any such fundamental transformation; leaving aside the mystique of revolution, it is merely the direct use of force to counter unjust force being used for exploitation.

A contractual relationship stands midway between exploitation and community. It can be described as a kind of benign, mutual exploitation: each party gives up something to the other or others in order to get something in return. In a fair contractual relationship that which each surrenders is roughly comparable in value to that which each receives. If—or to the extent that—contracting parties are mutually committed to fairness, their relationship already has about it an element of genuine community. However, an initially just contractual relationship can degenerate into a sort of sanctioned exploitation when one of the parties begins to give less and get more.

This can come about in either of two ways. Either one of the parties more or less deliberately violates the terms of the contract or else the conditions to which the contract applies change significantly, so that the balance shifts and one party finds himself or herself having to give a great deal and receive very little, while the other gives very little and receives a great deal. When a contractual relationship changes in this way, it ceases to be a true contract and becomes ordinary exploitation.

That being so, the means of redress are those outlined above when exploitation occurs: appeal by the injured party to the sense of justice of the exploiter, appeal to an authority which has the power to enforce contracts, and in extreme cases recourse to violence in order to counter the violence of the exploiter. The moral problem with resort to violence is that often there is no act which the exploited can do that will in and of itself lessen the violence being done to them; violence, therefore, is likely to be directed against some human good as a means to an ulterior end and is morally excluded for that reason.

When a contract is violated by one party, the injured party is of course no longer morally obliged to observe its terms, but this is often of little help. For in such cases it often happens that injured parties have already carried out their end of the bargain or, if they fail to do so, can be made to suffer more loss than gain, even though it is not just that they should now have to honor a contract which the other party has violated.

For the most part, though, it is less difficult to correct exploitation resulting from a contractual relationship which has gone sour than to rectify an exploitative situation which has never involved anything except exploitation. For in the case of what started out as a contract there was at least an initial commitment on both sides to a rough kind of equity, and if this commitment has not entirely vanished, it may be possible to reconstruct the relationship on its basis.

At the same time a contract can be a more impersonal kind of relationship than either direct exploitation or community. It is arguable, for instance, that some nineteenth-century plantation slaves enjoyed a more "human" relationship with their owners than did some nineteenth-century factory workers with the owners of their factories. This suggests that in a concrete situation of mixed exploitation and community—a real-life situation which one encounters with some frequency—it may not be advisable to attempt to change the relationship to a purely contractual one. Instead, it may be better in particular cases to seek to correct the situation by building upon such elements of community as already exist rather than eliminating community along with exploitation by making the relationship exclusively contractual.

For example, the solution to the problems of a family in which the parents, although basically loving, are habitually exploitative of their children might better be sought in counseling, encouragement, and mutual efforts of understanding and charity than in legal action, which can end by separating the children from their parents and making them wards of the state.

C. Reform of Community

As we have seen, communities are based on a shared commitment by their members to the realization of some fundamental good or goods. Communities can go wrong in their constituting act (the original Constitution of the United States, for instance, made provision for slavery), in the institutions which express constitutional purposes, or in particular actions.

The institutions of a community are corrupt when, as a result either of design or accident, they embody exploitation. Tax loopholes which unjustly favor some individuals or groups at the expense of others are a good example of this. As for the injustice which exists in communities as a result of particular actions, this comes about when individuals fail to carry out the duties which are properly theirs by reason of their roles in society. As we have seen, an individual faced with a genuine conflict of duties may morally be excused from performing some of them. But an individual cannot consistently claim the benefits of membership in particular societies and neglect the duties which arise from such membership without being guilty of injustice and irresponsibility.

Given the nature of a community, the only way to correct evil compatible with the principle of community itself is through communication, persuasion, an appeal to reason and good will (not excluding an appeal to emotion). Community can never be maintained by force, because the use of force by some members of the community against others is inherently destructive of community.

If, then, individuals in a community are guilty of evil actions contrary to the commitments which bind the community together, one must appeal to the institutions which embody the community's purposes in an effort to persuade such persons to live up to the duties which those institutions impose. And if the institutions themselves embody evil and injustice, one must appeal to the constitutional principles of the community in order to have the institutions brought into conformity with those purposes.

It is of course possible to use force at the operational level, and it may even be necessary at times to do so—for instance, people who break the law must sometimes be arrested and imprisoned. At the institutional level it is also possible to play politics (operate within the framework of the institutions as they are) in an effort to achieve an advantageous result without correcting what is wrong with the institutions. But to the extent that either of these things—using force, playing politics—is done, the principle of community has been abandoned, and the pattern of either exploitation or contract has been imposed on the relationship.

Where problems within a community concern fundamental constitutional principles, the methods of tackling the difficulty must essentially be philosophic. One may, for instance, attempt to demonstrate to other members of the community that a particular part of the constitution is inconsistent with other principles embodied there—for instance, toleration of slavery cannot very well coexist with commitment to the principle that human beings are fundamentally equal and possess equal rights.

If, however, there is no demonstrable urgency and the constituting principles are in fact mutually consistent, the only recourse is an appeal to basic principles of right and wrong which should govern action independently of any other commitments. Admittedly, the chances of success in such circumstances are not great. When the members of a community are bent on doing what is wrong, arguments intended to point out to them that there are other values which they ought not to violate are not likely to be heeded. Still, when something goes wrong in a community relationship, it is essential that one who would seek to set it right proceed on the assumption that the others are acting with good will. The opposite assumption—of ill will—undercuts the very possibility of community from the start.

While what we have been saying applies to political societies, it also applies, in one degree or another, to smaller communities. Here, too, the remedy for problems lies in procedures suited to building up community rather than in the adoption of contractual arrangements.

The radical difference between the two things becomes clear when, for example, people try to dissolve a marriage. Obliged to proceed as if marriage were a partnership (which it is not), they must attempt to divide the assets and make compensation for different contributions; but this does not work, inasmuch as the principle of fairness in a family is, not balance of value in exchange, but "from each according to ability, to each according to need." Every divorce settlement is more or less unsatisfactory, since a procedure appropriate to dissolving a partnership has been applied to a relationship too nearly organic to be divided and portioned out in that way.

In some cases it may be better to maintain an imperfect community—such as the unhappy but tolerable family situation described above—than to dissolve it. Even an imperfect community contains the seeds of growth in personal relationship; and often a careful, calm, honest articulation of their grievances by those wronged, together with insistence that those who are wronging them face up to the situation, can be quite effective (for example, the technique of "confronting" an alcoholic). If the wrongdoers retain some emotional bonds with those whom they have injured, the evasion and rationalization which have allowed them to persist in wrongful behavior up to now can sometimes be pierced in this way.

It is nevertheless difficult to bring about real reform in a community. No one is perfect, and reform—even if the means of effecting it is available—might bring to light other problems which most of those involved would prefer to leave unexamined. Thus there is a tendency for people to live resentfully with a bad situation rather than try to correct it. Moreover, those who might bring about reform—perhaps even have a responsibility to do so—may shy away from acting because they anticipate painful consequences and, in true consequentialist fashion, would rather shirk their duty than suffer these. Hence such phenomena as politicians who will not support an unpopular tax increase when increased taxes are needed, school administrators who will not confront erring students lest the students defy them, and parents who decline to discipline their children because they wish to avoid the hassle.

In a real sense violence is simply not a factor in community situations. For between those who do violence and those who have violence done to them there can be no community, at least not while the violence is occurring. Community depends on mutual self-commitment, and there is no sharing among people who do violence to one another. True, it may be justified to resort to violence in some complex communities—for instance, to overthrow an oppressive dictator (whose *de facto* government may have, in extreme cases, a relationship to the governed not dissimilar to that of an armed mob to an unarmed populace which it is terrorizing). In such cases those who employ violence are clearly not maintaining community with the individual or group against whom the violence is directed, but it may be that the use of violence is in fact the only way to preserve the possibility of community for everyone else.

Such cases are, however, rare. And, other things being equal, the larger the group to whom violence is done, the less likely it is that the violence is justifiable, at least as an instrument of preserving community.

As a practical matter, this suggests that the smaller the number of revolutionaries in a given society in relation to the society as a whole, the more likely it is that the revolutionaries are themselves would-be tyrants, obsessed perhaps by some scheme of transforming human nature by means which will turn out to be violent and exploitative in their turn. Whatever their rhetoric may assert, such people do not really have community in view; instead they are bent on imposing on everyone else their vision of how people should live and how society should function.

Social change brought about by violence will be no more stable than the ability of those who employed the violence to remain in power. As long as they have not received the consent of those they govern, they are only exercising a kind of tyranny. At best such a situation may represent a kind of contractual relationship; it can in particular cases be an improvement over a previously existing situation of exploitation. But it is far removed from community, and it may retard rather than advance the attainment of a truly communitarian relationship among persons.

Questions for Review and Discussion

1. To what extent, do you think, do the ills of society arise from moral evil and to what extent from other causes?

2. In practice how are the exploitative, contractual, and communitarian aspects of a society to be distinguished, when in fact they are mixed, in the same social situation?

3. Can you think of historical cases in which a nonideological rebellion of a genuinely exploited group of people succeeded in changing the situation of exploitation? How did the exploiters come to miscalculate?

4. We speak of a contractual relationship as midway between exploitation and community. This is an oversimplified, shorthand way of putting the matter. Can you think of more nuanced ways of defining the similarities and the differences of the various forms of relationship?

5. It has been said that in the United States there is a tendency for every great social issue sooner or later to come before the Supreme Court. Can you explain why this is so in terms of the analysis offered in this chapter?

6. Existing ways of treating criminals apparently tend, at least in many cases, to alienate them still further from society. But some proposals for reform are based on an at least implicit denial of freedom of self-determination. Assuming freedom of self-determination, is there any way to deal with criminals which would be better than present methods?

7. In this chapter we take a rather dim view of revolution, especially revolution on ideological grounds. Does this mean that our position is committed to a conservative or status quo stance on issues involving social justice?

8. The treatment here mentions civil disobedience but, for lack of space, does not say much about it. Investigate what is involved in civil disobedience and other tactics of confrontation politics and discuss the extent to which such activities might be justified and under what conditions.

9. To what extent is the present discussion applicable to relations between nations? Is permanent peace possible, or is war inevitable?

19. The Role of Religion

Is religion a help or a hindrance to morality?

The question seems odd. Religion and morality are often equated, so that a religious person is assumed to be a moral person. Hardly more sophisticated is the attitude which looks on religion as a bulwark of morality. How many tributes have been paid to "religion, the foundation of good citizenship and good conduct"? Yet the relationship between religion and morality is far from being that simple.

There are many different religions. All represent efforts to know and enter into a satisfactory relationship with the more-than-human source of meaning and value which monotheists call "God." Religions, however, cannot all be equally true and worthwhile, for many contradict one another, and some approve practices like human sacrifice which are plainly contrary to moral truth.

Although investigating the soundness of particular religions is beyond the scope of this book, well within its scope is the fact that Judaism, Islam, and Christianity—"monotheism" as we use the term here—make significant moral demands on people's lives beyond the sphere of religious activity itself. All three claim to hand on the revelation of a personal God who calls people into a covenant relationship with himself and one another, requires that they worship him and him only, directs them to show mercy toward others, and insists that they be faithful in their commitments to him and one another. These are demands with a significant ethical dimension.

But even among those who accept the claims of monotheism with faith there is no necessary connection between religious belief and morally good behavior. People who hold very strong religious beliefs can commit moral atrocities. People with no visible or identifiable religious convictions can lead morally exemplary lives. As we shall see, religious commitment can indeed provide strong support for ethically correct behavior; but there is no necessary connection between the two things.

Furthermore, as we remarked earlier, the effort to tie religion to morality can have unfortunate results: specifically, the result of making religion a handmaid of ethics. In its most simplistic form this comes down to reducing religion to a single formula: "Be good or you won't go to heaven."

It may be true that being good (trying to do what one regards as morally right) is a precondition to going to heaven (achieving a permanently satisfactory relationship with God). We personally believe the formula expresses a truth. But we are also convinced that reducing religion to this formulation debases both salvation and goodness by making one the payoff for the other. In this way of looking at things religion and moral goodness are placed in the context of second-level, means-end action rather than third-level action: action performed for the sake of a basic good in which one participates precisely in performing the action.

At this point it is perhaps necessary to state something both obvious and important. In using words like "God," "religion," "heaven," "salvation," and so forth we are not now departing from our established procedure and taking for granted the truth of a body of religious teaching. We merely assume that many of our readers are familiar with certain religious beliefs and will wish to explore how ethics relates to them. One need not assume that religious convictions are true in order to discuss how the subject matter of ethics relates, or should relate, to them.

While many people suppose there is a simple and self-evident relationship between religion and morality, others profess to have difficulty in seeing any positive relationship at all. Many objections are raised to religion on ethical grounds, but in different ways they say the same thing: not only does religion not necessarily foster good behavior, it actually hinders people in their efforts to do what is ethically right. Such objections generally take one of three forms.

A. *Religion: Evasion of Responsibility?*

First, it is said that by focusing attention on the transcendent—on God, salvation, heaven, the afterlife, and such—religion distracts human beings from the here and now and causes them to neglect their responsibilities in and to the world and the people around them. This is the argument against supernatural religion advanced by John Dewey and Karl Marx ("Religion is the opiate of the people"). Holding out the promise of happiness in a future life, religion seduces human beings from the task of correcting evils and injustices in this life.

It is nearly inevitable that religion should be open to this charge. As was suggested above, there is very often no way to motivate children—or people who, although beyond childhood, are still morally immature—except by promising them a reward for acting in a certain way. In a religious context this naturally leads to the formulation: "Be good, and you'll go to heaven." Some popular expressions of religion have tended to emphasize this point to the virtual exclusion of any other consideration.

Nevertheless, a true religious act is a third-level action: an act performed not simply to achieve a specific future objective (heaven, eternal life) but to participate in the good of religion now. A pattern of acts of this sort can be described as "living a devout life."

When one refers to people as living devout lives, one is speaking of them doing something here and now. Their action represents present participation in a good: in this case the good of religion. So one might speak of others as "living scholarly lives" (participating consistently in the good of truth or knowledge) or "living sociable lives" (participating consistently in the good of friendship).

Such expressions describe the pattern of life of people who are not merely pursuing particular objectives but participating in certain goods. Nor are these necessarily highly sophisticated persons who speak of "third-level action" and such, and have a well worked-out theory of human behavior and ethics. What is in question here are people's fundamental attitudes and commitments, not their command of ethical theory. In any case, whatever else one might say of persons who live devout lives (that is, participate consistently in the good of religion), one cannot accuse them of ignoring the here and now. They are participating here and now in the good of religion, and doing so to such an extent that their manner of living can be characterized by the expression "living devout lives."

Someone might object that this still leaves such people open to the accusation of ignoring other human goods. But if they are really doing what they are said to do—participating consistently in the good of religion—this cannot be the case. As we have seen earlier, the four basic goods focusing on harmony—which we have called for convenience's sake integrity, practical reasonableness, friendship, and religion, and which we grouped under the general heading of "reflexive" goods— are mutually dependent, so that insofar as one acts contrary to one of them, one undermines one's participation in all. Stated positively, this means that a person committed to and participating in one fundamental reflexive human good, such as the good of religion, will also act, so far as he or she can, to realize the other reflexive human goods.

"Very neat," those who criticize religious supernaturalism might say just here. "So religion as such need not be a distraction from the business of living responsibly in the world. But surely you have to admit that Christianity, with its promise of pie in the sky when you die, does undermine moral seriousness about the world and so buttresses a status quo which is unjust in many ways."

As a matter of fact, this is true, at least up to a point. Any interpretation of Christian teaching which reduces life in this world to a second-level act, with heaven as its goal, deserves such criticism and has no satisfactory answer.

There are, however, other interpretations of Christianity according to which "heaven" or "the kingdom" is not something separate and apart from life here and now but is already present, though hidden, in this life and this world. In this view morally good acts, including efforts to overcome social injustices and build up human community, have all the meaning they would have if there were no heaven to come, but they also have the further significance of helping build up a heavenly community which will last forever. Whether this is true is not an ethical question, but the possibility of understanding Christianity in this way is relevant to the ethical objection that religion is an obstacle to authentic morality.

B. Religion and Freedom

A second objection advanced against religion on ethical grounds is that it destroys human freedom. According to religion, it is said, human beings are good if they are obedient to God's will; but to make goodness contingent on obedience to God is to withdraw from human beings their autonomy and reduce them to a state of subjection. This complaint is found in the work of a number of writers, notably Nietzsche, for whom it is a major theme.

Like the first objection to religion, this one also has a kind of inevitability about it, given the need to present religious claims to children and others who are morally immature. It is virtually inescapable that religious purposes and imperatives be presented to such persons as a system of rules demanding obedience. And there exists in this an obvious danger: the danger of suggesting that the gulf between God and human beings is of the same sort as that between the parent and the small child or, even worse, between the exploiter and the exploited.

One way to try to answer this objection is by asserting that religion makes no demands on anyone: religion has no connection with morality, is in fact fundamentally amoral. But it is difficult to see how such religion could contribute anything to achieving reconciliation, which all forms of monotheism posit as necessary and desirable, between human beings and God. If reconciliation is needed, something must be *done* to bring it about. This implies acting in certain ways, not acting in others.

A better solution to the objection is found in the fact that, as we have seen, responsibilities are not imposed externally but instead arise naturally from reality—the reality of the human person. People are not morally responsible because God arbitrarily requires them to observe a merely external set of rules. Rather, people have a responsibility to respect and seek to participate in human goods because it is humanly right and good to do so. Those who act morally—as we have explained what it means to act morally—achieve fuller realization of their personhood by doing so: their humanity is enhanced, not debased. Since acting morally essentially means acting within the framework of a fundamental commitment or set of commitments, one might well speak of people who act in this way as acting with committed freedom, the freedom of self-determination. The contrary state of affairs—acting on the basis of *un*committed freedom—suggests either a merely premoral (or amoral) spontaneity or a "doing as one pleases," which is immoral.

Furthermore, even assuming a religious duty to do what God wills, the responsibilities associated with religion become moral responsibilities in precisely the same way as the moral responsibilities which arise from any other basic human good. That is, the moral responsibilities which arise from the good of religion are binding in the same way and for the same general reasons as the responsibilities which arise from the goods of truth and friendship. One has the responsibility of doing some things and not doing others because that is how one realizes more fully what it means to be human.

Whether to choose to accept something proposed as a matter of religious faith is itself a moral question, and clearly one ought to reject any religion whose acceptance would require one to do anything one believes to be immoral. Christianity, in fact, claims that God demands nothing contrary to human good, that most of his commandments simply call attention to moral truths which we could know even without faith, and that the rest are reasonable requirements God makes of his human friends, analogous to what we require of our friends and they of us. His commands are to be obeyed because what he commands is humanly, in the deepest meaning of that word, right and good; it is simply not the case that what is commanded becomes right and good from the fact that God commands it, in the sense of imposing it externally on us.

Today, of course, the more traditional forms of monotheism face the fact that their moral teaching, which they claim to hand on as valid and binding, is widely rejected on the grounds that it is rigid and oppressive. Still, these religions propose their moral doctrine as truth, not arbitrary rules, so that an honest investigator of their claims must answer the question: Is it true or not?

Although we shall not attempt an answer here, we note that the question can be approached in two ways: either by considering the moral teachings one by one or by considering the grounds for accepting or rejecting a particular form of monotheistic religion as a whole. If there were good grounds for accepting the claims of a particular religion in general, one would also have good grounds for accepting its moral teachings, regardless of whether it was possible to demonstrate conclusively and to everyone's satisfaction the truth of each one separately. On the other hand, in the absence of reasons for thinking one should accept the claims of a religion, there is no reason to be concerned with its claims for its moral doctrine, even though one might happen to agree with one or another point in it.

C. Religion and Evil

A third ethical objection to religion is based on the fact of evil. If God were all-knowing, all-powerful, and all-good, surely there would be no evil; but there is evil; therefore God must be something other than all-knowing, all-powerful, and all-good. This "problem of evil" is indeed a profoundly mysterious one, precisely from the point of view of monotheistic religion. It has no answer or solution which is totally satisfying in every respect, and a reasoned analysis itself runs the risk of seeming glib. The present writers have dealt with this question at greater length elsewhere (see the suggested readings for this chapter). So here we offer only a few thoughts in the context of the present discussion.

Some religious theories have attempted to solve the problem by speculating that God is in fact not powerful enough to prevent evil; the principle of good and the principle of evil, it is suggested, are more or less coequal, and the struggle between them results in victory sometimes for one, sometimes for the other. But such theories really fall outside the framework of monotheistic religion, for they point to two or more *ultimate* sources of meaning and value—a picture of reality itself freighted with problems.

A better solution emerges when one realizes that "good" has many different meanings, and there is no logical reason to suppose that our human understanding of what is good necessarily applies unequivocally to the transcendent being whom we call God. It is unreasonable to attempt to measure divine action or inaction according to the norms of human moral goodness. In an earlier edition of this book we suggested, by way of example, that God could hypothetically be a utilitarian—because, presumably, an all-knowing being would know what the "greater good" or "lesser evil" is and so be able to judge whether it is worth doing evil to achieve good. While it now seems to us that, even as a speculation, this is a misleading formulation and easily subject to misinterpretation, it does suggest the essential point we wish to make: it is unreasonable to try to apply simplistically a morality based on human goods to a being who is, by definition, nonhuman. One ought rather to take it for granted that what it means for God to be good will be radically different from what it means for a human being to be good.

But this does not really answer the fundamental question posed by the problem of evil: If God is all-knowing, all-powerful, and all-good, how can evil be? Rather than trying to state here what we think is the real answer (which we have offered elsewhere), we note only that the very terms of the problem—God is *all*-knowing, *all*-powerful, and *all*-good—come from monotheistic religious faith. If faith itself generates the problem, those who crave a solution must look to faith, not philosophy. And those who use the problem of evil as a challenge to religious faith should, in all fairness, allow faith to give its full answer in *its own terms* rather than demand an answer in purely philosophic terms to a question which can only be posed in terms of faith.

A related objection is the assertion that religion itself has been and remains a force for evil in human affairs. Religion is an outlet for fanaticism, an occasion and excuse for people to act cruelly and unjustly toward others. This accusation has been leveled against religion by such writers as Voltaire, David Hume, and, closer to our own times, Bertrand Russell.

Its impact comes from the fact that it is true, although it is not the whole truth. Logically, the problem can arise from any or all of at least three causes: defects in the religion itself, its abuse or exploitation by immoral people for their own ulterior purposes, and misunderstanding and misapplication of religion by its adherents. It is in the latter area that fanaticism enters the picture. A person can indeed practice fanaticism in the name of religion, since exclusive (and exclusivistic) concentration on one human concern at the expense of others is precisely what is meant by fanaticism. As there are fanatics in the pursuit of knowledge, fanatics in the pursuit of sensuality, fanatics in the pursuit of the whole range of human experiences, so also there are fanatics in the pursuit of religion.

There is no necessary reason, however, why religion should breed fanaticism. Those who suggest otherwise mistake an abuse of religion for its whole reality. One can give the central place in one's life to the human good of religion without making it an absolute to which all else must be sacrificed. The good of religion is not identical with God, and even in traditional religious terms the quest for union with God is seen as involving an effort to respect and participate in many different goods besides those in the category of religion.

In the Christian tradition, which we cite here only by way of example, even Jesus, whom orthodox faith believes to be God made man, acted as a human being according to the conditions of human good. And the individual Christian, it is further believed, must conform to God by conformity to Jesus in his human nature. Christianity proposes, in other words, that people respond to the call to share intimacy in divine life not by evading human responsibility, not by living inhumanly, but by fulfilling the requirements of what it means to be human. Christianity thus demands of its adherents that they be open to the fullness of human personhood, not that they be limited to the fanatical pursuit of one aspect or another of that personhood.

D. *Religion and Hope*

There is more to be said about the relationship between ethics and monotheistic beliefs than simply responding to ethical objections to religion. For there is, or can be, a positive relationship between the two, a relationship in which monotheism supports the individual in the effort to live a morally good life. To say this is not to assume the truth of religion, but only to point to the fact that hope, founded on traditional religious beliefs and attitudes, does strongly buttress the effort of many people to do what is ethically right.

The key word here is hope. And hope relates directly to the fact of evil.

Faced with evil in the world, one is tempted to respond in either of two ways: with a kind of technological-humanistic presumption which takes for granted that if only the proper techniques can be found and applied, evil will be eradicated from human life; or with a despair which takes for granted that evil is ineradicable and can never be fully overcome. The former attitude is illustrated by theories of progress and perfectibility which deny freedom of self-determination—the sort of theories, so prevalent in our Western culture, which we have criticized repeatedly. The latter attitude is illustrated by theories of fatalism and rejection of the reality of the world, which also deny freedom of self-determination; these theories have been prevalent in Eastern cultures. Hope—a hope founded in monotheism—makes it possible to avoid both extremes.

The object of hope is God's faithfulness in protecting humankind and bringing it to human fulfillment. Looking at it from an ethical perspective, hope comes down to the conviction that doing what is right will not be fundamentally at odds with human well-being. This is often difficult to see and accept, especially when "human well-being" is conceived in second-level terms as lying in some limited goal or objective, while "doing what is right" requires setting aside something of this sort in favor of respecting human goods. To those who believe that happiness means getting what they want, a morally good person may seem a bit of a dreamer, a good deal of a fool.

Even for those with hope the human condition is very difficult. Sooner or later we all must die. Not even those with ideals
live up to them perfectly. We often are thrown into competition with one another for what we need, and in this competition those who try to do the right thing are frequently at a
serious disadvantage in relation to the unscrupulous. It is easy
to see why people consider consistent reasonableness unreasonable, hold that it makes sense to look for relief from anxiety
in pleasure-seeking which is humanly unfulfilling, subscribe to
the code of looking-out-for-number-one, and truly believe
that when the stakes are high enough, the end justifies the
means.

Theistic hope offers an alternative: Doing what is right will
not in the end be at odds with human fulfillment, for God will
see to it that moral fidelity in the face of suffering and sin is not
pointless. Such hope enables those who have it to cope with the
facts of the human condition and, in coping, to continue to do
what is morally right. It does this by making it possible to hold
as a rational belief the conviction that evil will ultimately be
overcome, even though we cannot say how or when.

Only if one has such hope can one readily reject a morality
of consequences, which holds that it is right to do evil so that
good will come about. With such hope it is possible to say in
effect, "Even though I do not see the good consequences of
doing what is morally right in this difficult case, I will nevertheless do it, convinced that my responsibility as a free person is to
do what is humanly good—to respect all of the human goods—
not to achieve all human good consequences."

Utilitarians—and their contemporary proportionalist/con-
sequentialist cousins—are likely to object: "That sounds suspi-
ciously like the Stoic maxim 'Let right be done though the
heavens fall!'" However, Jews, Moslems, and Christians, who
believe in the God of Abraham, Moses, David, and Jeremiah,
can answer: "Not at all. Rather, let right be done that God may
be glorified *and* that his people may rejoice in the blessings he
has promised and will surely grant to those who hope in him."

Yet even such religion is no *solution* to the human moral
predicament. There are no panaceas for the problem of evil,
neither in psychoanalysis, social revolution, educational theo-

ries and techniques—nor religion. If religion or anything else is regarded as a panacea, the result will be frustration. We are not suggesting that religion is a solution for evil; instead, we are pointing out that religion can be, has been, and still is a support for many people in their efforts to do what is right in the face of evil.

Religion does no more and no less than place the paradox of moral evil in a perspective in which it is possible to live with it, neither rebelling nor despairing. To say one can live with evil does not mean that one regards it complacently or fails to do what one can, consistent with sound morality, to correct and remove it. It means that one recognizes that because human beings are free, moral evil is and will continue to be a reality in human life; but in the context of religious belief it also involves the conviction that evil will ultimately be overcome, although we do not know how this will come about.

Finally, speaking now as persons who hold the Christian faith, we add one further thought. Although Jesus is a divine person, he willingly accepted the responsibilities of human freedom and thus demonstrated that this freedom is compatible with divine personhood. The implications for the individual Christian are enormous. Christianity not only allows but demands that people approach the challenge of living with the intention of realizing as fully as they can all that it truly means to be human. Christianity need not stunt or degrade persons; on the contrary, understood as it really is, Christianity teaches humankind to respect the dignity of the human person and all that constitutes a person. And, finally, Christianity teaches that with God's help human freedom will be able to fulfill the responsibilities which freedom itself entails.

Questions for Review and Discussion

1. To what extent, do you think, has religion, as a matter of historical fact, distracted people from the here-and-now goods of this life?

2. Can you think of historical figures or people you know who you would say were really living devout lives and at the same time were committed to realizing human goods here and now?

3. Various types of religion have used various substantive goods as their vehicles. Show how life, esthetic experience, play, and speculative knowledge have been vehicles for religion in various forms of it.

4. Can you think of examples in which substantive goods, serving as vehicles for religion, have been perverted to the status of mere means? Does the same thing also happen when other reflexive goods become objects of strong commitment?

5. Do you see any reason why religion especially should give rise to fanaticism?

6. It has been said that the difference between martyrs and fanatics is that martyrs are willing to die for what they believe in, while fanatics are willing to kill for their beliefs. Discuss.

7. Relate Augustine's conception of happiness, discussed in chapter three, to the fear, discussed in the present chapter, that religion infringes on human freedom.

8. Why do most people assume that God should act in a morally good way according to human standards of morality?

9. What is the difference between hope and optimism?

10. Do you agree that there is a relationship between religious conviction and the ability to resist moral theories which put the emphasis on the visible, tangible consequences of action? If so, do you think the relationship is the one sketched out here, or is there more to it than that?

20. We Must Decide Who We Shall Be

To do the right thing it is not enough to have good will, to *mean* to do what is right. It is also necessary to make sound judgments about reality. A man gathering mushrooms as a treat for his family can kill everybody by collecting the wrong sort. A serious but misguided scholar can fritter his life away on a pseudoscience like astrology. Dedicated social reformers imbued with utilitarianism can wreak havoc with the fabric of commitments binding society together even as they try to solve society's problems.

The point is important to the subject to which we turn as we near the end of this book. Although we are not assuming the truth of monotheistic religion or acting as apologists for any sort of religion, precisely from the point of view of ethics it is necessary for each of us to make a fundamental "religious" commitment—that is, a commitment to some general world-view and way of life—within which other commitments can then be integrated. Religions and their functional equivalents are not all the same and, evidently, are not all suitable as the objects of this commitment; yet every person who wishes to live a good human life ought to pursue the religious quest, seeking the truth about the basic questions concerning meaning and value to which various worldviews provide answers.

A. *Religion and the Religious Quest*

Much earlier we saw that religion is one of the fundamental human goods. As such, religion is harmony with a more-than-human source of meaning and value. True, sophisticated people sometimes attempt to argue that nothing of the sort exists, but they are arguing against a conclusion reached by virtually all people of every time and place on the basis of the facts of the human situation. On the one hand, we are quite limited and are doomed to die, yet on the other hand we know ourselves to be part of a larger reality into which an upright person's pursuit of human goods must somehow fit. Moreover, the flat rejection of *every* more-than-human source of meaning and value would lead to ethical subjectivism or relativism. For it would mean that prior to human evaluation and choice there is no standard of genuine human fulfillment by which to measure the judgments and choices of individuals and societies.

Thus, rather than deny the place of religion entirely, sincere and thoughtful people who do not subscribe to a traditional religion generally look to some features of the world itself as the more-than-human source of meaning and value. This is the case, for instance, with Marxists who look to the dialectic of history, as it is with many Western liberals who look to the inevitable dynamic of evolutionary progress. Professedly nonreligious though they are, such worldviews are nevertheless religions, for they seek not only to explain life but to bring people's lives into harmony with the source of meaning and value which, as they see it, undergirds human goods and requires submission and respect.

Although this book is not concerned with settling ultimate religious questions, we can say that some worldviews will not pass muster. For worldviews conflict with one another, and so not all of them can be true. Thus, making all possible allowances for pluralism and tolerance, it is simply not a matter of indifference what worldview one happens to hold. It even makes a difference which form of monotheism one subscribes to (supposing one subscribes to any), since, although they are

alike in some ways, different monotheistic religions are also
more or less radically inconsistent with one another. Furthermore, one must bear in mind the logical possibility that all of
them are false and some other worldview is true.
We repeat: It is not our intention to settle these questions
here. But the questions are extremely important, including the
question of whether any form of monotheism is true. All
monotheistic religions demand a fundamental commitment of
faith, and for anyone who makes that commitment seriously
and attempts to carry it out faithfully it will have profound
impact on the rest of his or her life, both as an individual and as
a member of many different communities. If people subscribe
to some form of monotheism and it is not true, they shape their
lives by an illusion; but people who reject the possibility of
religious truth, whatever it may be, are no less out of touch with
reality.

This points to a fairly simple conclusion. People who wish to
live good lives should seek the truth about the religious question. The task is not merely to sort out the claims of various
religions and worldviews according to how congenial or un-
congenial they might be to oneself, but to determine which
gives a credible account of the source or sources of meaning
and value, offers a reasonable plan for living in harmony with
that more-than-human reality, and thus *deserves* to be accepted. If one finds a worldview which one has good reason to
believe is true, one should accept it and make the commitment
to shape one's life in accord with it, for this means living in
accord with one's best understanding of reality.

Even within the limits of our present inquiry it is possible to
eliminate certain worldviews from consideration. Those to
which determinism is essential are fundamentally mistaken.
Marxism, for example, denies the reality of human freedom of
choice, so that whatever truth there is in the Marxist worldview—truth which should be acknowledged and preserved
—Marxism itself cannot as a whole merit a reasonable person's fundamental commitment. Again, any worldview which includes among its essential requirements the
violation of any of the modes of responsibility is false and must

be rejected. One cannot properly make one's fundamental commitment to a system which commends revenge or partiality toward some persons at the expense of others or any other form of immorality.

Once one has engaged in this weeding-out, one finds that the remaining candidates—monotheistic and other possibly true worldviews potentially meriting one's fundamental religious commitment—have two interesting characteristics.

First, were one to opt for any of them, one would be making an authentically fundamental commitment. One would be taking a stance not only toward the more-than-human ultimate source of meaning and value but toward all the basic human goods and all people. In many cases these worldviews say, explicitly or implicitly, what human fulfillment would be like, and some insist that it is realizable, for example, in heaven or an afterlife. They likewise specify how to realize and participate in the various basic human goods—what forms of inquiry are worthwhile in pursuit of truth, what kinds of relationship among people constitute genuine community, even (in some cases) what practices are good for one's health.

But, second, all such worldviews nevertheless leave open many possibilities in life. Rarely, for instance, does one find a worldview which insists that all its adherents must marry or remain single, make their livings only in certain ways, cultivate some fine arts or crafts but not others, use leisure time for certain specific kinds of recreation, and so forth. Worldviews generally leave room for much personal diversity in choice and behavior.

At the same time they also demand unity. This is so precisely because most envisage their adherents as composing a rather large community in which different members play different roles for the sake of common purposes. Even commitments with respect to matters which do not bear directly on the fundamental religious commitment must be made with reference to it, for the fundamental religious commitment establishes requirements to be met by other commitments and indicates how the sum total of a person's commitments should mesh to form an integrated plan of life. It is obvious, for example, that committed membership in a peace church rules out service in a combat arm of the military, that devout sabbatarians will avoid jobs which require them to work on Saturdays, and so forth.

B. Making Commitments to Organize One's Life

Consistency is crucial in making commitments and organizing one's life. But consistency here does not mean mere predictability or always doing the same thing. Its meaning is more precise and more interesting than that.

To begin with, people whose attitude toward all the basic human goods is open and inclusivistic will not live for passing satisfactions or for specific future objectives. Such people are committed to the realization of basic goods with which they identify to such an extent that the free actions which realize these goods truly constitute them as persons.

Within the framework of a fundamental religious commitment—to a worldview which they judge to give the correct answer to questions about the more-than-human ultimate source of meaning and value—such people make a number of other commitments bearing upon human goods and the approach they will take to them. These are large, third-level actions like marrying or engaging in a profession. In doing so, moreover, they strive to make commitments which are consistent with the fundamental commitment and also with one another, so that taken all together they form a harmonious framework for their lives. This is the "consistency" of which we speak here.

It is not consistency over a period of time—which, although important, has more to do with fidelity, the living-out of commitments. What is in question instead is the internal consistency of one's commitments and purposes, of which it may be said, when consistency is present, that they "hang together" in an integrated way. Nor is this necessarily the outcome of highly sophisticated introspection. Quite simple people are as capable as others of the requisite consistency, which is achieved by, and reflected in, prudent long-range choices about matters like marriage and work. This does not require thinking deep thoughts about *The Meaning of It All,* and indeed most of us know people who think such thoughts—people, that is, apparently more taken up with speculation than with ordering and conducting their lives—who seem quite uncertain of who they are and what their lives are all about.

Negatively, consistency rules out a certain kind of premoral spontaneity, in which people place themselves at the service of desires or inclinations which have not been harmonized with their fundamental life-purposes. Many persons spend a great part of their lives in the service of such goals—pleasure, wealth, status, and so forth—which do not represent rational commitments but instead originate as mere wants or cravings. Such slavish and unreflective activity has no place in a life of free self-determination.

Yet there is a real place for spontaneity in such a life. For persons who have integrated their commitments into a consistent pattern, spontaneous action within the pattern can become almost second nature. Spontaneity in this case is in line with commitments, not something which precedes commitment. This is the case, for instance, with conscientious parents who spontaneously respond to new situations from the perspective of their commitment to parenthood, with serious-minded students who spontaneously know when to say Yes and when to say No to various proposed diversions and recreations, with ethical doctors and lawyers who rule out unethical conduct without giving the matter a second thought, and so on. From the perspective of consistency, immorality consists in using mature powers in the service of infantile goals, while morality means organizing life around morally sound basic commitments and acting within the pattern thus created.

Part of this pattern involves undertaking long term projects which are consistent with, and carry out, one's commitments. Such projects—for example, seeking a college degree—are not themselves commitments; rather, they are complex plans of action directed to specific objectives. But ordinarily they occupy and organize a great deal of a person's time and activity, and they either contribute to or interfere with the carrying-out of commitments. They should therefore be selected with care.

It is also important not to get too wrapped up in one's

projects. Projects serve commitments, but they are not the commitments themselves, so that the failure of one or another is not in itself a disastrous, definitive blow: "You win some and you lose some." This attitude makes it possible to work at projects as long as they really do serve commitments, and to give them up without regret when they no longer do so. In large measure it is a question of combining detachment with fidelity. The meaning of detachment is best illustrated by its contrary: the attitude of people so attached to one goal or purpose that its frustration or loss—for example, failure in school or in business—is a shattering experience which drains their lives of meaning. A person with a morally good attitude, of openness to and service of all human goods, will not be so totally destroyed by the loss, no matter how genuinely painful, of a particular instance of any one of them.

At the same time, while prepared to accept the loss of particular satisfactions and achievements without regarding this as a fundamental threat to their identity, people should nevertheless be firm in their commitments: they should practice fidelity. A person with such an attitude will persist in seeking to realize realistically realizable purposes consistent with his or her commitments; by contrast, a person without it will tend to give up in the face of problems and obstacles.

Fidelity or stability in commitment to purposes is not the same thing as mere constancy, much less rigidity. It is dynamic, implying continuing effort to explore new ways of better serving the purposes to which one is committed. It also involves refusal to narrow down a human good to those particular expressions of it with which one happens to be familiar. A creative and open approach to living is not only consistent with fidelity but essential to it.

Thus detachment and fidelity complement and balance each other. They enable people to strike a mean between the immoral extremes of fanaticism and noninvolvement. They also rule out unwillingness to risk failure by attempting difficult things. Morality does not require that one take needless risks or be unrealistic about circumstances, including one's own abilities and the chances of failing in an undertaking. But people with a morally good attitude will be inclined to push beyond what they and others have already accomplished and to take reasonable chances in doing so, aware that many good things in life will never be done except by those who are willing to risk failing.

C. Making Commitments: Right Ways and Wrong

No one can do everything well. True as that is, however, our culture sometimes pressures us to make the attempt. One enduring myth about self-determination and human development concerns the ideal of the well-rounded person, the individual who is developed in all respects.

This notion has its uses if not carried too far—if it means only that a person should not become so wrapped up in one area of endeavor that he or she completely neglects other matters which ought to receive attention (for example, the workaholic who has no time to spare for sociability, recreation, even intimacy with his or her family). But the myth of the well-rounded person becomes pernicious when it encourages people to expend vast amounts of time and energy trying to do a bit of everything, an enterprise whose actual outcome is that nothing is done really well.

People who are generous and altruistic are perhaps more prone than most to make this mistake. The classic do-gooder is into every cause and campaign, from human rights to "no nukes," and often fails to make a significant contribution to any. Granted, there are many good causes in the world—many situations of evil and injustice which cry out for redressing— but it does not follow that everyone should become extensively involved in crusading for them all. We must make choices, opting for certain areas of concentration in preference to others, and doing so precisely as our particular contribution to the common life of commitment to human goods which we share with those with whom we live in community; and this is not only not bad but positively good if it enables us to do well something which is worth doing.

As part of this whole process we should try to know as well as we can what possibilities are really open to us before choosing one. Too often even intelligent and well-educated people drift into extremely important commitments without making a careful investigation of the alternatives and without consulting others who could help them deliberate wisely.

A conspicuous example of this slipshod manner of organizing life is the careless way in which many people enter marriage, only to regret the decision within the first year, sometimes even before their honeymoon is over. To say that two responsible people considering marriage will make their decision for reasons other than the way they happen to feel about each other at the time is not to belittle romantic love but merely to recognize its limitations as a basis for making a lifelong commitment.

At the same time we should take our feelings into account in making commitments, for feelings often mirror something important about our deeper selves which should be part of our deliberations. Usually one makes a mistake in trying to force oneself into a commitment in the face of strong feelings to the contrary. It is hard to be very optimistic about the prospects of a young man who has had to wrestle with a strong antipathy to contact with sick people in order to become a physician or a thirty-five year old woman who has had to struggle against her emotions in order to bring herself to the point of saying Yes to a suitor.

Having assessed our abilities and also the possibilities which are open to us, we should then try to match our particular abilities to the possibilities we perceive. In doing so we should be quite deliberate and cautious (which is not the same thing as being merely timid and indecisive). In matters of fundamental importance one should never proceed simply on the basis of the information which happens to be immediately available. One should reflect on oneself and on the situation rather than simply follow the bidding of imagination and feeling.

In every case one's worldview will provide a point of reference for testing and validating particular commitments one is considering. This way of life, that occupation, this relationship—are they or are they not consistent with the fundamentally "religious" account of the world and way of life to which I subscribe? This testing, furthermore, as well as all the other aspects of the process of making commitments, occurs repeatedly throughout life as conditions change. One may, for instance, have made a commitment to a certain form of work rather early in life, but repeatedly over the years it will be necessary to specify that commitment further—for example, by choosing between particular jobs, adapting to promotions or changed working conditions. Or, if one's spouse dies, one may then face anew, after the lapse of many years, the question of whether to marry.

D. Character and Virtue

Many books have been written about character and virtue. As we draw near the end of this one, we can make only a few important points about this topic as it pertains to our theme.

In many ways choice is central to what we mean by character. In deciding that this or that is the right thing to do, a person is definite in a way that he or she is not while simply wondering what to do; in making a choice one determines oneself toward goods and other persons according to the implications of the choice; in carrying out a choice one brings all the various parts of the self involved in the action into the configuration required by that choice—one engages in self-determination, one makes oneself be a certain kind of person. A person who has made a consistent set of commitments in accord with reality and moral truth and then consistently carries them out becomes more and more completely integrated, for there are no underlying, insoluble conflicts in his or her life.

Obviously, in carrying out one's commitments it is necessary to seek and perform a variety of actions which further and express them in an expansive manner. And this has strong bearing upon character. For example, people who wish to further commitments involving the fundamental value of friendship will turn to the performance of kindly acts on behalf of those to whom they feel emotionally close (their "friends" in a narrow sense); but to achieve full self-integration they must go further, expanding kindly acts beyond the circle of immediate friends so as to include people who are not friends in any conventional sense.

Why does this foster self-integration? Because in seeking ways to deal in a kindly fashion with such persons—casual acquaintances, those with whom one is not on good terms, and indeed everyone with whom one comes into contact—and in actually dealing with them in this way one necessarily brings into play imagination, emotions, and other faculties in support of the effort to find ways of expressing the commitment and carrying it out. And this is precisely how one's whole self comes to be integrated around one's commitments, and one's character comes to be shaped, with the various virtues as its various aspects. Thus one's makeup becomes like that of a team which has thoroughly practiced playing according to a winning system: like the players smoothly working together and perfectly playing their positions, all the parts and aspects of the personality become a smoothly functioning whole.

But this is the most optimistic scenario. To the extent that one's fundamental commitment is not in accord with reality, or one's other commitments and choices are not in accord with that which is fundamental, one will be less than perfectly integrated and one's character will be more or less unsettled, with various unsolved tensions. And if some or all of one's commitments are morally defective, one will have a more or less bad character, more or less *dis*-integrated and torn by internal conflicts, whose various aspects are what are commonly called vices.

Quite simply, though, some people do not have much character to speak of, either good or bad. Their lives are disorganized and episodic. Sometimes they do good things, sometimes bad, but with no pattern or regularity to either. Their choices are their responsibility, morally speaking, and their fundamental lack of character and purposefulness is more or less their own fault; but their lives, taken as a whole, can hardly be said to have moral significance. Yet such people are likely to take full credit for their morally good acts while trying to evade ultimate responsibility for their bad ones by telling themselves that in their deepest heart, somewhere out of sight even when they examine their conscience, is hidden a good "fundamental option." They really intend to be good—with the sort of intention which paves the road to hell.

What is one to do if, on balance, one wishes to lead a life which has its moral significance as a unified whole? The answer must be obvious by now: Seek religious truth, strive to know moral truth, make a sound fundamental commitment, organize one's life by a harmonious set of commitments which implement the fundamental commitment, review and adjust commitments as changing circumstances open up new and different possibilities, carry out commitments faithfully and consistently, putting all one's skill and energy into the effort.

E. Finally . . .

We have come, then, to the end of this discussion, and in a sense we find ourselves at the point where we began. The fundamental responsibility of human freedom is the responsibility we all face to create our own lives—our own selves— through our choices. It is possible to use this freedom well or badly, but it is not possible to avoid using it. Using freedom well means choosing in ways which progressively open us to ever greater realization of what it means to be human persons. Using freedom badly means choosing in ways which stunt, and finally kill, the capacity for further growth.

Rather than inhibiting love by burdensome rules, ethics is human reason's effort to provide safeguards for love—guidelines for choices which make possible our continued growth as human persons. Only when we choose in this way and continue to grow as persons can we be truly fulfilled.

Such fulfillment is not the same as gratification or practical success. To live in a morally good way is always more or less difficult, all but inevitably involves us in pain, and may enmesh us in tragedy—if by tragedy we mean failure to attain our legitimate but limited goals and objectives. This, however, is the reality and dignity of human life. Freedom is both blessing and burden. In both aspects it lies at the heart of what it means to be human.

Questions for Review and Discussion

1. Do you agree that it is necessary to have some fundamental commitment which provides the framework for organizing and harmonizing all the other important commitments of one's life? Understanding the special sense of "religious" as we have used the word here, do you think it is possible for good people to integrate their lives through a fundamental commitment which is not "religious"? Where do convinced atheists fit in this scheme of things?

2. Would it be a fair summary of our position to say that one worldview and one fundamental commitment is as good as another? To say that *any* fundamental commitment is better than none?

3. In the view adopted here there are many different lifestyles from among which it is necessary and appropriate to choose. Does this introduce an element of subjectivism or relativism into this ethics?

4. Why must good people be nonconformists?

5. In stressing consistency and faithfulness in carrying out commitments have we made it impossible for people to change their minds and correct their mistakes? What advice would you give a student who is thinking about switching majors? A man or woman who is thinking about changing careers? A husband or wife who is thinking about changing marriage partners? If the advice would be different in some cases than in others, explain why.

6. Why does the ideal of the well-rounded person have such a strong hold on many people's minds?

7. Should counseling help people avoid drifting into important commitments without sufficient consideration? Has it done so for you or others whom you know?

8. To what extent do you take your feelings into account when making important decisions? Which emotion or emotions do you think it most important to pay attention to?

9. Do you think your friends and acquaintances are sufficiently willing to risk failure in life, or are they more likely to settle for greater security for themselves rather than run risks for important human goods? How would you distinguish between the right kind of risk-taking and mere rashness?

10. Some people seem to make their basic commitments mainly in response to adolescent rebellion: for example, they get married because their parents are opposed. Others seem to make commitments too much in response to parental or other influence: for example, they enter a certain profession because that is what their parents have always wanted. What signs would characterize a commitment which is really personal and not unduly influenced in either of these directions?

Suggestions for Further Reading and Research

These suggestions are not intended as a general bibliography for the field of ethics. Many of the topics we treat are discussed in articles in the *Encyclopedia of Philosophy;* these articles usually introduce various positions on a topic and provide rather extensive bibliography. R. B. Brandt, *Ethical Theories: The Problems of Normative and Critical Ethics* (Englewood Cliffs, N.J.: Prentice-Hall, 1959), summarizes and criticizes many ethical theories and provides very good bibliographies. W. T. Jones, Frederick Sontag, M. O. Beckner, and R. J. Fogelin, eds., *Approaches to Ethics,* 3rd ed. (New York: McGraw-Hill, 1977), is a good collection of selections from major philosophical works in ethics from Plato to the present. Vernon J. Bourke, *History of Ethics* (Garden City, N.Y.: Doubleday, 1968), is a useful history of ethics; this work also is available (1970) in two paperback volumes. Alasdair MacIntyre, *A Short History of Ethics* (New York: Macmillan, 1966), is a readable, interesting, and often arguable introduction to many of the major philosophical issues which have emerged in the history of ethics.

Henry B. Veatch, *For an Ontology of Morals: A Critique of Contemporary Ethical Theory* (Evanston, Ill.: Northwestern U. Press, 1971), systematically criticizes contemporary theories and points in the direction of an ethics something like ours; Veatch's book could be a useful introduction to ours for the more advanced reader. An even more difficult but very interesting book which could prepare an advanced student of ethics to consider our approach: Alasdair MacIntyre, *After Virtue: A Study in Moral Theory*, 2nd ed. (Notre Dame, Ind.: U. of Notre Dame Press, 1984).

Robert N. Bellah *et al.*, *Habits of the Heart: Individualism and Commitment in American Life* (New York: Harper and Row, 1985), approach the problems of ethics from a sociological viewpoint; by clarifying the experienced need for a reasoned solution to these problems their work is a useful preface to ethics as we understand it. John Finnis, *Fundamentals of Ethics* (Oxford: Oxford U. Press; Washington, D.C.: Georgetown U. Press, 1983), provides a sophisticated defense of many aspects of our theory through dialectic with Aristotle, Kant, and contemporary English-language work in ethical theory.

Our discussion of freedom in chapter 1 owes much to, but freely departs from, Mortimer J. Adler, *The Idea of Freedom: A Dialectical Examination of the Conception of Freedom*, 2 vols. (Garden City, N.Y.: Doubleday, 1958 and 1961). Joseph M. Boyle, Jr., Germain Grisez, and Olaf Tollefsen, *Free Choice: A Self-Referential Argument* (Notre Dame, Ind.: U. of Notre Dame Press, 1976), greatly expands the treatment given here and describes all the main arguments for and against free choice.

Hannah Arendt, *The Human Condition* (Chicago: U. of Chicago Press, 1958), pp. 79–247, distinguishes labor, work, and action—roughly corresponding to our three levels of action. Gabriel Marcel, *Being and Having: An Existential Diary* (New York: Harper and Row, 1965), pp. 154–74, distinguishes being and having—roughly corresponding to our third and second levels of action, respectively. Aristotle, *Nicomachean Ethics*, book 6, distinguishes between art and prudence —roughly corresponding to our second and third levels of actions, respectively. Regarding fundamental option and other matters an unsubtle but easily accessible presentation of views in Catholic moral theology which are at odds with our theory: Timothy E. O'Connell, *Principles for a Catholic Morality* (New York: Seabury, 1978).

Mortimer J. Adler, *The Time of Our Lives: The Ethics of Common Sense* (New York: Holt, Rinehart, and Winston, 1970), pp. 3–63, sees the ethical problem as one of giving meaning to life; he does not distinguish the second and third levels of action sharply but does (pp. 86–97) explain that neither pleasure nor a technical end can give meaning to life. Robert Nozick, *Anarchy, State, and Utopia* (New York: Basic Books, 1974), pp. 42–45, argues against equating pleasure with fulfillment much as we do; although his book ultimately defends positions with which we do not agree, it contains many clever arguments and useful clarifications. St. Augustine, *City of God,* book 19, presents the classic doctrine of heaven as a principle of meaning for human life. Germain Grisez, "Man, the Natural End of," *New Catholic Encyclopedia,* vol. 9, pp. 132–38, criticizes traditional conceptions of the natural end of human persons. Vatican Council II, *Gaudium et spes,* part 1, chapter 3, moderates the Augustinian emphasis on heaven as future as it stresses that the kingdom of God is already present in mystery. For a theological treatment of heaven: Germain Grisez, *The Way of the Lord Jesus,* vol. 1, *Christian Moral Principles* (Chicago: Franciscan Herald Press, 1983), chapters 19 and 34. Also see John Finnis, "Practical Reasoning, Human Goods, and the End of Man," *Proceedings of the American Catholic Philosophical Association* 58 (1984), pp. 23–36, for a comparison of the ideal of integral human fulfillment with the ultimate end as Aquinas understands it.

Our references to Aristotle in chapter 4 are to *Nicomachean Ethics,* books 1 and 10. A good, succinct critique of Aristotle: B. A. O. Williams, *Morality: An Introduction to Ethics* (New York: Harper and Row, 1972), pp. 59–67. Henry B. Veatch, *Rational Man: A Modern Interpretation of Aristotelian Ethics* (Bloomington, Ind.: Indiana U. Press, 1964), pp. 148–54, introduces freedom, which alters Aristotle's position in the direction of ours. Gabriel Marcel, *Creative Fidelity,* trans. Robert Rosthal (New York: Farrar, Straus, 1964), pp. 104–19, presents the life of a person as a unique act. Charles Fried, *An Anatomy of Values: Problems of Personal and Social Choice* (Cambridge, Mass.: Harvard U. Press, 1970), pp. 87–101, introduces the concept of "life plan" and considers life as an ordered set of rational acts. John Rawls, *A Theory of Justice* (Cambridge, Mass.: Harvard U. Press, 1971), pp. 551–67, argues against hedonism and against any theory which tries to reduce human good to a single good.

Our treatment of community in chapter 5 owes much to, but freely departs from, Aristotle, *Nicomachean Ethics,* book 5 (justice) and books 8 and 9 (friendship); the distinction between friendship of utility and friendship based on virtue corresponds to our distinction between contract and community. Charles Fried, *An Anatomy of Values*, pp. 105–15, outlines a concept of society similar to our idea of community. Yves R. Simon, *Philosophy of Democratic Government* (Chicago: U. of Chicago Press, 1951), deals with democratic society as a potential form of community.

A classic statement of the subjectivism we discuss in chapter 6 is Bertrand Russell, *Human Society in Ethics and Politics* (London: Allen and Unwin; New York: Simon and Schuster, 1955). A good example of relativism is W. G. Sumner, *Folkways* (Boston: Ginn, 1934). A classic, frequently anthologized treatment of cultural relativism: W. T. Stace, "Ethical Relativity," in *The Concept of Morals* (New York: Macmillan, 1937), pp. 1–68. J. D. Mabbott, *An Introduction to Ethics* (Garden City, N.Y.: Doubleday, 1969), pp. 70–102, criticizes subjectivism. Williams, *Morality*, chapters 1 through 4, offers a very useful critical treatment of subjectivism and relativism. Vernon J. Bourke, *Ethics in Crisis* (Milwaukee: Bruce, 1966), pp. 102–19, takes up the problem of objective values in light of recent work in anthropology. Morris Ginsberg, *On the Diversity of Morals* (London: Mercury Books, 1962), pp. 26–40, 97–129, criticizes cultural relativism. An important contemporary form of subjectivism is "prescriptivism," best presented by R. M. Hare, *Freedom and Reason* (New York: Oxford U. Press, 1965). For a critique of prescriptivism: Joseph M. Boyle, Jr., "Aquinas and Prescriptive Ethics," *Proceedings of the American Catholic Philosophical Association* 49 (1975), pp. 82–95.

Also relevant to chapter 7 is an analysis of human needs by Peter A. Bertocci and Richard M. Millard, *Personality and the Good: Psychological and Ethical Perspectives* (New York: David McKay, 1963), pp. 157–72. A. H. Maslow, *Motivation and Personality* (New York: Harper and Row, 1954), pp. 80–106, provides a psychological approach to basic needs roughly corresponding to our fundamental purposes. William K. Frankena, *Ethics*, 2nd ed. (Englewood Cliffs, N.J.: Prentice-Hall, 1973), p. 88, gives a list similar to but longer than our list of intrinsic goods.

Erich Fromm, *Man for Himself* (New York: Rinehart, 1947),

presents a theory of human goodness which reduces it to health. Thomas Aquinas, *Truth*, vol. 3, trans. R. W. Schmidt (Chicago: Henry Regnery, 1954), question 21, presents a tight treatise on good, which really amounts to an entire value theory. Compare with Georg Henrik von Wright, *Varieties of Goodness* (New York: Humanities Press, 1963). Germain Grisez, "The First Principle of Practical Reason: A Commentary on the *Summa theologiae*, 1–2, question 94, article 2," *Natural Law Forum* 10 (1965), pp. 168–201, provides a technical expression of our value theory with some critique of alternatives.

Chapter 9's treatment of the basic principle of morality has few parallels in other literature. Among them are Rudolf Allers, *The Psychology of Character*, trans. E. B. Strauss (London: Sheed and Ward, 1933), pp. 206–40, which represents "true and false ideals" of character corresponding to our distinction, but in psychological terms. Joseph de Finance, S.J., *Essai sur l'agir humain* (Rome: Université Grégorienne, 1962), pp. 304–48, locates moral value in the openness of free commitment to the transcendent, moral disvalue in being closed upon a particular value. For Grisez's theological treatment of the first principle, see *The Way of the Lord Jesus: Christian Moral Principles*, chapter 7. For the most adequate technical presentation of our view of moral and practical principles: Germain Grisez, Joseph Boyle, and John Finnis, "Practical Principles, Moral Truth, and Ultimate Ends," *American Journal of Jurisprudence* 32 (1987). An interesting work, offering a criticism of our account of the first principle and a defense of the "respect persons" alternative: Alan Donagan, *The Theory of Morality* (Chicago: U. of Chicago Press, 1977).

The utilitarianism discussed in chapter 10 received a classic formulation in Jeremy Bentham, *An Introduction to the Principles of Morals and Legislation* (New York: Hefner, 1948), pp. 1–42. Also John Stuart Mill, *Utilitarianism* (New York: Library of the Liberal Arts, 1954). John Dewey develops his situationism in *Reconstruction in Philosophy* (Boston: Beacon, 1957), pp. 161–70. Joseph Fletcher, *Situation Ethics: The New Morality* (Philadelphia: Westminster, 1966), offers a popular presentation of situation ethics. A very accessible debate: J. J. C. Smart and B. A. O. Williams, *Utilitarianism: for and against* (Cambridge: Cambridge U. Press, 1973). Consequentialism or proportionalism is a closely related view, developed in recent Catholic moral theology. See *Readings in Moral Theology: No. 1: Moral Norms and Catholic Tradition,* Charles E. Curran and Richard A. McCormick, S.J., eds. (New York: Paulist Press, 1979). A representative work is Josef Fuchs, "The Absoluteness of Moral Terms," pp. 94–137. Also important: Richard A. McCormick, S.J., "Ambiguity in Moral Choice" and "A Commentary on the Commentaries," in *Doing Evil to Achieve Good,* Richard A. McCormick, S.J., and Paul Ramsey, eds. (Chicago: Loyola U. Press, 1978), chapters 1 and 6. For criticisms of utilitarianism, consequentialism, or proportionalism: G. E. M. Anscombe, "Modern Moral Philosophy," in *Collected Philosophical Papers,* vol. 3, *Ethics, Politics and Religion* (Minneapolis: U. of Minnesota Press, 1981), pp. 26–42; Donagan, *Theory of Morality,* pp. 172–209; Bartholomew M. Kiely, S.J., "The Impracticality of Proportionalism," *Gregorianum* 66 (1985), pp. 655–86; Germain Grisez, "Against Consequentialism," *American Journal of Jurisprudence* 23 (1978), pp. 21–72; "Moral Absolutes: A Critique of the View of Josef Fuchs, S.J.," *Anthropos* 1, no. 2 (October 1985), pp. 155–201; *The Way of the Lord Jesus: Christian Moral Principles,* chapter 6. The technical argument is presented most adequately, however, in John Finnis, Joseph M. Boyle, Jr., and Germain Grisez, *Nuclear Deterrence, Morality and Realism* (Oxford and New York: Oxford U. Press, 1987), chapter 9.

Many works could be cited to illustrate the philosophical development of one or another of the modes of responsibility in chapter 11. Ancient and medieval writers who attempted to identify and clarify various virtues actually were dealing with what we treat as modes of responsibility. Several of the modes, treated as virtues, are defended by P. T. Geach, *The Virtues* (Cambridge: Cambridge U. Press, 1977), pp. 88–170. Among modern writers, Immanuel Kant, *Foundations of the Metaphysics of Morals,* trans. Lewis White Beck (Indianapolis: Library of the Liberal Arts, 1959), p. 50 and *passim,* provides a classic formulation of the univeralizability principle, which is the most widely recognized mode of responsibility. Josiah Royce,

The Philosophy of Loyalty (New York: Macmillan, 1908), develops a balance of self-control and fortitude; he also has some understanding of the idea of commitment, and his thinking is not far from the idea of openness to all the goods and all people as the criterion of morality. Grisez's theological treatment of the modes: *The Way of the Lord Jesus: Christian Moral Principles,* chapters 8 and 26. A philosophical treatment of the ethics of sex and marriage, using our theory: Robert E. Joyce, *Human Sexual Ecology* (Washington, D.C.: University Press of America, 1980). A theological treatment: Ronald Lawler, O.F.M.Cap., Joseph M. Boyle, Jr., and William E. May, *Catholic Sexual Ethics: A Summary, Explanation, and Defense* (Huntington, Ind.: Our Sunday Visitor Press, 1985).

Chapter 12's treatment of the eighth mode of responsibility will be illustrated in the concise traditional statement of Thomas Aquinas, *Summa theologiae,* 1–2, question 20, article 2. Eric d'Arcy, *Human Acts: An Essay in Their Moral Evaluation* (Oxford: Clarendon Press, 1963), does not go as far as we do but presents an analysis helpful as far as he goes. Much the same position as ours is approached in an enlighteningly different way by Charles Fried, "Part I: Wrongs," in *Right and Wrong* (Cambridge, Mass.: Harvard U. Press, 1978), pp. 7–78.

A more historical treatment of the problem in chapter 13: Germain Grisez, "Toward a Consistent Natural-Law Ethics of Killing," *American Journal of Jurisprudence* 15 (1970), pp. 64–96. Also see Joseph M. Boyle, Jr., "*Praeter Intentionem* in Aquinas," *Thomist* 42 (1978), pp. 649–65, for a clarification of the notion of side effect; "Toward Understanding the Principle of Double Effect," *Ethics* 90 (1980), pp. 527–38, for a defense of the principle of double effect, with a clarification of the theory of agency it presupposes.

The theory treated in chapters 12 and 13 is laid out and applied technically to life-and-death issues in two studies: Germain Grisez and Joseph M. Boyle, Jr., *Life and Death with Liberty and Justice: A Contribution to the Euthanasia Debate* (Notre Dame, Ind.: U. of Notre Dame Press, 1979), pp. 336–441; Finnis, Boyle, and Grisez, *Nuclear Deterrence, Morality and Realism,* chapters 10 and 11. These works include extensive bibliographies of the relevant literature. Perhaps the best philosophical presentation of the utilitarian view of the life-and-death issues: Jonathan Glover, *Causing Death and Saving Lives* (New York: Penguin, 1977).

Chapter 14's treatment of duties can be supplemented by a close study of Aristotle, *Nicomachean Ethics*, book 5 (justice). An ethics of duty is F. H. Bradley, *Ethical Studies* (Indianapolis: Library of the Liberal Arts, 1951), esp. pp. 98–112. For a very helpful treatment of authority: Yves Simon, *A General Theory of Authority* (Notre Dame, Ind.: U. of Notre Dame Press, 1980). Relevant both to our chapters 14 and 18 is a major work which develops a philosophy of law based on our theory: John Finnis, *Natural Law and Natural Rights* (Oxford: Clarendon Press, 1980).

Chapter 15 will be supplemented by Eliseo Vivas, *The Moral Life and the Ethical Life* (Chicago: U. of Chicago Press, 1950), pp. 185–267, who treats the person as constituted by free commitment and objective values. Abraham H. Maslow, *Toward a Psychology of Being*, 2nd ed. (New York: Van Nostrand Reinhold, 1968), pp. 149–85, gives a psychological account of establishing self-identity that parallels our ethical account; note his treatment of values as objective potentialities. Erik Erikson, *Insight and Responsibility* (New York: W. W. Norton, 1964), pp. 83–134, offers another psychological account close to our view; his wholeness/totality distinction corresponds to our inclusivity/exclusivity distinction.

Chapter 16 owes something to G. C. de Menasce, *The Dynamics of Morality* (New York: Sheed and Ward, 1961), a remarkable effort to show how human goods provide sufficient reason to be good. Our educational theory is closest to that of Montessori; see E. M. Standing, *Maria Montessori: Her Life and Work* (New York and Toronto: New American Library, 1962), esp. chapter 17, for an introduction. Gilbert C. Meilaender (a Protestant philosopher), *The Theory and Practice of Virtue* (Notre Dame, Ind.: University of Notre Dame Press, 1984), presents views on moral education and virtue in many ways close to ours.

Chapter 17 on progress draws on but departs from Charles van Doren, *The Idea of Progress* (New York: Praeger, 1967), who surveys theories of progress. John Passmore, *The Perfectibility of*

Man (New York: Charles Scribners' Sons, 1970), offers a full critique of moral progress theories; he is not always fair to religious views. Herbert Spencer, *Illustrations of Universal Progress* (New York: Appleton, 1889), exemplifies evolutionary optimism. A sympathetic presentation of Marxist views: John Somerville, *The Philosophy of Marxism: An Exposition* (New York: Random House, 1967), pp. 121–59. A striking critique of utopian theories in general and Marxism in particular: Hans Jonas, *The Imperative of Responsibility: In Search of an Ethics for a Technological Age* (Chicago: U. of Chicago Press, 1984), pp. 136–204. On Teilhard de Chardin see R. C. Zaehner, *Dialectical Christianity and Christian Materialism* (London: Oxford U. Press, 1971).

Chapter 18 may be supplemented by Michael Walzer, *Obligation: Essays on Disobedience, War, and Citizenship* (Cambridge, Mass.: Harvard U. Press, 1970), who discusses the problems of revolution and reform, and related issues, in an ethical context based on the concept of responsibility as communitarian. Norman Cohn, *The Pursuit of the Millennium* (New York: Harper and Row, 1961), pp. 307–19, sums up the implications of history for the idea that revolution is a panacea. Hannah Arendt, *The Origins of Totalitarianism* (New York: Meridian, 1958), pp. 460–79, develops the idea of ideology in relation to efforts to transform humanity radically. Lewis A. Feuer, *The Conflict of Generations: The Character and Significance of Student Movements* (New York and London: Basic Books, 1969), offers a historical and psychological study of student movements, suggesting that much of their energy is wasted. H. L. A. Hart, *The Concept of Law* (Oxford: Clarendon Press, 1961) and Lon L. Fuller, *The Morality of Law*, rev. ed. (New Haven and London: Yale U. Press, 1969), present philosophies of law based on contrasting ideas of the national community. The two authors think they disagree, but Hart's theory emphasizes the contract aspect, while Fuller's attends to the community aspect. Grisez and Boyle, *Life and Death with Liberty and Justice*, deal with certain questions of philosophy of law in chapters 2, 10, and 13. John Finnis, *Natural Law and Natural Rights*, most fully uses and develops our theory in treating these matters.

Chapter 19's reference to Nietzsche can be illustrated in

Friedrich Nietzsche, *The Portable Nietzsche,* ed. Walter Kaufmann (New York: Viking, 1954), pp. 197–200. E. H. Madden and P. H. Hare, *Evil and the Concept of God* (Springfield, Ill.: Thomas, 1968), state and develop the objections based on evil. A brilliant reply to such atheology: Alvin Plantinga, *God, Freedom, and Evil* (London: George Allen and Unwin, 1975), pp. 7–64. Germain Grisez, *Beyond the New Theism: A Philosophy of Religion* (Notre Dame, Ind.: U. of Notre Dame Press, 1975), provides (pp. 274–324) a technical treatment of the existential objections to the existence of God and religion; this work articulates the metaphysical foundations of the ethics we present here. Grisez, *The Way of the Lord Jesus: Christian Moral Principles,* chapter 34, provides a theological treatment of the relationship between this life and everlasting life. The problem of evil treated (as we think it ultimately must be) within the perspective of faith: Russell Shaw, *Does Suffering Make Sense?* (Huntington, Ind.: Our Sunday Visitor, 1987). Gabriel Marcel, *Homo Viator: Introduction to a Metaphysic of Hope* (New York: Harper and Row, 1965), pp. 29–67, develops the concept of hope. Richard L. Purtill, *Reason to Believe* (Grand Rapids, Mich.: Eerdmans, 1974), deals with ethical objections to religion; Bertocci and Millard, *Personality and the Good,* pp. 677–97, present a somewhat similar view.

A basic set of readings introductory to religion conceived with the breadth we assume: Whitfield Foy, ed., *Man's Religious Quest: A Reader* (London: Croom Helm and Open U. Press, 1978). Dietrich von Hildebrand, *Christian Ethics* (New York: David McKay, 1953), pp. 161–66 and 453–63, deals with religious commitment as basic in life. For Christians the act of faith is the fundamental commitment, and the organization of life according to faith is a question of discerning and committing oneself to one's personal vocation; see Grisez's theological treatment of personal vocation: *The Way of the Lord Jesus: Christian Moral Principles,* chapters 23, 27, and 31.

Index

The contents of the "Suggestions for Further Reading and Research" are not indexed.

Abortion, 112, 141, 146–47, 200
Absolutes, moral, 108, 129–39
Action: ambiguous, 9, 140–53; community and, 57–64, 156–61; first-level, 18, 24–33, 35–37, 41; freedom and, 8, 12–22; fulfillment and, 37–42; goods and, 77–87; second-level, 13–14, 18, 25–35, 50, 56, 59, 106–7, 112, 116, 137, 155, 159–61, 186, 188, 217, 219; technique and, 197–98; third-level, 8, 17–20, 26–34, 41, 53, 56, 58, 77–78, 106, 112, 156–61, 217–18, 233
Adolescence, 5, 176, 181
Aesthetic experience, 44–45, 80, 82–88, 197
Animal behavior, 24
Anthropology, 67–70
Aristotle, 43–45, 53, 84, 169
Art, 80, 93–96, 196
Augustine, St., 37–40, 115, 228
Authority, 14, 74, 157–61, 189, 208–9

"Bad": meaning of, 89–96; and moral evil, 105–7
Barth, K., 30

Basic human goods, 41, 44, 77–87, 110, 118, 132, 143–45, 162–63, 219, 232–33; community and, 61–62, 156–58, 162, 165; ends in themselves, 78, 131; first moral principle and, 98–104; goals and, 18, 47, 57–59; God and, 84; love and, 115; moral ideals and, 175; not Platonic ideas, 80; relativism and, 68–71; third-level action and, 29–32. *See also* Good(s).
Bentham, J., 111

Calculation, 13, 28–29, 34, 45–50, 112–13, 135–36
Capital punishment, 53, 149–50
Character, 29, 34, 50, 144, 184, 238–39
Children, 57, 60, 62–64, 69, 79, 156, 158, 160, 174–76, 210–11, 218; raising of, 4–5, 182–93
Choice, 17–22, 45–52, 85, 197–200, 231–32, 238–40; ambiguous action and, 141–46; decision and, 73; experience of, 21, 186; first principle of morality and, 97–107; personhood and, 25–31; proportionalism and, 130–33;

252